Fascism and Big Business

Fascism and Big Business

Daniel Guerin

PATHFINDER

New York   London   Montreal   Sydney

ISBN 978-0-87348-878-5
Library of Congress Catalog Card Number 73-80854
Manufactured in the United States of America

First edition, 1939
Second edition, 1973
Thirteenth printing, 2010

Translated from the French by Frances and Mason Merr.
Revisions in the 1965 French edition translated by Dan Stewart and Francoise
Collet.

Pathfinder
www.pathfinderpress.com
E-mail: pathfinder@pathfinderpress.com

CONTENTS

PREFACE TO THE 1945 FRENCH EDITION

Fascism and Big Business was begun in 1934 shortly after February 6, and appeared in July 1936. Was it necessary to reprint the book in its present form or continue the investigation to the start of 1945?

The date on which we stopped writing was undoubtedly premature. The phenomenon of fascism was then still in the full course of development (above all in Germany). Certain of its traits had not yet been sufficiently revealed. It was necessary to probe further.

But perhaps there was an impediment in probing too extensively. The object of this book, if we can so express it, is the study of fascism *in its pure form.*

After 1939, the phenomenon of fascism tends to become confounded with the great upheaval of the imperialist war. Nothing so resembles a country at war as another country at war. The characteristic traits of fascism are, in large part (not completely) blurred by those now familiar traits, namely, universally unleashed militarism and war economy. Undoubtedly a materialist explanation of the war should be undertaken as well as the materialist explanation of fascism. But whoever embraces too much grasps too little. We leave this task to others. We have consciously limited the scope of this work to the study of the phenomenon of fascism by itself.

An objection might perhaps be raised that fascism and war are inseparable, that the present war is the monstrous product of fascism. But that's precisely what we deny. There is, certainly, a direct link between war and fascism. They grow out of the same dungheap; they are, each in its own way, the monstrous products of the capitalist system in decline. They both flow from the fundamental vice of the system: first, the incompatibility between the tremendous development of the productive forces, and private ownership of the means of production; second, the partitioning of the world into national states. They both aspire, by different roads, to break the iron ring of the contradictions in which this system is henceforth enclosed. They both aim to restore endangered capitalist profits. Moreover, beyond these general ties, a more direct interconnection can be observed between fascism and war in Italy and in Germany: because these two countries lack raw materials and markets, because they are in the category of "hungry nations" as opposed to the "sated" nations, the crisis in which the whole capitalist system is convulsed takes on in their case a particularly acute character, and imposes upon them, in advance of the others, a "strong state." They act as "aggressive" powers with the aim of seizing part of the plunder from the "sated" nations. They aim at a new division of the world by force of arms, while their adversaries, opposing this redivision, assume the attitude of "peace-loving" powers.

Thus fascism and war are, to be sure, related. But the relationship *is not one of cause and effect.* Eliminate fascism (assuming that could be done) and the causes of rivalries and of imperialist wars will not in the least thereby be eliminated. For four years, from 1914 to 1918, two groups of great powers fought over possession of the world market. In neither camp was there a "fascist" country. In reality, fascism and war are both the effects, *different* effects, of the same cause: though the two phenomena criss-cross, though, at times, they seem to be confounded with each other (and every conscious effort is made to confuse them) still each has a distinct existence and demands a separate study.

Do the events since 1939 cast a new light on the phenomenon of fascism? At the risk of disappointing the reader, we reply in the negative. At the risk of appearing presumptuous or of clinging to outlived positions, we will say that the events of these last years, in our opinion, do not modify to any marked degree the conclusions of our book. The only thing that fascism has brought, since 1939, is renewed proof of its barbarism. But who can be surprised at this, after witnessing the manner in which it crushed the Italian and

German proletariat before crushing Europe? And can this barbarism which is "fascist" in its most hideous traits, be considered solely "fascist"? The whole war is barbarous.

Apart from that, the war and the German occupation, by giving us the opportunity to observe the phenomenon more closely, taught us, as we had already suspected, that the fascist regime, despite its "totalitarian" pretensions is not homogeneous. It never succeeded in dissolving the different elements of which it was composed into one single alloy. Its different wheels did not function without friction. Despite Hitler's attempts for several years to find a compromise formula between the party and the army, the Wehrmacht on the one hand, and the Gestapo and the SS on the other, continued their cat and dog fight. Behind this conflict is a class question. The fascist regime, despite appearances, appearances that it delighted in maintaining, never domesticated the bourgeoisie. When we upheld this thesis several years ago, that fascism is an instrument of big business, it was objected that in Italy as in Germany (in Germany above all) big business marches in step. This is not exactly true.

The bourgeoisie remained an autonomous force, pursuing its own ends in the totalitarian state. It made others don the brown shirt, for the Hitler bands were indispensable to crush the proletariat, but thus far it has not donned the brown shirt itself (or, if it has, it was only for the gallery). Hermann Rauschning led us into error with his thesis according to which the ruling class was eliminated by the Nazi plebeians, people who respected nothing, "nihilists." Undoubtedly there have been individual cases where big capitalists have been ill-treated or forced to emigrate. But big business, taken as a whole, was not engulfed by the brown tide. Quite the contrary.

At all times the army is the instrument par excellence of the ruling class. The relative independence of the army with regard to the regime, its refusal to permit itself to be thoroughly nazified, makes clear the autonomy of big business (and the big landlords) towards the fascist regime, its refusal to be brought into line. We will be told: Hitler dealt some secret blows within his General Staff; insubordinate generals were successively eliminated. No doubt; but this continual "purge" was only a confirmation of the resistance that the army, backed by the big bourgeoisie, put up against complete nazification.

But what about July 20, what about those generals, those big capitalists, those country squires who were hung or shot, following the attempted assassination of Hitler? July 20, 1944, in Germany, just like July 25, 1943, in Italy (the day that Marshal Badoglio and the King had Mussolini arrested) carries striking proof that the capitalist ruling class was never absorbed by the self-styled totalitarian state. After subsidizing fascism and pushing it into power, the bourgeoisie tolerated, in spite of minor inconveniences, the overrunning of the state by the Nazi plebs: this conformed to its interests. But from the day when it appeared that the inconveniences of the regime outweighed the advantages, the bourgeoisie, with the support of the army, did not hesitate to throw it overboard.

As early as 1936, in the conclusions of our book, we set forth this hypothesis. The move succeeded in Italy. It has failed, for the time being, in Germany. But since the attempted assassination of July 20, Hitler is virtually finished. Big business, the top circles of the army, do not follow him any longer. He only survives artificially by means of unheard of terror that the police and Himmler's SS exercise within the very midst of the army and the population as a whole. He survives only because the plans for the dismemberment of Germany, agitated from abroad, have aroused in the masses a desperate reflex of the instinct of self-preservation. The regime, although abandoned by the people, has been able to take momentary advantage of this. He survives only because the ruling class fears to let loose open civil war in the midst of total foreign war. This last episode proves that the redoubtable instrument of repression forged by fascism can prolong the life of the latter for a moment, even after it has been abandoned by big business. The bullet destined for the workers can also serve to make a hole in the skin of a few capitalists. But not for long.

No political regime can govern against the class which holds the economic power. Although it may not please some naive people, the old laws which have always governed the relations of classes have not failed this time either. Fascism has not suspended them, as with a wave of the magic wand. The link between fascism and big business is so intimate that the day when big business withdraws its support is the beginning of the end for fascism.

We pointed out, in the conclusion of this book, fascism's extraordinary *will to endure*. The desperate tenacity with which it defends itself today, although knowing itself lost, evidently surpasses all expectations. Nevertheless the phenomenon is comprehensible if one remembers that fascism is not only an instrument at the service of big business, but, *at the same time* a mystical upheaval of the pauperized and discontented petty bourgeoisie. Although a large part of the middle class who had helped fascism to power is cruelly deceived today, such is not the case with the *militant* sector. There are many playboys and corrupt people in the enormous bureaucratic apparatus of the Fascist state, but there are also some *real fanatics*. These not only defend their social position, even their lives, in defending the regime—they also defend an idea to which they firmly cling to the death. (Let us note in passing: it is not by brute force, much less foreign bayonets, that one loses faith. Only the powerful wind of the proletarian revolution in Germany would be able to clear their brains.)

Fascism, in the countries where it attained power, stands a chance of surviving for another reason: in its decline, as at its birth, it owes much to the complacence of its "adversaries": the "democratic" state which succeeded it remains completely infected with the fascist virus (just as the "democratic" state which had preceded it was entirely infected with the fascist virus). The "purge" is nothing but a shameful comedy, because to really disinfect the bourgeois state, it is necessary to destroy it. The administrative tops, the army, the police, the judiciary remain staffed with auxiliaries and accomplices of the former regime, the same personnel for the most part who, a short time ago, delivered the keys of power to fascism. In Italy, Marshal Badoglio is the man who once placed the cadres and resources of the army at the disposition of the "black shirts." Who can be surprised if, as Mussolini's successor, he lets the Duce escape from prison?

Perhaps in the conclusions of this book, there is a point which has not been sufficiently stressed: the underground development of the class struggle beneath the fascist lid. We stressed, and it was necessary to stress, the formidable methods employed by the totalitarian regimes to break up, to "atomize" the movement of the working class, to scientifically track it down, if one can so express it, and to destroy in the embryo every form of opposition. But gradually and to the extent that the fascist lid is lifted, we perceive that beneath it, the class struggle, supposedly destroyed forever, continues right on its way. As we are writing these lines, Northern Italy has not yet been liberated. But we have already heard many echoes of the extraordinary fighting power displayed in these last years by the workers of Milan, of Turin, within the great industrial combines on which the red flag waved in 1920. More than twenty years of fascist dictatorship have not succeeded in changing the Italian worker.

In Germany, the grip of the regime and the police terror have been infinitely stronger. But, in spite of the savage muzzling of the German people, we find once more traces of a revolutionary vanguard, especially in the concentration camps and the prisons. Fascism has not halted humanity's continuous march toward emancipation. It has only delayed it temporarily.

Is it necessary to reissue this book at the moment when the fate of Mussolini and Hitler would appear to discourage their imitators in other countries? Outside of its retrospective interest, does it retain its timeliness?

Re-reading it, we are impressed with the fact that its real subject is *socialism* much more than it is fascism. For what is fascism, at bottom, but the direct product of the failure to achieve socialism? Behind fascism, the shadow of socialism is ceaselessly present. We have only studied the first in relation to the second. More than once, in the course of these pages, fascism has served us simply as a counterpoint with which to define better by contrast certain essential aspects of socialism. When, as we hope, the day comes in which nothing remains of fascism but a bad memory, this book will remain an attempt to contrast socialism to what was, at one time, its most redoubtable opponent. On this score perhaps *Fascism and Big Business* will not become outdated too quickly.

But, as a matter of fact, is it really certain that the fascist epidemic has been definitively checked? We can only hope so, but we cannot at all be certain of it. It is a widespread illusion that the defeat of "The Axis" sounds the death knell of fascism in the entire world.

The big "democracies" do not always tell the truth. They fought Hitler, not, as they claim today, because of the authoritarian and brutal form of the National Socialist regime, but because German imperialism, at a given moment, dared to dispute with them the hegemony of the world. It has been too generally forgotten that Hitler was hoisted to power with the blessings of the international bourgeoisie. During the first years of his rule, Anglo-American capitalism from the British aristocracy to Henry Ford gave him, according to all evidence, their support. They viewed him as "the strong man," who alone was capable of reestablishing order in Europe and saving the continent from Bolshevism.

Only much later, when the capitalists of the "democratic" countries found their interests, their markets, their sources of raw materials menaced by the irresistible expansion of German imperialism, did they start to preach against National Socialism, to denounce it as "immoral" and "un-Christian." And, even then, there were capitalists and princes of the Church, who, more anxious to ward off the "red peril" than the German peril, remained partial towards the policeman of Europe.

Today the big "democracies" proclaim themselves "anti-fascist." That's the word they're always mouthing. In reality, anti-fascism became necessary as a platform for them to overcome their German competitor. They could not gain the full allegiance of the popular masses in the struggle against Hitlerism solely by exalting national sentiment. Despite all appearances, we are no longer in the age of national wars. The struggle of the classes, the social war, dominates our epoch. The toiling masses could not have been brought to sacrifice themselves to liberate Europe unless sentiments of a social order were aroused in them, unless an appeal was made to their class instinct. They were told that it was necessary to finish off fascism. And as they understood more or less clearly, that fascism is the exacerbated form of detested capitalism, they consented to all sacrifices. The Parisian barricades of the end of August 1944, the exploits of the various Maquis [underground partisans], will live as admirable examples of proletarian devotion.

But tomorrow the big "democracies" may very well put *antifascism* back on the shelf. Already, this magic word, which inspired the workers to rise up against Hitlerism, is considered by them undesirable as soon as it becomes the rallying point of the adversaries of the capitalist system. Already in Belgium and Greece, the Allies did not hesitate to brutally crush the very resistance movement which they had been only too happy to utilize for their own purposes. To reestablish "order," they will sooner or later be compelled (as is already the case in Greece) to find points of support in the midst of the liberated populations. Against the people's vanguard they will support formations of a clearly fascist character. Naturally they will be baptised with another name, for the word *fascist* is definitively "played out." But, under the new label, the old merchandise will remain the same. Fascism, by whatever name it is called, will remain the reserve army of decaying capitalism.

Thus our basic conclusion is seen to be confirmed by the most recent developments, namely, that fascism, outgrowth of the failure to achieve socialism, can be effectively fought and vanquished definitively only by the proletarian revolution. All "anti-fascism" that rejects it is but vain and deceitful babbling. The misfortune is that we have permitted the bourgeois-democrats to seize hold of anti-fascism. These gentlemen fear the fascist whip for their own skins, but they fear the proletarian revolution at least as much. They conjured up a bastard solution to reconcile these two fears, that of the "Popular Fronts." The "Popular Fronts" declaim against fascism but without taking a single thoroughgoing measure to attack its material roots. They refrain from laying a hand on capitalism despite their demagogic tirades against the "two hundred families," against the "trusts," and, an even graver crime, by their economic and social policies, they deepen the causes of friction between the proletariat and the middle classes; and thus they push the latter towards the very fascism from which they pretend to divert them.

The fascist menace has made many people discover the problem of the middle classes. Only recently, the parties of the left saw in them only an easy, faithful and stable electoral clientele. But from the day when it was demonstrated that in the course of their oscillations, amplified by the economic crisis, the middle classes could enter the opposite camp, that they could be seized with collective madness, that they could don the fascist uniform, these same parties have known the anguish of the mother hen menaced with losing her chicks; the question has become an obsession with them— *how to retain the middle classes?*

Unfortunately, they have understood nothing (nor do they wish to understand anything) of the problem. We must apologize for only having, in this book, skimmed the surface of this problem. In effect, the logic of our analysis has led us less to research concerning how socialism could have been able to turn the middle classes away from fascism than to showing why and how it, fascism, succeeded in conquering them. The reader will therefore permit us a brief digression here.

The middle classes and the proletariat have common interests against big business. But there is more involved than common interests. They are not "anti-capitalist" in the same fashion. Undoubtedly the bourgeoisie exploits, sharpens at will these differences of interests, but it does not create them out of the whole cloth. It is therefore impossible to bring together the proletariat and the petty bourgeoisie around a common program which will completely sat-

isfy both. One of the two parties must make concessions. The proletariat, naturally, can agree to some. Whenever possible, it must
see that the blows it directs against big business do not strike at the
same time the small investors, artisans, merchants, peasants. But
on certain essential points, it *must remain intransigent,* for if it yields
on these points in order to retain influence over the middle classes,
to reassure the small shopkeepers or peasants, it would renounce
dealing capitalism the decisive blows.

And every time that it failed in its mission to destroy capitalism,
every time it has not pushed its advantage right to the end, the
middle classes, caught between menacing big business and an aggressive working class, have become enraged and turned toward
fascism.

In short, the proletariat cannot win over the middle classes by
renouncing its own socialist program. The proletariat must convince the middle classes of its capacity to lead society onto a new
road; by the strength and firmness of its revolutionary action. But it
is precisely this that the inventors of the "Popular Fronts" do not
wish to understand. They have but one idea in their heads: to catch
the middle classes on bait-hooks, and they do this with so much
skill that they eventually throw them back towards the fascist bait.

Anti-fascism cannot triumph as long as it drags along as the tail
to the kite of bourgeois democracy. Beware of "anti" formulas. They
are always inadequate because they are purely negative. One cannot conquer a principle except by opposing to it another principle—
a superior principle. The world of today, in the midst of its convulsions, is not only looking for a form of property that corresponds
to the collective character and gigantic scale of modern production; it seeks also a form of government capable of substituting a
rational order for chaos, while liberating man. Bourgeois
parliamentarianism offers only a caricature of democracy, ever more
impotent and more corrupt. Deceived and disheartened, the world
turns towards the strong State, the heaven-sent man, towards the
"leader principle."

On the plane of ideas, fascism will be defeated only on that day when we present to humanity and when by example we make triumphant a new form of government of men, an authentic democracy, complete, direct, in which all the producers take part in the administration of things. This new type of democracy is not a chimera, an invention of the spirit. It exists. The Great French Revolution—as we will demonstrate in another work—let us hear its first birth cries. The Commune of 1871 was the first attempt at its application, as Marx and Lenin have shown in a masterly manner. The Russian soviets of 1917 provided the model to the world in unforgettable fashion. Since then, soviet democracy has gone through a prolonged eclipse in Russia itself, for reasons too numerous to outline here. This eclipse coincides with the rise of fascism.

Today fascism lies crippled. We will give it the finishing blow by proving in action that true democracy, democracy of the Commune or soviet type, is viable and superior to all other types of government of men. *All Power to the Soviets*, said Lenin. Mussolini shamefully caricatured this slogan, making of it the slogan of the totalitarian state: *all power to fascism*.

The totalitarian state is a tottering monster. We shall be forever rid of it by assuring the triumph of the antithesis: the Republic of the Workers' Councils.

PREFACE TO THE 1965 FRENCH EDITION

After Hitler came to power in the beginning of 1933, and after the attempted fascist putsch in Paris on February 6, 1934, I let myself be persuaded by friends, and particularly by Simone Weil, to fight fascism by means of "learned" research. To expose the real reasons for the fascist victory; to unsparingly expose the failings of the defeated workers' parties, which others persistently covered up; to convince the reader that fascism could not be combatted by grasping at the straw of bourgeois democracy, that one must therefore choose between fascism and socialism—that was my plan.

But in carrying this undertaking through it was first of all necessary to diagnose the *true nature* of fascism. In my view, fascism was a disease. To describe a new and little-known disease the doctor has no recourse but to minutely compare the symptoms observed in various patients. This is what I tried to do. My patients were, appropriately, Italy and Germany. Setting aside the particular divergent traits of the two countries under study, I tried to retain only the common traits of the fascist phenomenon.

In this immense comparison I was undertaking, the writings of Leon Trotsky on Germany and France served as a guide.[1*] They helped me understand the complex problem of the middle classes, who wavered between the proletariat and the bourgeoisie, and who were propelled by the economic crisis on the one hand, and the default of the working class on the other, towards the gangsters of the ultraright. These writings likewise steered me towards my description of how fascism, once in power, eliminates the most left-wing of its "plebeians," and, having carried out this purge, ends

---

* References will be found at the end of the volume.

up at least to a certain extent in a classic military and police dictatorship.

Two other works were a great help to me. The first was a theoretical analysis of Italian fascism—noteworthy for its precision, lucidity, style, and wealth of facts—that Ignazio Silone, exiled in Switzerland, published in German under the title *Der Faschismus.* The second was a work by Trotsky's Spanish disciple Andres Nin: *Les dictatures de notre temps* (Contemporary Dictatorships), which Pierre Naville had translated into French and which he entrusted to me in manuscript (still unpublished). It was Nin who taught me the respective roles of light and heavy industry in fascism's march to power and the reasons why "big business" needs the fascist "strong state" more than other economic pressure groups do.

As for the innumerable facts I had to collect in the course of the evolution of the fascist disease, I drew them from the columns of the daily paper *Temps,* conservative but well-informed, and from two abundantly documented periodicals, one "Stalinist" and the other "reformist": the monthly bulletins published by the "Institute for the Study of Fascism" in Paris under the title *Etudes sur le fascisme,* and the newsletter published in Amsterdam by the International Federation of Transport Workers (under the leadership of its Secretary-General Eddo Fimmen) entitled *Fascism.*

FOREWORD

To define fascism—how can this be better done than by studying that phenomenon in the countries in which it has manifested itself in an altogether characteristic form, those countries where it has, so to speak, assumed its classic form—in Italy and in Germany?

This book is not a history of fascism in either country. Nor is it a *comparison* of the two examples—that is, a balance sheet of their similarities and differences. Such distinctions have been intentionally disregarded in favor of an attempt to define, above and beyond accidental factors peculiar to one or the other nation, a certain number of general traits. If scientific terms were valid in politics, one might write: a certain number of laws.

But "laws" are of interest in politics only in so far as practical conclusions may be drawn from them. It is hoped that the reader will be convinced that there is only one way to bar the road to fascism, namely, to overthrow capitalism. "Fascism," Clara Zetkin wrote as far back as 1923, "is the punishment inflicted on the proletariat for not having continued the revolution begun in Russia. . . ."[1]

Fascism could be our punishment tomorrow if we let the hour of socialism pass.

I

Big business finances fascism

The state has always been the instrument by which one social class rules over other social classes. When a state changes its outward features, when one political regime yields to another, the first thought that comes to mind is: what is going on behind the scenes? Is a new class coming into power? But when a number of unequivocal signs indicate that it is the same class in the saddle, the question instead becomes: *what interests of the ruling class are served by this upheaval?*

Up until now, the political system in most of the advanced industrial states was "democracy"—pseudo-democracy, that is: parliamentary democracy not direct democracy, bourgeois democracy not proletarian democracy, adulterated democracy not pure democracy. On close examination, it often even turns out to be half-breed Caesarism. But on the whole, even today one may say it is the most usual political form in the advanced countries.

In two great Western European powers, Italy and Germany, democracy has been superseded by a new political system, quite different from democracy: namely, *fascism*. Because it first appeared in

23

Italy, this new system is usually given an Italian name.* But it is by no means specifically Italian. The problem it poses is universal. Since the rise of capitalism, the dominant bourgeoisie has considered democracy the most desirable political system. Now in two countries, and those by no means the least important, the bourgeoisie has changed its mind. Why?

Revolutionaries have a perfectly natural tendency to see everything as it relates to themselves. They are under the impression that the bourgeoisie resorts to fascism only to smash the imminent threat of proletarian revolution. There is a certain grain of truth in this explanation, but it is oversimplified. The wealthy certainly fear revolution and finance bands of gangsters to teach the workers good manners. But it is not so much to stifle the revolution that they hand state power over to the fascists. Neither in Italy nor in Germany was revolution in the offing at the moment fascism took state power. The bourgeoisie resorts to fascism less in response to disturbances in the street than in response to disturbances in their own economic system. The sickness they aim to banish is within, not without.

The keystone of capitalism is profit. As long as capitalism was growing, the bourgeoisie was able to tap ever new sources of profit through the ceaseless development of production and the constant expansion of domestic and foreign markets. After World War I, capitalism as a whole began to decline. To the periodic economic crises of the past there has been added a chronic crisis, involving the whole system and threatening capitalist profit at its very source.

Up to the war, democracy suited capitalism perfectly. Everyone knows the old refrain: Democracy is the cheapest form of government . . . The spirit of free enterprise can flower only in the benign

---

* In ancient Rome, certain public officials were preceded by officers called "lictors" who carried bundles of willow sticks tied around an axe as a symbol of power. In modern Italian political jargon, the name *fascio* (pl. *fasci*) was applied to various militant political and social groups, many of which were politically very advanced. But then Mussolini's fascist movement took the word over.

climate of liberty . . . The political rights which democracy grants to the masses act as a sort of safety valve and prevent violent clashes between rulers and ruled . . . Democracy enlarges the capitalist market by encouraging the masses to want more goods and by giving them, to some extent, the means of satisfying their needs. All true enough—when the feast is abundant, the people may safely be allowed to pick up the crumbs.

In the present period of capitalist decline, however, the ruling class is impelled to put democracy into the scales, carefully weighing its advantages against its drawbacks. Like Buridan's ass, it eyes the two bundles of hay—and hesitates. Cruel dilemma! In certain countries and under certain conditions, the drawbacks seem to outweigh the advantages. *Seem*—for on this point, it is not yet certain that the bourgeoisie has correctly calculated its own interests. Time alone will tell.

When the economic crisis becomes acute, when the rate of profit sinks toward zero, the bourgeoisie can see only one way to restore its profits: it empties the pockets of the people down to the last centime. It resorts to what M. Caillaux, once finance minister of France, expressively calls "the great penance": brutal slashing of wages and social expenditures, raising of tariff duties at the expense of the consumer, etc. The state, furthermore, rescues business enterprises on the brink of bankruptcy, forcing the masses to foot the bill. Such enterprises are kept alive with subsidies, tax exemptions, orders for public works and armaments. In short, the state thrusts itself into the breach left by the vanishing private customers.

But such maneuvers are difficult under a democratic regime. As long as democracy survives, the masses, though thoroughly deceived and plundered, have some means of defense against the "great penance": freedom of the press, universal suffrage, the right to organize into unions and to strike, etc. Feeble defenses, it is true, but still capable of setting some limit to the insatiable demands of the money power. In particular, the resistance of the organized working class makes it rather difficult to simply lower wages.

And so, in certain countries and under certain conditions, the

bourgeoisie throws its traditional democracy overboard and con-
jures up with its invocations—and its subsidies—that "strong state"
which alone can strip the masses of all means of defense, tying their
hands behind their backs, the better to empty their pockets.

The phrase "in certain countries under certain conditions" is
important. These are those nations which have put in their claim
for a place in the sun too late, and so find themselves lacking raw
materials and markets. In richer, more fortunate countries, the bourgeoisie seems to have succeeded, not in escaping the crisis perma-
nently, but at least in extricating itself for the time being from its
difficulties. They have been able to start up again, after a fashion,
the mechanism of profit, resorting to expedients which at least have
not required the substitution of dictatorship for democracy. But
they used basically the same methods in both cases: the state refloated private capitalism, revived it with great public works and
huge "defense contracts." But thanks to the wealth accumulated by
preceding generations, in the latter case there was no need for the
fascist club to empty the workers' pockets. In the U.S.A., Roosevelt's
New Deal sufficed.

It is not enough to say that the bourgeoisie in certain countries like
Italy and Germany financed fascism and brought it to power for
the above reasons. That would be imprecise. Contrary to common
belief, the capitalist bourgeoisie is not completely homogeneous.
To any general threat against its class interests, it presents a face of
granite. But in less crucial matters, the rock betrays deep fissures.
Each capitalist group, in defending its own economic interests,
comes into conflict with the interests of other capitalist groups. It is
quite true that such groups are closely interrelated, and that the
lines of demarcation are not always very sharp. But this by no means
prevents the existence of violent conflicts of interest. And so it is
important to ask whether, in Italy and in Germany, fascism was
invoked and subsidized by the bourgeoisie as a whole or by certain
particular groups of capitalists. Since the various bourgeois political parties are simply the mirrors, or rather the tools, of the various

capitalist groups, unless one knows the attitude of these groups towards fascism, it is impossible to understand the shifting, complex, and puzzling interplay of political parties in the period which precedes fascism's seizure of power.

This chapter will show that fascism, in Italy and Germany alike, has been subsidized above all *by the magnates of heavy industry (iron and steel, mining) and by bankers with a stake in heavy industry.* Let us anticipate for a moment the conclusions we shall later draw: the detailed and objective study of fascism in Italy and Germany will show clearly that the heavy industrialists, the "big business men" are the *chief,* and one might even say the *only,* beneficiaries of the fascist dictatorship.

But to return to our analysis. Why, in the early stages, are the heavy industrialists almost alone in subsidizing and egging on the fascist movement? Why are other capitalist groups—and those, notably, which may be lumped under the heading of *light industry or finished goods industry*—why are they, in the beginning, noncommittal and sometimes even hostile towards the growing fascist movement?

One does not have to go to Italy and Germany to observe that heavy and light industry do not have the same economic interests and do not use the same social and political strategy. Conflicts are constantly breaking out between the two groups. Light industry often complains about the overlordship of heavy industry, which makes it pay through the nose for raw materials and machines. In foreign policy, heavy industry, living in great part off munitions orders (originating in its native state as well as in "friendly" powers), is characteristically for a policy of "prestige," force, and imperialistic adventure. Light industry however, interested in exporting non-military products, has nothing much to gain from war or from autarky. Besides, it is much more closely tied up with international capitalism and international finance than heavy industry. It favors, therefore, a policy of international collaboration.

In dealing with labor, heavy and light industry usually rely on quite different methods. The chiefs of steel and mining enterprises

are noted for their authoritarian attitude, their "tough boss" psychology. Their will to power is explained by the vast scope of their
enterprises and the dominant role they play in the economy and in
the state. But the explanation must also be sought in what Marx
calls "the organic composition" of the capital invested in their enterprises: the ratio of "fixed capital" (invested in plant, raw materials, etc.) to variable capital (i.e., wages) is much higher in heavy
than in light industry. The result is that the limits within which
production is profitable are especially narrow in heavy industry.[1]
Whenever the steelmasters are unable to run their works at a sufficiently high percentage of capacity, the "fixed charges" (interest,
depreciation) on their plants are distributed over an insufficiently
large quantity of products, and profits are impaired.[2] When a strike
breaks out, the least stoppage of production means losses mounting into the millions.[3] If the economic crisis sharpens they are unable to cut their fixed costs, and can only reduce their wage bill;
brutal wage cuts are for them an imperious necessity.

The light industrialists follow a rather different labor policy. The
organic composition of their capital is lower, their fixed costs less
burdensome, their arrogance less overpowering. Furthermore, the
fact that they produce goods for consumption makes them fear that
the too brutal measures of deflation demanded by heavy industry
during a period of crisis will have a disastrous effect on the purchasing power of the masses, that is to say, of their consumers. So
most of them prefer, in place of strong-arm tactics, what they call
"class collaboration" and "industrial peace" and what is actually only
a more hypocritical and insidious way of taming, and corrupting,
the proletariat.

It is, then, hardly surprising that in Italy and Germany, heavy
and light industry should have looked on the growth of fascism
with quite different feelings. Heavy industry wanted to pursue the
class struggle until the proletariat was crushed; light industry still
believed everything could be patched up by "industrial peace" and
political horse trading. Heavy industry called for a "dynamic" foreign policy; light industry leaned toward a policy of "internal co-

operation." Heavy industry wanted to strengthen its economic hegemony with the aid of a dictatorial state which should be *its* state; light industry feared this development.

But—the point cannot be too strongly underlined—the capitalist groups in light industry put up no serious resistance to fascism. They did not want its triumph, its "totalitarian" dictatorship, but they did nothing effective to block its progress. Why not? First, because fascism was a "national" movement, that is to say, in the service of the owning class and deserving, by this token, the sympathy, or at least the tolerance, of all property owners. Again, because they did not think a "totalitarian" fascist dictatorship was possible. They saw fascism as just one more political movement, which they could manipulate and even make use of. And so in both countries, "liberal" politicians closely connected to the light industry groups temporized with fascism. Faithful to their customary tactics of "industrial peace" and political jockeying, they imagined that, once it was housebroken and parliamentarized, fascism would serve as a useful counterweight to the forces of the proletariat. They succeeded only in putting it into the saddle.

And on that day when fascism, to their amazement, had become a considerable political force in its own right, a popular movement which could no longer be checked without the use of armed force, light industry and its liberal politicians put class loyalty ahead of the conflict of interests. They were loath to shed the blood of "patriots." They resigned themselves to the triumph of fascism. The entire capitalist class united to put fascism into power.

This should be a warning to those anti-fascists who think they can rely not on themselves but on "left-wing capitalism," on the "liberal" bourgeoisie to block fascism's road to power.

We shall see in detail, first in Italy and then in Germany—according to the scheme of this book—what the various capitalist groups thought of fascism.

For clarity's sake, this analysis will be presented in two parts:
1) At first, it does not occur to big business to launch fascism

toward the conquest of power. Business uses its hired fascist gangs for nothing more than *anti-labor militia.*

After World War I, in the two countries under consideration, it was necessary to make important concessions to the working class in order to avoid a real social revolution. Determined to take back these concessions some day, big business had the quite original idea of entrusting to armed, militarized gangs the task of harassing the organized proletariat and smashing its resistance. The great landed proprietors joined in the game. They drew their income from the unlimited exploitation of the rural proletariat, and they, too, had been forced to make concessions and were anxious to regain the ground they had lost.

Their backers assigned another task to the armed bands of Mussolini and Hitler. After the war, Italy and Germany found themselves in the position of powers that were either conquered or humiliated, in contrast to the great "satisfied" powers. Hungry for munitions orders, the heavy industrialists subsidized the fight against "unjust treaties." And they used the fascist gangs to carry on the fight over the heads of the legal governments.

2) But as soon as a serious economic crisis threatened to destroy its profits and a "strong state" alone seemed able to make its enterprises profitable again, big business decided to go a step further and launch its fascist troops towards the *conquest of political power.* With their aid, big business moved to set up a new kind of dictatorship.

In Italy

In Italy, after World War I, there was a real revolutionary upsurge of the masses. Workers and peasants, although they were not mature enough to address themselves to the conquest of power, at least were militant enough to force big concessions. Industrial workers got better wages, the eight hour day, general recognition of collective contracts, and a voice in production through "factory committees." One strike followed another—1,663 in 1919; 1,881 in 1920. In Genoa and other big seaports, the solidly organized dock workers won out over the shipowners. The steel workers did even better:

in September, 1920, they broadened a simple wage dispute into a large-scale class struggle. When the big industrialists resorted to a lock-out, 600,000 Italian metal workers occupied the mills and carried on production themselves through their own elected "shop committees." They did not hesitate to violate the holy of holies of the bosses. They opened their safes and discovered secrets, so closely guarded, of cost prices and profits . . . They won the fight: they were given—on paper, anyway—the right to check up on management, and "workers' control."*

The peasantry showed no less fighting spirit. Returning from the trenches, they demanded the "division of the land" which had been promised them, and, when it was not forthcoming, they occupied the coveted soil. A governmental decree sanctioned the *fait accompli:* on condition that they organize themselves into cooperatives, they obtained the right to remain four years on the lands they had spontaneously occupied (Visochi decree, September 2, 1919). The tenant farmers also succeeded in improving the terms of their leases. The agricultural day laborers formed strong unions, the famous "red leagues," backed up by the rural communes, won over to socialism, which had become so many proletarian fiefs. They bargained with the great landowners as one power with another, forcing from them union agreements, etc.

These conquests threatened directly both the interests and the authority of the two dynastic powers that ruled Italy: the industrial "dynasty" and the landowning "dynasty."

The industrial dynasty was very young. Not until the first decade of this century did the steel industry arise in Italy. In a country barren of iron ore and coal, such an industry could not but be parasitic, could become profitable only by subjugating all the economic and political forces of the country, only by levying a heavy toll on

---

* *On paper,* because the law drafted on "workers control" never went into effect. The magnates used the sharp economic crisis at the end of 1920 as a pretext to obtain its postponement to better times. And the better times were . . . the triumph of fascism.

the manufacturing and consumption industries, only by living off tariff protection and government orders. The Tripoli expedition (1911–1912) and then World War I put steel in the saddle. Certain steel magnates who had piled up insolent fortunes in the manufacture of instruments of death—the Perrones, the Agnellis, etc.—aspired, when the armistice was signed, to dominate the whole economic life of their country. Grudgingly, and to avoid a revolution, they made certain concessions to their workers, but they were determined to take them back as speedily as possible. The occupation of the factories, in particular, was for them a danger signal. They felt the chill of expropriation pass over them. Once the crisis was past, they and their allies, the shipowners—notably those of Genoa—were ready to go to any lengths to escape "workers' control" and the meddling of employees in management. Spurred by their strong class consciousness, they organized the powerful *Associazione Agraria* in 1908, and they were reinforced during the war by a new layer of landed proprietors.

In Genoa, at the beginning of April, 1919, the big industrialists and landowners sealed a holy alliance for the fight against "bolshevism." "This gathering," Rossi wrote,[4] "is the first step towards a reorganization of capitalist forces to meet the threatening situation." On March 7, 1920, the first nationwide conference of industrialists was held at Milan, and the *General Federation of Industry* was created. An all-embracing and detailed plan of joint action was drawn up, covering everything including the strategy of the campaign against the labor unions. Shortly after, on August 18, the *General Federation of Agriculture* was formed. "Industrialists and landowners will no longer enter the battle with scattered forces."

But neither the industrialists nor the landowners could themselves undertake the fight against the organized proletariat. For this job, they called in the armed gangs, the *fasci* of Benito Mussolini, which styled themselves the "united front against bolshevism." These gangs were to harry the working class, to weaken its ability to fight and resist, so as to allow the bosses to recapture their lost ground as speedily as possible. In April, 1919, Mussolini hailed the gathering of the economic "congregations" and offered his cooperation, which was not rejected. But it was above all in the fall of 1920, after the workers' occupation of the factories, that the subsidies of the industrialists and the landowners rained into his coffers.

2

Italian big business had still another reason to subsidize the fascist gangs. The youthful Italian imperialism had arrived too late in a world where all the best places were already preempted. It had been lucky to get a crumb from the feast—the sandy deserts of Tripoli. The Italy of 1914 was, in the words of the nationalist Corradini, "the great proletarian." And she remained just that after the armistice was concluded. As the price of her entry into the war, the Allies had promised her certain territorial concessions; but the promises were not kept. The big industrialists had a direct interest, as we have seen, in an aggressive foreign policy which would enrich them with munitions orders and open by force new markets for their production. And so they financed and armed extra-legal gangs of war veterans and adventurers. Because the Versailles Conference had denied Italy the little city of Fiume on the Adriatic,* they had these gangs carry out a symbolic gesture: they sent them, under the command of the litterateur d'Annunzio, to occupy the city (September 17, 1919). Later, at the end of 1920, they furnished Benito Mussolini the means to carry on in his paper, the *Popolo d'Italia*, now a journal with a big circulation, a noisy campaign for naval and air armaments. In the issue of December 23, Mussolini announced that he was going to campaign "for a foreign policy of expansion."[5]

3

This policy of heavy industry was opposed by light industry, textiles in particular, which in Italy antedated heavy industry. The op-

---

* After July, 1919, Fiume, awarded to neither Italy or Yugoslavia, was turned over to an international military commission.

position was financed by the powerful *Banca Commerciale.* On the eve of Italy's entrance into the war, and during and after the hostilities, the struggle between the two groups had been especially sharp. It was the Perrone brothers and their great metal-working trust, *Ansaldo,* against Toeplitz, head of the *Banca.* Light industry feared the domination of heavy industry, which would mean excessively high tariff duties and monopoly prices for machinery. Following the traditional labor policy of light industry, its political leader, Giolitti, exerted all his ingenuity to tame the proletariat through "class collaboration."

In 1915, light industry—and Giolitti—had unsuccessfully opposed the entrance of Italy into the war. But in July, 1919, Giolitti returned to power. He proposed to the Chamber an investigation of war profits, a measure openly aimed against heavy industry. He liquidated the Fiume adventure (end of December, 1920). He carried out a policy of international collaboration. Finally, during the occupation of the factories, he played a middle-of-the-road game, giving his complete support neither to the lock-outers nor to the locked-out, restraining the revolutionary impulses of the one and forcing concessions from the other party. For their part, the directors of the *Banca Commerciale* assured the FIOM (the strikers' union) of their "friendly neutrality."[6]

4

It was not long before the big industrialists began to look beyond merely weakening the organized proletariat by means of fascism. They began to think of launching fascism towards the conquest of power, they longed for the "strong state," through which they could directly impose their will.

During 1921, a serious economic crisis relentlessly dried up the wellsprings of profit. Under the hot sun of war, their enterprises had burgeoned prodigiously. Giant trusts had arisen, such as *Ansaldo,* a huge combination of metal-working and iron plants, and *Ilva,* which brought together a number of mining, metal, and shipping companies. During this period, *Ansaldo* had a par stock value of 500,000,000 lire and bonds outstanding in the amount of 100,000,000 lire. *Ilva* had a par stock value of 300,000,000 and bonds outstanding to the tune of 146,000,000.[7] The very idea of cost of production was forgotten. Artificial, parasitic industries were created. Mines long abandoned were exploited again. Munitions orders led people to believe that markets and profits were both without limits.

But when the hour of peace struck, war orders ceased overnight, the domestic market vanished, and the established foreign outlets disappeared. Italy was cheated out of the "compensations" promised by the Allies, and, worse yet, she lost the markets she had won with such difficulty before 1914 in Eastern Europe and the Near East. How could the enormous capital invested in heavy industry be made to yield a return? How could the productive capacity of so mushroom-like an industry be reduced? One after another, "dinosaurs" like *Ansaldo* and *Ilva*, and their bank, the *Banca di Sconto*, went under. In January, 1921, there were 600,000 unemployed.

The big business interests had reached the point where only the aid of the state could make their enterprises profitable again. It was up to the state to help them break working-class resistance and cut wages; it was up to the state to refloat their sinking enterprises, grant them subsidies and tax exemptions, assure them greater tariff protection, and keep them going with armament orders. "Among those involved in the failure of that big bank [the *Banca di Sconto*]," Rossi writes, "were several financial backers of fascism . . . who wanted to be rescued at the expense of the state."[8]

But the state was not an utterly obedient tool in their hands. The politicians in power (Giolitti and his colleagues) represented the interests of light industry rather than their own. Above all, democratic liberties allowed the toiling masses some means of defending their standard of living. Even though the working class organizations had been weakened, and their members demoralized by the savage "punitive expeditions" of the fascist gangs, the Socialist Party and the CGT (General Confederation of Labor) still represented a force which had to be reckoned with.

One solution remained: completely blot out democratic liberties, smash the labor organizations, and hand over the state to completely subservient politicians. The fascist gangs no longer played
merely the part of anti-labor militia. At their Rome congress (November 7–10, 1921) the *fasci* turned themselves into a political party.
At the national council meeting in Florence (December 20–21,
1921), Mussolini gave its marching orders to the new party: On to
the *conquest of power!*

5

As we have seen, light industry by no means wanted the triumph of
fascism. But the politicians in its pay temporized with fascism, because it was a "national" movement. Giolitti imagined that, having
tamed the proletariat and having prevented the occupation of the
factories from turning into a revolution, he would be able, in the
same way, to tame fascism. Once it was "parliamentarized," fascism
would serve as a useful counterweight to the forces of the proletariat.

In the spring of 1921, he dissolved the Chamber of Deputies and,
preparing for the new elections, incorporated fascism into a "national bloc" of government parties. All through Italy, fascist candidates presented themselves with governmental support. In this way
Giolitti caused the election of thirty fascist deputies, Mussolini
among them. "I consider this a fine stroke," Giolitti wrote in his
Memoirs, "for fascism already represented a real force in our national life, and, according to my old principle that every political
force in the nation should express itself in parliament, it was desirable that fascism should have parliamentary representation." Believing he had brought both the socialists and the fascists under
control, Giolitti tried to reconcile them. His lieutenant, Bonomi,
got them to sign on August 3, a "peace treaty."

But Giolitti's scheme had a result precisely the opposite of what
its author had planned. Far from bringing fascism to heel, he supplied it, by endorsing its candidates in the elections, with the best of
springboards. Far from ending the civil war, the "peace treaty" gave

Mussolini an invaluable breathing spell, which he used to reassure public opinion, antagonized by fascist violence, and to discipline a movement which had grown too fast. Once this double result was attained, Mussolini hastened to denounce the pact (November, 1921). "It had been useful and necessary to make it," writes the historian Volpe. "It was now useful and necessary to break it."[9] The civil war began again, more implacable than ever.

By the beginning of 1922, the leaders of light industry as well as the Crown, intimately linked to the *Banca Commerciale,* realized that fascism had become an independent power which could only be checked by force of arms. But the general interests of the owning classes required that "national" forces should not tear each other apart. Moreover, a new economic factor had entered into the situation: after the foundering of the great metal trusts and the *Banca di Sconto,* the *Banca Commerciale* had taken over part of the latter's industrial holdings, thus acquiring an interest in heavy industry. From then on, not only the big industrialists but also the *Banca Commerciale* pushed Mussolini into power: the magnates of the "Federation of Industry" and Toeplitz came together in October, 1922, to supply the millions necessary for the March on Rome. On October 28, according to Rossi, "some very lively conferences took place between Mussolini . . . and the heads of the General Federation of Industry, Sig. Benni and Olivetti. The chiefs of the Banking Association, who had paid out twenty million to finance the March on Rome, the leaders of the Federation of Industry and of the Federation of Agriculture, telegraphed Rome that in their opinion the only possible solution was a Mussolini government." Senator Ettore Conti, a big power magnate, sent a similar telegram. "Mussolini was the candidate of the plutocracy and the trade associations."

6

In Germany

Here, too, when the war is over, we see a revolutionary upsurge of the workers and peasants. When Prussian militarism collapsed in November, 1918, a new order sprung up spontaneously in a few hours: the workers' and soldiers' councils, a German version of the Russian soviets. For some days, these councils were the only legal authority in the Reich. In each city, the councils delegated their powers to an executive committee. In Berlin, the central government of "people's commissars" was merely a reflection of the executive committee of the Berlin workers' and soldiers' councils.

The experiment was cut short, partly by the treachery of the Social Democracy, partly by the lack of education and revolutionary tradition on the part of the masses. The republic of the "councils" had to give way very soon to a bourgeois democratic republic. But, under this republic, the workers and peasants won vital economic and political advantages: the extension of universal suffrage to both sexes, the eight-hour day, general recognition of union agreements, unemployment insurance, elected "shop committees," etc. The farm laborers, employed by the great landowners of the East, won for their part the right to organize and they crowded into the unions. The Federation of Farm Workers increased from 10,000 members in the middle of 1918 to 700,000 in 1920. They extorted better working conditions, union agreements, unemployment insurance, and the right to elect shop committees. Nevertheless, the gains of the farm workers were much more limited than those of the industrial workers. To be allowed to elect a "shop committee," for instance, they had to have at least twenty workers in the same establishment (as against only ten in industry). The agricultural work day was fixed at ten, not eight, hours. Part of the farm laborers were practically excluded from unemployment insurance, and farm servants were excepted from union agreements.[10]

These gains impaired the interests and the prestige of both the industrial and the landowning dynasties of Germany.

The industrial dynasty was much older in Germany than in Italy. Long before the war, the Krupps, the Thyssens, the Kirdorfs and

Boersigs and the rest played the part of "tough bosses," treating their exploited workers like serfs. "The military and bureaucratic state," writes Professor Bonn, "did not negotiate with its subjects. It commanded. Likewise German capitalism, once it had come into power, sought to rule its subordinates with authority and to impose on them, from above, the viewpoint of the masters."[11] Krupp told his employees: "We want only loyal workers who are grateful from the bottom of their hearts for the bread which we let them earn."[12] Long before the war, the big iron and steel masters were giving huge subsidies to the "German Union to Fight Against the Social Democracy."

For a few days, the magnates of heavy industry felt the chill of expropriation pass over them. But they recovered quickly and their fright merely intensified their desire for revenge, merely strengthened their determination to take back the concessions they had been forced to make. In February, 1919, Stinnes said: "Big business and all those who rule over industry will some day recover their influence and power. They will be recalled by a disillusioned people, half dead with hunger, who will need bread and not phrases."[13] Fritz Thyssen said (1924): "Democracy with us represents—nothing."[14] The former minister Dernberg spoke out for the big employers: "Every eight-hour day is a nail in Germany's coffin!" Big business remained deeply hostile to the "shop committees," pale caricature though these were of the "councils" of 1918. It sabotaged the so-called "socialization" laws. It gave lip service only to the idea of "collaborating" with its employees. The industrialists looked forward to the time when each would be "master in his own house."

More ominous still was the point of view of the Junker proprietors of the great estates east of the Elbe. In Germany, as in Italy, the old aristocracy still owned the land. Preserving a medieval idea of their authority, the Junker landlords were accustomed to treat their farm laborers like serfs. Up to the war, these laborers were deprived of the most elementary rights. They had to vote alongside their masters for the conservative candidate, or else "pack their bundles."[15]

A German writer has given an impressive description of this region east of the Elbe, this *terra incognita* where feudal rights, such as the *jus primae noctis,* still hold sway.[16] One must have felt this atmosphere if one is to understand the rage of the post-war Junker at the few concessions he was forced to give to his serfs.

But neither the industrialists nor the Junkers could themselves carry on the fight against the organized proletariat. This task they confided to the "volunteer corps" or "combat leagues," armed gangs specializing in "bolshevik fighting." These bands became, as Professor Gumbel puts it,[17] "the bodyguard of capitalism." They were trained to fight the organized proletariat, to weaken and subdue it. One such gang in Munich took the name, "National Socialist Party," and, from 1920 on, hailed as its chief, Adolf Hitler.

7

German big business had still another reason for financing these armed bands. German imperialism, arriving on the scene too late, had failed to carve out a new division of the world by force of arms. The Versailles Treaty had robbed it of raw materials and vital industrial regions (Lorraine, Silesia, the Saar, etc.) as well as of its colonial empire. Germany had been forced to disarm and to pay to the victors, under guise of "reparations," the astronomical sum of 132 billion gold marks. The magnates of heavy industry pushed Germany into an aggressive and chauvinist foreign policy, (1) to recapture their lost markets, (2) to get rid of disarmament, which cut them off from a major source of profit, (3) to shake off the burden of reparations which weighed so heavily on their production costs. Acting over the head of the Reich government, they paid and armed gangs of war veterans and adventurers. In June, 1919, for example, they sent the "Baltikum" corps, 50,000 strong, to fight in Lithuania against the Soviet army. In 1923 their "volunteer corps" resisted the French occupation of the Ruhr. The "Black Reichswehr"—as these different squadrons were called—was formed to transform the official "passive resistance" of big business to democratic gains into "active resistance." On September 25, 1923, all these "combat leagues" were merged into a single organization, at the head of which was put Adolf Hitler.[18]

8

The policy of the magnates of heavy industry was opposed, as in Italy, by the leaders of the *Fertigindustrie* (finished goods industry), particularly the electrical goods and chemical industries.

After the war the antagonism was particularly violent between the two groups—Stinnes and Thyssen, magnates of heavy industry, versus Rathenau, president of the powerful AEG (the General Electric Association). The *Fertigindustrie* rose up against the overlordship of heavy industry, which forced it to pay cartel prices for the raw materials it needed. Rathenau publicly denounced the dictatorship of the great metal and mining industries: just as medieval nobles had scoffed at the German Emperor and divided Germany into Grand Duchies, the magnates of heavy industry were dividing Germany into economic duchies "where they think only of coal, iron, and steel, and *neglect, or rather absorb, the other industries.*"[19]

The social policy of the *Fertigindustrie* was built around class collaboration. While the Stinnesses and Thyssens were dreaming of taking back from the proletariat the concessions made, and subsidizing anti-labor militias, Rathenau worked out plans for "corporatism," for collaboration between employers and wage earners.[20] While the former accepted only grudgingly the Weimar republic and dreamed of dictatorship, Rathenau entered the cabinet of the democratic government of the Reich. In foreign affairs, heavy industry, though also dependent on exportation, had mainly nationalist and protectionist tendencies. The *Fertigindustrie,* oriented chiefly toward export trade, and closely connected with the powerful American company, General Electric, which had an important interest in the German AEG, was for free trade and international collaboration. Rathenau signed the Wiesbaden agreement with France, the treaty of Rapallo with Russia, and accepted the principle of reparation of German capitalism. A significant detail: when he was assassinated in June, 1922, by young nationalists, it was proved that the car used by the murderers had been put at their disposal by a great industrialist in Saxony.[21]

9

From 1924 to 1929 the big business interests subsidized the fascist bands just enough to keep them from disappearing. They did not, in fact, have immediate need for them, and merely wanted to keep them in reserve. For during these years they were engaged in an enormous industrial reorganization with the aid of foreign capital. This enterprise demanded, temporarily, a policy of collaboration—collaboration abroad with the Entente, with Anglo-Saxon finance, and collaboration at home with the workers' organizations. When the mark was definitely stabilized and the Dawes plan came into effect, American capital began to flow into Germany. Until 1931, the "most enormous investment operation in financial history"[22] was taking place. It reached the figure of 30 billion gold marks.

But this audacious operation ended in an economic catastrophe also without precedent. With the dollars borrowed at very high rates, German industry expanded its productive machinery by a third; she equipped herself to supply the needs of the whole world. But one thing was lacking: the consumer. At home, the purchasing power of wages rose much more slowly than the productive capacity; on the other hand, an increasingly large number of workers had been eliminated by "rationalization" and reduced to idleness. (This technological unemployment appeared as early as 1927, and in January, 1929, there were already more than two million unemployed). Finally, the ever-widening trustification, by permitting the big monopolies to raise sales prices arbitrarily, overwhelmed the consumer and reduced his purchasing power. But the magnates were counting above all on the foreign market; they cut their export prices to the bone and, at the expense of the domestic consumer, prepared to dump on a gigantic scale.

And, suddenly, at the moment the new means of production were put into operation, when the finished products were beginning to pile up in the factories, the foreign buyer disappeared; the world crisis began. While the index for production (1928: 100) dropped sharply in the United States from 106.3 in 1929 to 64 at the end of 1931, there was a parallel drop in Germany from 101.4 in 1929 to 60 at the end of 1931. By February, 1930, the number of unemployed rose above four million. The gigantic machinery was soon operating at only half its capacity.

The industrial crisis was accompanied by a financial crisis. While America had prudently granted most of its credits on *short terms,* the German banks reissued them to their clients on *long terms.* The announcement of the Austro-German Anschluss (customs plan) on March 19, 1931, which aroused the opposition of French imperialism and its satellites, precipitated a series of crashes. First came the failure of the Vienna *Credit-Anstalt* (May 11), which shook the credit of the German banks. Like Panurge's sheep, foreign short-term capital rushed out of the Reich. And the banks, which had themselves made long-term loans to industry, could not continue their payments (failure of the *Danatbank,* July 13). The rise of the discount rate to absolutely prohibitive heights completed the paralysis of German economy. The accumulation of capital was interrupted. Corporations no longer paid dividends, and a number of them were practically in bankruptcy; the rate of profit tended toward zero.

The great industrialists were particularly hard hit: their enormous fixed capital burdened them with extremely high fixed costs which they had to carry even when their plants lay idle. They reached the point where only state aid could artificially revive their profits. It was up to the state to help them reduce the workers' wages, raised during the deceptive prosperity of "rationalization." But in order to lower wages, they first had to smash the system of union contracts, which in 1931 applied to ten million workers and almost two million office employees. Hence they had to reduce to impotence not only union organization but its projection in the factory, the "shop committee." It was up to the state to restrict "social expenditures," which resulted in excessive taxation. It was up to the state to refloat the sinking enterprises, grant them subsidies and tax exemptions, and nourish them on its orders. The crisis was no less severe in agriculture, and the great landed proprietors demanded one state "emergency subsidy" after another, and import duty piled on import duty.

But the state was not an altogether docile tool in the hands of the magnates and the Junkers. Men like Chancellor Bruening and Chancellor von Schleicher represented more the interests of the *Fertigindustrie* (in particular the chemical products industry, which depends largely on exports) than those of heavy industry. Bruening was still recommending "collaboration" with the organized proletariat. Schleicher humored the reformist union leaders, and, contrary to the interests of heavy industry, he advocated plans for "state socialism" more or less inspired by Rathenau. Bruening would not heed all the demands of the Junkers, and he prepared a "colonization" plan which threatened, however slightly, their privileges. Schleicher refused to grant them the import quotas they demanded, and which von Papen's government (June–November 1932) had promised the Junkers. But the electrical goods and chemical industries, fearing reprisals that would endanger their foreign markets, rose up against von Papen's plans, forcing him out of power. By way of making himself even more disagreeable, Schleicher exploded the scandal of the *Osthilfe* ("emergency subsidies" in East Prussia), which had been dispensed a little too generously to the landed aristocracy, at the instigation of President Hindenburg, himself now a country gentleman.

To be sure, Bruening had promulgated a number of decree-laws reducing wages and restricting "social expenditures." But these measures were not enough. Papen tried to revive activity by subsidies and tax exemptions for industry. Still it was not enough. Moreover, the leaders of the Social Democracy and the unions, who had "swallowed" the decree-laws, had reached the extreme limit of concessions. They risked being overwhelmed by the masses if they yielded more.

One solution remained: The great industrialists and the landowners must subjugate the state completely to themselves and hand its direction over to entirely subservient politicians. That is why they brought National Socialism out of the obscurity in which they had let it vegetate for a number of years, and launched it towards the conquest of power. Fritz Thyssen, who had never "let down" his friend Hitler; old Emil Kirdorf, master of the powerful *Gelsenkirchen* metal trust, who had been Hitler's "admirer" since 1927; and others increased their subsidies.

Later, on May 1, 1936, Emil Kirdorf made this statement: "When I think back over my life, I cannot be too thankful to God for giving me a long life . . . and thus making it possible for me to come to the assistance, at the opportune moment, of our beloved Fuehrer."[23] On April 8, 1937, Hitler visited Kirdorf in Duisburg on his ninetieth birthday and bestowed on him the order of the German Eagle, the Reich's highest distinction. Finally, on July 16, 1938, the Fuehrer-Chancellor was present in person at Kirdorf's funeral in Gelsenkirchen and placed a wreath on the coffin.

By the summer of 1930, most of the great industrialists and bankers associated with them were underwriting the National Socialist party. They gave it the formidable material resources that permitted it to win the electoral victory of September, 1930, and gain 107 seats in the Reichstag. Much later, in a speech evoking the memory of that "astonishing campaign," Hitler begged his listeners to think of "what it means when a thousand speakers each has a car at his disposal and can hold in a year a hundred thousand meetings."[24] In 1931 and 1932 the subsidies of the great industrialists continued to rain, always more abundantly, into the coffers of the NSDAP.

The *Fertigindustrie* did not want the triumph of National Socialism. It still feared above all else the hegemony of heavy industry. But the statesmen who were connected with the *Fertigindustrie* temporized with National Socialism, because it was a "national" movement. Chancellor Bruening imagined that, having tamed the socialists, he could tame National Socialism the same way. The latter, once "parliamentarized," would serve as a useful counterbalance to the proletarian forces. In the spring of 1930 he dissolved the Reichstag. But he succeeded only in putting Hitler in the saddle by giving him the opportunity for his great electoral success. Still, he persisted in his error. He flattered himself that he would trap Hitler in his net, sober him, "lay at the feet of the President of the Reich, like a rare catch, this masterpiece of his policy."[25] In January, 1932, he had an interview with the Fuehrer and tried to bring him around. But his plan failed. Schleicher was no more successful a few months later in taming the moderate wing of National Socialism (Gregor Strasser) and in reconciling it with the moderate wing of the labor movement (Leipart).

The *Fertigindustrie* understood finally that National Socialism had become an independent force that could not be restrained—except by the use of armed force. But the general interests of the owning classes forbade that "national" forces tear each other to pieces.

On January 4, 1933, Hitler's coming to power had been decided upon at an interview between Papen and Hitler, in the house of a big Cologne banker, von Schroeder, who had connections with Rhenish-Westphalian heavy industry.[26]

Thus on January 30, 1933, Chancellor Schleicher gave up the game, and German capitalism united to hold the Third Reich over the baptism font.

2

The middle classes considered as fascism's mass base

Fascism is not born solely from the desire and subsidies of capitalist magnates. "To declare," Silone correctly observes, "that these organizations are only a diabolic invention of finance capital, wishing to preserve its rule, is not enough for an understanding of the nature of these forces which rise from the depths of society."[1] Doubtless, in the beginning, when they are still playing merely the role of "anti-labor militia," the fascist bands recruit many adventurers with the mentality of mercenaries. But as fascism orientates itself towards the conquest of power and becomes a great mass movement, the motives that bring thousands of human beings to it become more complex and require painstaking analysis. The capitalist magnates could never, in spite of all their gold, have "set marching"[2] such human forces if the masses had not previously been in a state of instability and discontent that conditioned them for conquest.

As a matter of fact, in Italy as in Germany, the various social layers *intermediate between big capitalist bourgeoisie and organized proletariat*, who were victims of both the developments and the crisis of capitalism, were profoundly discontented with their condition,

47

material as well as moral. They dreamed of a radical change. At once the question arises: why did they not turn to socialism? This is what we are going to try to explain.

Let us first consider the urban middle classes.

1

The backbone of the fascist troops was the urban "middle classes."

Socialism long believed that these middle classes were doomed to disappear as a result of capitalist development itself; competition and the concentration of industry and capital would destroy their economic roots. "The lower strata of the middle class—the small tradespeople, shopkeepers, and retired tradesmen generally, the handicraftsmen and peasants," the *Communist Manifesto* of 1848 declared, "all these sink gradually into the proletariat . . . they even see the moment approaching when they will completely disappear as an independent section of modern society . . ." In actuality, the development has been somewhat different or, at least, much less rapid than socialism had expected. The middle classes have, it is true, suffered from competition and capitalist concentration. Their condition has grown worse; they have been impoverished, but they have not disappeared. The individuals making up the class have not all "sunk into the proletariat." They have not been *proletarianized* but only *pauperized*. They stubbornly persist, even today, in attempting to constitute "an independent section of modern society." The more they suffer, the more they cling to their existence as a class. Toward the end of the last century, Eduard Bernstein[3] noted that the small manufacturers, artisans, and tradesmen succeeded in maintaining themselves and even in increasing their numbers absolutely if not relatively. This does not mean of course that capitalist concentration is slowing down. The big enterprises are expanding more rapidly than the little producers or small tradesmen are increasing. The latter find the competition of the great monopolies ever harsher, *but they continue to exist.* Why this resistance? Because the independent producer prefers his condition, even though it becomes more precarious every day, to that of the proletariat—just as, for the same reason, proletarians continually escape from their own class and come to join the starving ranks of the middle classes.

The course of evolution predicted has been checked by still another factor. At a certain stage of its development, capitalism itself engenders middle classes of a new kind. Their characteristic, in comparison with older ones, is economic dependence. Unlike the independent petty bourgeois, the newcomers no longer control the greater part of their *instruments of production*. If they are not, properly speaking, *wage earners*, they live from salaries, fees or commissions.[4] Kautsky was the first to draw attention to them.[5] He showed how the heads of modern enterprises delegate a part of their functions to appointed workers—engineers, designers, technicians, doctors, lawyers, attached to the company. Furthermore, the great industrial combinations organize their own commercial outlets; they set up an army of distributors, agents, garage managers, repairmen, etc. The small artisan and little tradesmen can survive only by renouncing their independence and indirectly becoming wage earners. The small retailer becomes a branch manager for a chain store; the craftsman is reduced to the role of skilled worker, etc.

Although they have no economic independence, the individuals composing the "new" middle classes have by no means "sunk into the proletariat." As Lucien Laurat has written, "the work they do is of a particularly skilled nature and, although their remuneration takes the form of salary or wages, the fact remains that their directing function in the economic process brings many of them close to the capitalist class . . . An extremely large section of this social category . . . continues for the present to consider themselves *above* the proletariat."[6]

Long before the war, the condition of the *old* middle classes was growing constantly worse. As for the rapidly growing *new* middle classes, they painfully felt their economic dependence and saw, with apprehension, the day approaching when they would be reduced to the status of the wage earner, pure and simple.

2

The war accelerated both the *pauperization* of the "old" middle classes and the *proletarianization* of the "new." The war was financed in great part by the holders of small savings. Monetary devaluation and the funding of government debts cut off the income of small investors; the little taxpayers were crushed by tax levies; the salaries of functionaries and office employees were not increased proportionately; the shrinkage in buying power of the masses diminished the business of the little merchants; the competition of monopoly capital remorselessly drove the small independent manufacturers to the wall; technicians came more and more to feel themselves the slaves of the corporations that employed them. These symptoms, observable in all the postwar capitalist countries, appeared with particular violence in Italy, and still more in Germany.

In Italy

The fall of the lira (1919–1920) cruelly squeezed the owners of fixed income. Their condition appeared all the more painful to the small investors, the holders of pensions, and those retired, because the proletariat had obtained, thanks to union action, a partial readjustment of its wages. At the same time the economic crisis had driven many artisans and small merchants into bankruptcy. Industrial concentration, which had already whipped up, was going on faster than ever. As to the lot of the middle classes, Russo writes: "receiving incomes much lower than those of wage earners, and forced to support much greater expenses both for their living and their education, their life after the war became a daily torture. Too refined to adapt themselves to the narrow existence of the proletariat, too poor to bear the burden of continually increasing prices, they felt themselves caught in pincers that were slowly crushing them . . . Mistreated by governments whose least concern was to satisfy their needs, exploited by the newly rich who had built its fortunes on the ruins of their own . . . the middle classes felt they were losing every day a little of their rank and former superiority."[7]

In Germany

The fate of the German middle classes was still more tragic. While under the Empire they enjoyed "appreciable material security and moral prestige,"[8] the total collapse of the mark bled them white. Those with fixed incomes and savings were reduced to the blackest misery. After the stabilization of the mark, the public loans of the Reich, the states, and the municipalities, were revaluated at only about 12.5 percent of their original value (law of April 1925).[9] "Whole social strata of respected professions fell to the level of the proletariat in spite of the desperate resistance by individuals to their fate," writes Moeller van den Bruck.[10] The salaries or fees of functionaries or office employees were reduced far more than the wages of workers in industry. A professor was paid less than a proletarian. After the inflation, 97 percent of the Germans were without capital.

Then came the "rationalization," which took the form of accentuated concentration and trustification. The middle classes suffered as consumers. They had to pay artificially raised prices for manufactured products; the little manufacturers and artisans were put out of business by the competition of the trusts and cartels, and the banks gave them credit only at exorbitant rates; the small merchants were hard hit by the increase in big stores and chain stores, and by the appearance of "one-price stores."

Big stores such as Tietz, Wertheim, and Karstadt embarked on an increasing number of activities (hair dressing parlors, bathing establishments, food shops, fish shops, butcher shops, tea rooms, restaurants, dressmaking shops, manufacturing and repair shops of all sorts). After 1925 the one-price stores multiplied in all the large and medium sized towns. In 1931 three companies (one founded by Karstadt, another by Tietz, and the third by the American Woolworth Company) alone owned 250 shops. The one-price stores were very successful owing to the cheapness of their goods, made possible by the purchase of stocks at advantageous prices and by the rapid turnover of their capital.[11]

Technicians and members of the liberal professions came more and more to feel themselves the house servants of big capital. Reduced to the rank of intellectual laborers, they were nothing but "a number in the factory."[12] As for the small shareholders, they were increasingly swallowed up by the capitalist magnates. The creation of new preferred stocks with multiple voting power took from them all means of control and expression; they no longer had a voice and were forced to be content with the miserable dividends alloted them.

In 1929 the minister Stresemann cried out: "If we go on this way much longer, we shall have nothing but the trusts on one side and millions of employees and workers on the other. . . . It [the middle] is today almost completely proletarianized."[13]

With the crisis of 1930, the third station of the cross began for the middle classes. They suffered more severely from it than did the proletariat, which was protected to a certain extent by union contracts and unemployment allowances. The situation of small commerce and industry became desperate. Office workers and technicians often saw their salaries sink lower than those of skilled workers. They were thrown into the street like authentic proletarians. Some of them were the sons of investors already ruined by the inflation— the "old" and the "new" middle classes were united in a common distress.[14] As the stock market quotations continued to fall, the small fortunes, rebuilt after the stabilization of the mark, were dissipated.

3

In Italy, as in Germany, the sufferings of the middle classes drove them to revolt. The petty bourgeois is ordinarily of a peaceful temperament. As long as his economic situation is endurable, or he has hope that it can be improved, he is respectful of the established order and looks for the improvement of his condition through *reforms*. But when he must abandon all hope of improvement by legal and peaceful methods, when he perceives that the crisis from which he is suffering is not passing but is a crisis of the whole social system, and one that can be resolved only by a radical transformation of this system, then "he is easily enraged" and "ready to give himself over to the most extreme measures."[15]

But it is a known fact that the middle classes are prevented by their heterogeneity and their position between the two fundamental classes of society—the bourgeoisie and the proletariat—from having a political policy of their own. Their revolt does not have an autonomous character. It can be exploited by the bourgeoisie or the proletariat.

Here we find ourselves faced with the crucial question: *Why do not the middle classes, ruined and despoiled by big capital, hold out their hands to the anti-capitalist class par excellence, the proletariat? Why do they not become socialist?*

We must first remember that between the middle classes and the organized working class there has long been a certain amount of antipathy and disagreement which the bourgeoisie has not failed to maintain and aggravate cunningly, to its advantage.

1) From the dawn of capitalism, the interests of the middle classes have been in sharpest conflict with the industrial and financial big bourgeoisie, and after the war the middle classes became frankly *anti-capitalist*. But their anti-capitalism was somewhat different from that of the proletariat. Proletarian socialism aims straight at the heart of capitalism. It wishes to destroy its motive force—the exploitation of labor power and the theft of surplus value. Hence it attacks the capitalist system as a whole, and proposes as a goal the socialization of the means of production. But the middle classes are not the victims of the exploitation of labor power but chiefly of competition and the organization of credit. Hence, when left to themselves, when their anti-capitalism is not given direction by proletarian socialism, they tend to have *reactionary* aspirations. They do not demand that capitalist development be pushed to its ultimate conclusion, the socialization of the means of production. They want "to roll back the wheel of history."[16] "They call for an economy that is not dynamic or progressive but a routine economy. They want the state to regulate economic freedom and activity in order to restrict the competitive capacity of their rivals."[17] They dream of a modified capitalism, freed from the abuses of concentration, credit, and speculation.

On the other hand the technicians and office employees of the big industrial consortiums have anti-capitalist aspirations closer to those of the proletarian. "Many wish," writes Herisson, "for the nationalization of those big enterprises that have not succeeded in winning their loyalty. They hope that as functionaries they would achieve material advantages, moral prestige, and security. Their anti-capitalism is much more socialistic than that of the tradesmen."[18]

While proletarian socialism is breaking the framework of private property, now grown too narrow, the middle classes cling to an archaic conception of property. And the capitalist bourgeoisie, while daily expropriating them without pity, poses before the middle classes as the defender of sacrosanct property and erects as a scarecrow, socialism . . . that denies property."

2) Furthermore, the middle classes are passionately attached to their class privileges, and after the First World War their increasing impoverishment only aggravated that attachment. The petty bourgeois has an invincible repugnance for the working class and the condition of the proletariat. In *Mein Kampf*, Hitler makes this characteristic confession: "For people of modest situation who have once risen above that social level, it is unendurable to fall back into it even momentarily." The middle classes were not resigned to being *proletarianized*. "The more their belief in their own social value is threatened, the more they attempt to consolidate their position. The most poverty-stricken functionary, the most debt-ridden shopkeeper, continues to consider himself a member of a class superior to the proletariat, even if he makes less than the majority of industrial workers."[19] The "white-collar proletarian," whose employer has imbued him with "a false feeling of bourgeois respectability,"[20] is likewise hostile to the industrial workers. He envies them for earning more than he, and tries at the same time to differentiate himself from them by every means. He does not understand why proletarian socialism speaks of destroying classes; he trembles for his illusory class privileges. Wishing to escape at any price from the proletarianization that lies in wait for him, he has scarcely any sympathy for a socialist regime which, according to him, would complete his

proletarianization. He is ready, on the other hand, to listen to those who promise to save him from that fate—or, if it has already taken place, who promise to "de-proletarianize" him.

3) The capitalist bourgeoisie tries to align the middle classes against the organized proletariat. It utilizes the fact that any wage increase obtained by union action raises costs for small enterprises more than those of big corporations, and that taxes necessary for the state's "social expenditures," also have more effect on the costs of small producers than on those of the big companies. Finally the capitalist bourgeoisie incites the small shopkeeper against the workers' cooperatives (this was particularly true in Italy and Germany, where socialist cooperatives reached a sizeable growth after the First World War).

4) The idea of the class struggle, the basis of proletarian socialism, is at first not understood by the petty bourgeois. For him, unlike the worker, the capitalist exploiter "remains anonymous, unperceived, hidden behind the curtain of free transactions."[21] When he defends his threatened interests, he does it with the same mentality as the capitalist he opposes: one individual struggling against another individual. There is a conflict of interests; there is no class struggle. The position of the middle classes between the bourgeoisie and the proletariat explains why they tend to condemn all class struggle—that waged by the bourgeoisie against the proletariat as well as that waged by the proletariat against the bourgeoisie. They are persuaded that class collaboration is possible, that there is a *general interest* above all antagonistic interests. And by general interests they mean their own interests, intermediate between those of the capitalist bourgeoisie and those of the proletariat. They dream of a "state above classes," which will not be in the service of either the proletariat or the bourgeoisie, and consequently will be in their own service. But while the proletariat proclaims the reality of the class struggle between capital and labor, the capitalist bourgeoisie carries on the class struggle behind the mask of "class collaboration," and often succeeds in turning the middle classes away from socialism.

5) Another misunderstanding between the middle classes and the proletariat is found in the idea of the *nation*. While the worker, rootless and owning only the strength of his arm, "has no fatherland," the petty bourgeois gives what he possesses the name of fatherland. To defend the fatherland is for him to defend his property, his workshop, his merchandise, his government bonds. But while the proletariat is inclined towards internationalism, the capitalist bourgeoisie, for whom money has no fatherland, decks itself out in the "national" mask, and succeeds in duping the middle classes.

Particularly after the First World War, the chauvinism of the middle classes was fanned, in Italy, by the disappointments of the "mutilated victory," and in Germany by the humiliation of defeat. The Italian and German middle classes were successfully persuaded that the principal cause of their misery was the "unjust treaties," or the *Diktat* of Versailles. These good people came to hate, not the capitalist system, which was really responsible for their wretchedness, or the representatives of this system in their own countries, but the "international plutocracy." Anti-capitalism and chauvinism, national liberation and social liberation, became confused in their minds. On the other hand, during this same period, the workers, tired of the war and full of enthusiasm for the Russian Revolution, rejected the gory idol of the "fatherland" and placed all their hope in the International.

However, despite these misunderstandings and antipathies, so skilfully fostered and inflamed by the capitalist bourgeoisie, proletarian socialism in both Italy and Germany could have neutralized or even won over a large section of the suffering and rebellious middle classes. It could have done so—not by disowning itself and making concessions that would render its program unrecognizable. The middle classes' hand is easily forced: had the working class shown itself bold and determined to transform the social order from top to bottom and to show them a way out of their distress, they would have overcome their reluctance. But in both Italy and Germany the working class parties did not want, or did not know how, to struggle against the existing system.

In Italy

After the war a rather large section of the battered middle classes placed their hope in socialism. In the 1919 election, the ballots of the petty bourgeois were cast with those of the workers in greater numbers than ever before. When the metal workers occupied the factories in 1920, they had the sympathy of a great part of the petty bourgeoisie. But the Socialist Party showed itself absolutely incapable of leading the revolutionary upsurge of the masses. Instead of placing itself at their head, it dragged in their wake. In Mussolini's own words, it did not know how "to profit from a revolutionary situation such as history does not repeat."[22]

In Germany

Large layers of the middle classes voted for the Social Democracy in 1919 for the first time, while office workers and functionaries joined the unions. In 1923, at the time of the Ruhr occupation and the monetary collapse, many ruined and desperate petty bourgeois came over to communism. But big capital was not defeated in Germany either in 1919 or 1923. In January, 1919, the Social Democratic leaders crushed the *Spartakist* insurrection in blood; in October, 1923, a new betrayal by the Social Democracy, to which was added the vacillating and zigzagging policy of the Communist International, paralyzed the fighting spirit of the masses and led to another fiasco. Finally, after 1930, neither of the two parties claiming to be working class profited from the crisis of capitalism by destroying the "system" and conquering power.

The working class disappoints the middle classes by showing itself incapable of finding a way out of the crisis. In addition, it exasperates the middle classes by its day-to-day economic struggles, which are too fragmentary and timid to even maintain past gains, but which are quite sufficient to maintain a state of instability without curing any of the ills of society as a whole. So the middle classes do an about-face and blame not only the trusts, but also the workers for their economic stagnation. The organized Right then only has to exploit this resentment against the workers. But the traditional bourgeois parties, such as the Nationalist Party in Italy or the German National Party in Germany, can hardly play this role since their avowed program is preservation of the status quo. So the bourgeoisie changes its methods. It disguises itself and subsidizes a political formation of a new kind—fascism. Fascism, far from declaring itself in the service of the existing order, claims to seek its overthrow. The better to dupe the middle classes, it professes to be anti-capitalist, even revolutionary. Thus capitalism accomplishes the *tour de force* of channeling for its own benefit the revolt of the middle classes, which should have been directed against it, and of enrolling its own victims in organizations whose real aim is the defense of its privileges!

4

Let us now consider the rural middle classes.

It is well known that the peasants, although they constitute a homogeneous class with identical interests, seldom have a political policy of their own. Their intermediary position between the fundamental classes of society, the fact that they are scattered, which prevents them from having contacts with each other and from assembling, and also their individualism, are unfavorable to the formation of a purely peasant political movement. The peasant oscillates between two poles of attraction, the socialist proletariat and the great landed proprietors.

Unlike the urban middle classes, they do not feel that they belong to a different class from the workers. Was not the worker himself a peasant yesterday, or the son of a peasant? The peasant is conscious of belonging, like the worker, to the *people*. He is not far from being a socialist in his hatred of the landed feudalism that monopolizes the land, and the great capitalism to which he pays tribute (fertilizer trusts, agricultural machinery trusts, seed trusts, electric power companies, big speculators, banks, insurance companies, etc.). But the capitalist bourgeoisie tries to arouse the peasant against the worker. It claims the proletarian socialist program would socialize the land, and it makes the peasant tremble for his bit of soil. It utilizes the fact that under the capitalist system higher wages in industry bring increased living costs, and that governmental "social expenditures" call for higher taxes. Finally, the bourgeoisie seeks to convince the peasant that he and the big landowner have common interests. It utilizes the conflict that exists under capitalism between the interests of agriculture and industry. Agriculture wants to be protected by higher tariffs and to sell its products as dearly as possible. Industry is hostile: first, to the high prices of agricultural commodities which increase living costs and consequently burden its own cost prices; and second, to an excessive protective tariff which would deprive it as a result of reprisals, of its foreign markets. Hence an attempt is made to persuade the peasant that as a farmer he has common interests with the big landowner to defend against industry.

The peasant can, then, according to circumstances, be drawn into either of the two "blocs," that of all agriculturalists from the poor peasant to the great landed proprietor, or that of all the victims of capitalism from the poor peasant to the proletarian. If the socialist proletariat knows how to resolutely wage the struggle against the feudal landowner and the great capitalist monopolies; if it shows itself to be the most "dynamic," it can clear up all the misunderstandings and draw large masses of poor peasants behind it. If, on the contrary, the initiative comes from the big landed proprietors; if these show themselves to be the most audacious and appear to energetically defend the interests of the poor peasantry, they will draw into their wake the masses of small landowners.

The latter is what happened in Italy and Germany.

In Italy

The independent peasants were in a minority. Italy has remained a country of large estates. About 60 percent of the agricultural population has no economic independence and can be assimilated into the proletariat; they are agricultural laborers or tenants. As for the "independent peasants," their independence is entirely relative; they are either farmers who, while owning their instruments of labor, their cattle, their working capital, do not own land; or they are very small landowners, so poor that many of them have to work outside their own morsel of land as hired laborers.

After the First World War, socialism could have conciliated or at least neutralized this rather thin layer of independent peasants. The small landowner and farmer are eager to increase their holdings or to achieve ownership of the land. By demanding "division of the land," they directly attack the great landed proprietors. But the Socialist Party did not dare fight the big landowners, and concealed its inertia under ultraleftist phraseology. Not only did it fail to support the peasants in their struggle for the land, but it warned them on the contrary that the proletarian revolution would take the land from them.[23] Hence at one congress, a leader of the Federation of Agricultural Workers declared that the Italian Socialists were "more revolutionary than the Bolsheviks, who had betrayed socialism by giving the land to the peasants."[24] The congress of the Federation of Labor in February, 1921, adopted, purely as a matter of form, a plan for "socializing the land," which they very well knew would never be passed by parliament and which offered the small farmers and tenant farmers on the land intended for expropriation only the prospect of "becoming proletarians." This plan, as Rossi wrote, turned "millions of peasant families, the great majority of the rural population of Italy" against socialism.[25]

The result was that the peasants turned away from the socialist proletariat. The poorest rallied to the Catholic party (*Popolare*), which easily controlled their spirit of revolt until it was time to hand them over to fascism. The others passed directly into the camp of the big landowners, the defenders of property.

But if the latter had shown their real faces and sponsored a conservative party of the traditional type, they would not have won the peasants so easily. Hence they disguised themselves and subsidized a new kind of political formation, the *fasci*. The latter declared themselves revolutionary and even took for their own the demagogic slogan "land for those who till it." They went even further: in certain regions, Rossi relates, they succeeded in persuading the big landowners' association to lease some tens of thousands of hectares of land—the poorest of course—directly to individual farmers, thus enabling the fascists to boast: "You see, the socialists promised you everything and gave you nothing; they prevented you even from becoming independent farmers. The *fasci* have installed hundreds of families on their own land, which they can work all year round."[26] Thus the great landed proprietors succeeded in enlisting the peasantry in defense of their own privileges.

In Germany

Small landholdings are much more widespread than in Italy. They go back to the beginning of the nineteenth century (legislation of von Stein and Hardenberg). About 28 percent of the rural population is without economic independence (agricultural laborers), but approximately 55 percent are small peasants owning not more than five hectares. These small proprietors predominate in the South and West. On the other hand, in the East (Pomerania, East Prussia, Brandenburg, Silesia) big estates predominate; some 18,000 Junkers own 20 percent of the German soil.

After World War I, the socialist movement could have won over or at least neutralized a large part of the German peasantry. In January, 1919, the small peasants voted in large numbers for the Social Democracy and set up "peasants' councils," after the pattern of the "councils of workers and soldiers." As in Italy, their essential demand was the division of the big estates—*Siedlung* (colonization). Rosa Luxemburg and the first German Communists advocated an alliance of the proletariat and peasantry on the basis of division of the big estates and the elimination of the landed aristocracy.[27] But their Spartakus League was crushed, and the Social Democracy was careful not to wage a struggle against the landowners. In its passion to destroy Communism, it enlisted the aid of all the forces of reaction and especially the army, which means the aristocratic caste.

A "colonization law" was promulgated April 11, 1919, by the terms of which the state could buy two-thirds of estates larger than a hundred hectares. But the state bureaucracy sabotaged the law, and the Social Democracy did not even attempt to force its application. Likewise a Prussian law of March 10, 1919, dissolved the entailed seignorial domains, but that law was almost cancelled out by a decree in November 1921. By 1933, only one-third of the hereditary domains had been broken up.

Thus at a decisive hour the proletariat did not succeed in attaching the peasantry to itself, and later the indifference of the peasants was transformed into open hostility. After 1929, in fact, German agriculture fell into an extremely serious crisis. To understand this crisis, it must be remembered that Germany was not originally an agricultural country. Good land is rare. Costly efforts are necessary to make the northern plains profitable, where forests, sand, and marshlands alternate.[28] In this country of astounding industrial development, the unevenness of development between agriculture and industry is more marked than in other capitalist countries. On the eve of the war this lack of balance found, on the one side, industry at the zenith of its development, and on the other, agriculture more than sixteen billion marks in debt.

Although during the war and the inflation, German agriculture had an artificial boom and freed itself from the greater part of its debts, the old differences between agriculture and industry soon reappeared, and the agriculturalists began to go into debt again. While industry advanced with giant strides, agriculture strove in vain to follow it. "Rationalization" of farming was on the order of the day; foreign capital was offered in abundance. The tillers of the soil, who had emptied their woolen stockings during the period of inflation, had to borrow at high rates. After having paid tribute to American lenders and German banks, they paid a heavy toll to the big national fertilizer and farm machinery trusts. The yield from cultivation continued to increase, the herds to multiply; but these improvements were profitable only in appearance. "Every year the burden weighing on agriculture grew heavier, and the hope of amortizing the debt became fainter."[29] The least favored farmers could not even embark on an attempt at "rationalization." They continued to employ the same backward methods of cultivation and borrowed, not in an attempt to increase their return, but simply to pay their daily expenses and their taxes.[30]

The result? The sum of agricultural debt rose regularly every year, from a billion and a half in 1925 to almost six billion in 1928 and to twelve billion in 1930. As long as market prices—although none too profitable—held up, and the abundance of foreign capital made it possible to pay off debts by contracting new loans, the farmers were not aware of their real situation. But during the summer of 1929 farm prices began to weaken much faster than industrial prices. German agriculture entered the crisis, and—a vital fact—*the little and middle peasants were harder hit than the big landowners.* It is one of the peculiarities of German agriculture that feed and grain are grown chiefly by the large landowners, while the small peasants have specialized more in raising cattle and producing dairy and poultry products—butter, eggs, milk, cheese, etc. The Junkers had succeeded in obtaining, especially after 1930, strong tariff protection on grains, which prevented the market quotations from collapsing. On the other hand, the small cattle raisers were not protected because industry was opposed to raising the duty on secondary products for fear of foreign reprisals. Not only were the small farmers in an unfavorable position in comparison with the big landowners, but they had to buy the feed and grain necessary to feed their cattle at prices that had stayed high. Finally, the landowners were maintained by all sorts of state subsidies, particularly the famous *Osthilfe,* while the small peasants were abandoned to their fate. The agricultural taxes (a billion marks in 1932 as compared with 750 million in 1929) hit the small and middle peasants almost exclusively.

Hence the German peasants were literally ruined. Would their sufferings bring them closer to the proletariat? In Weimar Germany, the Social Democracy was a government party; in Prussia it was even in power. It was the Social Democracy, the "system," the "social expenditures," that the peasants considered responsible for their misery. Overwhelmed with taxes, pitilessly pursued by the treasury, driven to forced sales, they arose against the existing order. After 1928, in Schleswig-Holstein, the peasants, taking as their emblem the black flag, revolted against the state apparatus, the tax collector, and the sheriff. They first used the weapon of passive resistance, of "non-cooperation." The tax strike started in Schleswig and spread throughout the North of Germany, as far as Silesia and East Prussia. The Socialist government of Prussia replied by imprisoning the principal instigators of the movement, which then turned to terrorism. Tax offices were attacked, bombs thrown.

That was the moment the big landowners chose to suggest to the small peasants that all "agriculture" was in solidarity against "industry" and should defend itself. They promised the small cattle raiser to help him to obtain the same tariff protection from which their own grain already benefited. They tried to enlist him in a "peasant defense" association, the *Gruene Front* (Green Front).

But the Green Front was an organization too openly dominated by the big landowners, too frankly serving their interests. Consequently it was unable to attract the mass of revolting peasants. Then the Junkers, who had more than one trick in their bags, disguised themselves; they subsidized a new kind of political formation, the National Socialist Party. National Socialism claimed to devote itself particularly to the defense and rescue of the small peasantry and even demanded the "colonization" of the big estates. By means of this subterfuge, the Junkers succeeded in enlisting the small peasants for the defense of their own privileges.

5

Fascism also recruits from two other social categories composed of individuals belonging to different classes but having certain economic interests and moral aspirations in common: the *war veterans* and the *youth*.

The war veterans have in common certain material claims against the state (payment of war pensions), and this community of interests leads them to organize. But there are other sentiments and memories that also help to unite them—what has been called the "comradeship of the front," and the "spirit of the trenches."

Demobilized and back home after the war, they were prey to deep discontent; many of them could not adapt themselves to civilian life. Even when they got back their former employment, they were "weary, restless, disappointed."[31] It was painful for them to "return to the monotony of average existence, divided between work, the family, and a game of cards in the corner cafe."[32] The most disoriented were those who could not find a job again or, because they had not completed their studies, lacked a profession. To them must be added the former commissioned and non-commissioned officers who were retired (160,000 officers were put on the retired list in Italy in 1920; and many more in Germany). And finally, there were those who carried back from the war a physical need for violence, a need they could no longer satisfy in the prosaic existence of peace times.[33] All were hostile to the existing order of things; they were irritated because the nation, which they had defended at the cost of their blood, did not give them the rank they expected. They felt a confused need for political and social regeneration.

These aspirations might, in certain respects, have brought them closer to the organized proletariat and socialism. But between them and socialism there were a number of differences. The comradeship of the front, born of equality before death, was of a quite different nature from proletarian comradeship, and was unwilling to recognize the class struggle. The war veteran reproached socialism for insisting on the reality of the class struggle. Furthermore, the confused hatred the war veteran preserved for "those behind the lines" was two-edged—almost socialist when its target was the war profiteer and the bourgeois politician responsible for prolonging the great slaughter, but anti-socialist when its target was the militant workers labeled "defeatist" and "pacifist."

Nevertheless, socialism after the war could have guided the discontent of the war veterans. It was certainly impossible for it, without self-betrayal, to make concessions to the "trench spirit" and to give "the fraternity of the front" precedence over class solidarity. Nor could socialism, in order to pamper the war veterans, renounce its internationalism. But if it had displayed audacity, had it known how to link hatred of war and the war profiteer to the revolutionary idea, and had it shown itself determined to overthrow the capitalist system responsible for the great butchery and bring on that "better human civilization" for which so much blood had been shed— doubtless socialism could have attracted many war veterans. But it did not do so. It showed itself incapable of action. To these men eager for a new order, it appeared to be a superannuated and fossilized movement.

It was fascism which offered satisfaction to the aspirations of the war veterans (Chapter 3).

6

Similarly, the *youth* have in common both a tragic material fate— unemployment—and an aspiration of a sentimental order: that youth should be considered an autonomous factor in society.

In so-called "normal" times, the bourgeois youth and the young proletarian have little in common. The student, of a bourgeois or petty bourgeois family, remains in the college or university classroom until he is fairly old, often well beyond his twentieth year. During the long years of study, he is not integrated into the productive process, and he has no economic independence, for instead of supporting his family, his family supports him. He is a sort of parasite, not yet a productive citizen. Hence he has the illusion of belonging to a special category. He differentiates himself from adults and believes he has interests to defend against them. He talks a great deal about the "aspirations of youth." In all periods, the common trait of this student youth has been impatience and envy. The young doctor, lawyer, or artist must wait for many years before entering his chosen career. They form a union of malcontents against the elders who bar their road.

Thus in Italy, around 1910, the intellectual and student youth was *futurist*, with the poet Marinetti. These young people could differentiate themselves only by stressing their youth, and inscribing the word "youth" on their banners. They knew only one thing: their impatience in the face of the future. Their bugbear was the adult, the man in office, the "has-been." "The oldest among us is not yet thirty! Let us hasten to make everything over. We must go against the stream!"[34] Such was their *leitmotiv*.

In Germany, from 1900 to 1914, the intellectual and student youth was organized in the *Jugendbewegung* (youth movement), in order to assert, in opposition to the "mature in years," the autonomy and mission of youth. Very characteristic is the letter of invitation to the congress of 1913, held on the Hohen Meissner, near Kassel, by 10,000 young people: "For the older generations, youth has been up to the present only an accessory. It has been excluded from public life, reduced to the passive role of learning while mured away in stupid sociability. Now it is beginning to become conscious of itself and is striving to build its own life, independently of the cowardly habits of its elders . . . *It aspires to act as an autonomous factor in the social community.*"[35]

With the young worker, on the contrary, the idea of class is more important than the idea of age. As soon as he comes from the elementary school, there is nothing to distinguish the youth from the adult. On the job, young and old are subjected to the same exploitation. Often the young worker is the support of the family. He has passed, without transition, from childhood to maturity; he is already a man.

But after the war, in both Italy and Germany, the lot of the young bourgeois (or petty bourgeois) and young proletarian was almost identical: all young people, *without distinction,* were victimized by the crisis.

1) As a result of the economic crisis, the position of the intellectual and student youth became most precarious. Their particular "aspirations" were thereby intensified.

In Italy, the demobilized youth, whose studies had been interrupted, as well as the new graduates, had the greatest difficulty in finding or getting back a position. Their families were severely affected by the monetary depreciation and the high cost of living. Furthermore, the war, which they had experienced either as soldiers or behind the lines, had given them a taste for adventure. Their quality of youth had been exalted: "Youth, youth, springtime of beauty," sang the Arditi in their hymn *Giovinezza* ("Youth") which was adopted by the fascists. Now they were idle, rudderless, eager for action.

In Germany, the economic crisis which began at the end of 1929 plunged young students and intellectuals into terrible distress. Their ruined families could no longer afford to pay for their studies, and they could not work with their hands. As for the graduates, they had no hope of finding positions. The candidates for government employment had to wait until they were twenty-seven or even thirty years old, and only 20 percent of the applicants were examined. For 24,000 diplomas granted, there were 10,000 positions offered. These young people, demoralized and rebellious, hated a society that forbade them to use their talents and condemned them to inaction.

2) Unemployment crushed the proletarian youth. Rootless and declassed, rejected by the productive process, and transformed into a parasite, the young unemployed was placed in an economic and moral position quite similar to that of the young student. The solidarity of age brought closer together all the youth reduced to idleness and despair. They rebelled against the injustice of their lot, and demanded a social system under which youth would no longer be sacrificed.

The phenomenon was especially striking in Germany where, in 1932, 26 percent of the unemployed were less than twenty-four years old. Large numbers of young proletarians had to abandon the family roof and wander through the streets and the highways, without hope of finding work again, or without having ever worked. Uprooted, declassed, often delinquent, these young vagabonds no longer expected their salvation from the action and triumph of their class. They joined the army of unemployed young intellectuals.

In Italy, and especially in Germany, socialism could have won over a great part of this desperate youth. It was obviously impossible for socialism—without self-betrayal—to take a stand on the fallacious ground of "youth in itself" and to give the idea of age precedence over the idea of class. But it would have been sufficient for it to display strength and audacity. Youth naturally has a love for risk and sacrifice, and a contempt for danger. The boldest, most idealistic movement, the one demanding the greatest sacrifice, and showing itself the most capable of overturning the existing system which is responsible for their distress, would be the one to win them. If socialism had shown itself the most "dynamic," it not only would have prevented the young workers from deserting their class, but it would have attracted a number of young intellectuals and students into the proletarian army.

But the socialist movement did not show itself revolutionary and ceased to be a pole of attraction. It was fascism, playing skilfully on the youth mystique, which won over not only the intellectual youth, but also—what was far more serious—many declassed unemployed youth.

Finally, fascism recruited a certain number of proletarians. Although it did not succeed in making an impression on the great masses of the proletariat (Chapter 8), it did succeed in detaching from the working class certain categories of workers who, for various reasons, lacked class consciousness. In a period of crisis, a strong and daring working class vanguard gathers around it all the peripheral layers of the proletariat. But if the vanguard lacks energy and dynamic force, the class decomposes and falls apart. That is what happened in Italy and Germany.

The corruption took place both from *above* and *below*. From *above*, fascism recruited from those known as the "aristocracy of labor." It succeeded in attracting a certain number of proletarians who had become "bourgeoisified," and who already considered themselves above their class. These persons remain faithful to labor organizations as long as it is necessary to belong to them in order to get work, or as long as they insure a decent living standard. But when labor organizations lose their influence or are no longer capable of insuring this living standard, these workers abandon and betray them. In Germany, especially, National Socialism gathered in those formerly privileged wage earners who blamed the Social Democracy and the unions for not having been able to achieve their petty-bourgeois ideal.[36]

From *below,* fascism recruited those who had recently become proletarian—peasants' sons freshly arrived from the country, who had not had time to acquire class consciousness, and workers transformed by modern technique into unskilled labor, moving indiscriminately from one branch of industry to another, no longer having a trade or professional pride, remaining on the fringe of the labor organizations and, consequently, predisposed to desert their class.[37] Through them, in Italy as in Germany, fascism was introduced into the factories.[38]

From *below* also fascism recruited the unemployed. The unemployed rejected by the productive process is on the fringe of his class, the ties uniting him to his brother workers are loosened and soon there is no longer an identity but an opposition of interests between him and the worker on the job. Poverty and inactivity demoralize him, frequently even degrade him. He despairs for himself and his class. He is ready to betray his class for a mouthful of bread.

Finally, fascism recruits a certain number of *outcasts* from the working class—the "scabs," those eternally rebelling against labor organization, who are always ready to lick the boss's boots, to act as stool-pigeons, to accept wages below union rates, to break strikes: and on the other hand, those that Marx called the *lumpenproletariat,* that is, the ragged bums—those who are voluntarily declassed, who remain outside their class and betray it because they do not want to work and because they hate a revolution that will force everybody to work.

In Italy, tramps and ex-convicts met in Mussolini's "squadrons of action." There they took characteristic nicknames: "The Savages," "The Damned," "The Desperate."[39] There they could freely satisfy their depraved instincts while feeling assured of absolute immunity from punishment.[40] A former fascist, Aniante, evoking memories of 1924, writes: "On that day I truly felt that Mussolini and fascism had called upon the dregs of society."[41]

In the Hitler storm troops there was the same stench of refuse. The case of Horst Wessel, a vulgar pimp transformed into a national hero, is symbolic. "All who live on the outskirts of the law," write D. and P. Benichou, "the adventurers, gangsters, and procurers, are drawn into the fascist movement . . . They are found from top to bottom in the Hitler organizations."[42]

The fascist leaders, in all ranks of the hierarchy, are in the image of their troops. For the most part they are *plebeians,* whether petty bourgeois or declassed proletarians. Out of 308 Italian fascist leaders of the party and of the "unions," 254 come from the petty bourgeoisie.[43] Mussolini began his career as a functionary; he was a country schoolteacher. "At the age of twenty," he told the Lombard steelworkers, "I worked with my hands. I was a laborer, and then a mason."[44] But Benito Mussolini is a proletarian of a very peculiar sort. Angelica Balabanoff, who knew him, defined him as a "declassed vagabond." A thwarted individualist, at heart he had only scorn for the class to which he temporarily belonged.

Hitler too is the son of a functionary, a customs officer. He dreamed of becoming an architect, but he was temporarily forced to work with his hands. "In Vienna," his panegyrists relate, "as a building laborer and mason's helper, he lived with the workers, worked, and struggled with them."[45] But he was an odd proletarian. His working companions—he himself confesses in *Mein Kampf*—inspired in him only disgust, and he was almost "dumped" off a scaffold for refusing to comply with union discipline.

The Duce and the Fuehrer are certainly grown in the image of their troops. Even in their success, they effortlessly preserve a plebeian manner and aspect which flatters and reassures their supporters. Hear the eyewitnesses: "The overall impression I received and which persists," wrote Daniel Halevy after a visit to Mussolini, "was that of a rather rough man, still very much of the people, scarcely well dressed and badly shaved . . . His vigor is great, strong as the beard that blackens his face in a few hours . . . .[46] And Georges Suarez, after having seen Hitler: "He went back to the station with a heavy step . . . He looked kind and vulgar . . . He was nothing more than a good mountaineer embarrassed by his hands . . . His heavy step, his ungraceful gesture, and his incredible lock of hair are so many signs in which a whole nation recognizes itself."[47]

From their origin, the fascist leaders from top to bottom of the hierarchy retain not only a plebeian aspect but a plebeian mentality. They are parvenus. They cordially hate and despise the big bourgeoisie who subsidize them. They try to supply the shortcomings of their own upbringing and education by demanding all sorts of deference for their persons. That is why, when the capitalist magnates entrusted them with the guidance of the state, they pitilessly eliminated the old political staff of the bourgeoisie and demanded *all the power* for themselves.

3

Fascist mysticism: the man
of destiny, the fatherland

Before all else, fascism offers its followers mysticism. Why is mysticism put first?

In the first place, because the fascist troops are not homogeneous; each social category to which fascism appeals has its own demands and aspirations. No doubt it uses anti-capitalist demagogy as a "pass-key," but it adds formulas intended specifically for the conscious proletarians, the peasants, et al. (Chapter 4). But this demagogy, often contradictory, is not enough to unite all these malcontents. First must be found the cement that will bind them together, an intentionally vague *mysticism* in which all, whatever their divergencies of interests or conceptions, can commune—a mysticism through which, in the words of a National Socialist, "the many individuals of an assembled crowd are amalgamated in spiritual unity, in a sentimental union."[1]

Moreover, fascism would rather arouse faith than address itself to the intelligence. A party supported by the subsidies of the propertied classes, with the secret aim of defending the privileges of property owners, is not interested in appealing to the intelligence of its recruits; or rather, it considers it prudent not to appeal to their understanding until they have been thoroughly bewitched. The moment the faithful *believe*, nothing is easier than to play with truth and logic. They will notice nothing. And if, by chance, they open their eyes, there will be no difficulty in closing them immediately with the argument: *It is so because the Leader says so!* Fascism, furthermore, is fortunate enough to address its appeal to the miserable and discontented. It is a psychological phenomenon, as old as the world, that suffering predisposes to mysticism. When man suffers, he renounces reason, ceases to demand logical remedies for his ills, and no longer has the courage to try to save himself. He expects a miracle and he calls for a savior, whom he is ready to follow, for whom he is ready to sacrifice himself.

Finally, fascism has the advantage—if we may say so—over socialism in that it despises the masses. It does not hesitate to conquer them through their weaknesses. Mussolini (he has boasted of it publicly) has had experience with the people which "has helped him very much," and "permitted him to know the psychology of crowds and have, so to speak, a tactile and visual perception of what they want and can do."[2] In addition to his personal experience, he knows by heart Doctor Le Bon's *Psychology of Crowds*, which is one of his bedside books: "Crowds are always feminine . . . They are incapable of having any opinions except those imposed on them . . . They are not led by rules based on pure theoretical equity but by seeking what can impress and seduce them . . . Crowds understand only simple and extreme sentiments . . . and can be impressed only by images."

Hitler has made the same observations: "The great majority of the people," he writes, "have a disposition so feminine that their opinions and actions are determined much more by the impression produced on their senses than by pure reflection. The masses . . . are little receptive to abstract ideas. On the other hand, they can be most easily taken hold of in the domain of the emotions. Whoever wishes to win the masses must know the key to their hearts. In all periods, the force that set in motion the most violent revolutions on this earth has lain less in the proclamation of a scientific idea which took possession of the crowds, than in a driving fanaticism and *a real hysteria which madly excited them.*"[3]

1

Thus fascism presents itself, above all, and even before trying to define itself, as a *religion.*

Religion seems to have originated among primitive peoples in the fear and anguish in the face of natural forces which man did not yet know how to control and which overwhelmed him. Subsequently, when he began a social existence, the need to believe in the supernatural is maintained by the misery that the exploiting classes force him to live in. Hope for life in heaven is compensation for the privations of life on earth.

In modern times, as man has learned to rule nature to lighten the burdens of everyday life, religion has concomitantly lost ground. But the crisis of capitalism plunges the masses into dismay and confusion analogous to what their distant ancestors must have experienced in the face of the incomprehensible unchained forces of nature. And since traditional religion, threadbare and too discredited by its ties to the wealthy, no longer always has any appeal left, an ersatz religion is manufactured, modernized and cut to the latest style. But even if the form is new, at bottom it is still the same old opium.

"Fascism is a religious conception," Mussolini states.[4] "If fascism were not a faith, how could it give its adherents stoicism and courage?"[5] "Nothing great can be accomplished except in a state of loving passion, of religious mysticism."[6] In Milan, a "School of Fascist Mysticism" was inaugurated, and a newspaper stated on this occasion: "Fascism is a reaction of the divine."[7] "I believe," enunciates the *Credo of the Balilla* "in our Holy Father, fascism."

Believe! is also the alpha and omega of the National Socialist religion. After taking power, Hitler thus addressed his troops: "You were the guard that formerly followed me with a *believing* heart. You were the first partisans who *believed* in me . . . It was not hair-splitting intelligence that led Germany out of her distress, but your *faith* . . . Why are we here? By command? No, because your *heart* ordered it; because an *inner voice* dictated it; because you *believe* in our movement and its leadership. Only the *force of idealism* could accomplish this . . . Reason would have advised you against coming to me, and only *faith* commanded you to do so!"[8]

Like all religions, this one consoles its followers for their miseries by preaching absolute scorn of the "material" and by giving "spiritual" nourishment precedence over that of the stomach. Fascism here, in short, only plagiarizes the Catholic Church: "What would it profit [man] to find . . . material abundance," asks Pope Leo XIII, "if a spiritual famine imperiled the salvation of his soul?"[9]

Mussolini writes that "fascism believes in saintliness and heroism, that is to say in deeds in which there is no economic motive, immediate or ultimate." He "rejects the idea of economic well-being which . . . would transform men into animals thinking of only one thing—being fed and fattened."[10]

Hitler likewise asserts: "The man who, for his satisfaction in life, needs nothing but to eat and drink has never understood him who sacrifices his daily bread to appease the thirst of his soul and the hunger of his spirit."[11]

2

But asceticism in itself is not enough consolation. Fascism's great discovery is merely the revival—again borrowing from the Church—of the oldest form of religious feeling, the cult of the *Man of Destiny.* Under the thin varnish of civilization, men remain idolaters. Those of old, imagined gods who were merely the "distorted reflection of their own being."[12] Those of today feel the need of creating, in the words of Marcel Martinet, "a redeeming myth which is only the projection of themselves, but which in return assumes the burden of their grievances, their needs, their thoughts, and their very life."[13] They abdicate before the divinity they have made in their own image, and await their salvation from the Man of Destiny, the Duce or the Fuehrer.

But this mythical being is not created spontaneously by the

masses. Fascism helps them along with a long and laborious process of suggestion. At first we see skillful charlatans, among them the future idol himself, working to bring to birth in the people's soul the obscure need for a messiah. Mussolini wrote in 1921 that during the coming decades "men would necessarily feel the desire for a dictator."[14] We await a savior who will lead us out of our misery, but nobody knows from where he will come," Thyssen states in 1922.[15] "We need a Fuehrer," sighed Moeller van den Bruck in 1923.[16] And Hitler himself: "Our task is to give the dictator, when he shall appear, a people ready for him."[17]

Then the Man of Destiny appears. But he is still only a mortal like the rest. He will be deified by degrees. He cannot, obviously, achieve this by himself, and, happily for him, those around him lend a hand. Every morning and evening his flatterers present him to the crowd as the Elect. At first they are not believed. Their attempts at canonization are really too crude, and arouse laughter. But they are patient, and time works for them. Ten times in succession they propose—without success—their messiah, but the eleventh time, the petty bourgeoisie begins to wonder: "After all, perhaps he is the savior!" Thus in Italy, Farinacci and a few others tirelessly *wove a myth* (the expression is Count Sforza's)[18] around Mussolini. In Germany, as early as February, 1921, Esser consecrated his friend Hitler as Fuehrer. Rosenberg and Goebbels carried on for years the work begun by Esser.

The man is then (still according to Sforza) "promoted to the rank of a demi-god." He is proclaimed infallible and omniscient. "Mussolini is always right," we read in the *Decalogue of the Militia Man*. And in the *Credo of the Balilla*, "I believe in the genius of Mussolini." "Adolf Hitler is a personality of universal genius," asserts Wilhelm Kube. "There is unquestionably no domain of human activity that the Fuehrer does not supremely dominate."[19] Goering said to a representative of the *Morning Post*, "Just as Catholics consider the Pope infallible in all questions of religion and morality, we believe with the same profound conviction that the Fuehrer is infallible in all matters concerning the moral and social interests of the people."[20] "One person is above all criticism, the Fuehrer!" exclaimed Rudolf Hess. "Everybody knows that he has always been right and that he always will be right."[21]

From this to worship, there is only a step, and it is quickly taken. In Italy, the official publication, *Milizia Fascista*, offers this instruction: "Remember to love God, but do not forget that Italy's God is the Duce."[22] Gentizon, Rome correspondent of the *Temps*, relates: "Peasants and their wives knelt on perceiving on a distant hill the tower where the Duce had just arrived for a brief stay . . . Already a halo of idealism and poetry envelops him. For some he has become a legendary figure. When he appears at a demonstration, the faces of many spectators seem to be illuminated."[23]

In Germany, Goebbels made himself the high priest of the new cult. "Faith in the Fuehrer," he said, "is surrounded, one almost might say, with a mysterious and enigmatic mysticism!"[24] He addresses Hitler in the style of a Father of the Church: "In our profound despair, we found in you the one who showed the road of faith . . . You were for us the fulfillment of a mysterious desire. You addressed to our anguish words of deliverance. You forged our confidence in the miracle to come."[25] When "his" Fuehrer had become master of Germany, he went still further and spoke to him as to God himself. On April 20, 1930, Hitler's birthday, he sent him this prayer over the radio: "Today *Thou* must know that behind *Thee*, and if necessary before *Thee*, stands a compact army of fighters who at any moment are ready to sacrifice themselves for Thee and Thy idea. . . . We promise Thee solemnly that Thou wilt always be for us what Thou art today: *Our* Hitler!"[26] Roehm called him a "new redeemer."[27] Hess affirmed that "this man will lead the German people without concerning himself with earthly influences."[28] "His will is in fact the will of God," wrote a panegyrist.[29]

3

There is something else this religion must have if it is to exercise its full attractive force on the masses. Fascism superimposes on the old cult of the Man of Destiny the more recent one of the father-land—the fatherland, "the terrible idol of our age," as Martinet says, "pseudonym for the masses themselves, in which the crowd adores its own power as a crowd."[30] We perceive how fascism profits from identifying the two cults. The leader henceforth appears as the nation incarnate, materialized; to worship the Man of Destiny is to worship the fatherland; to serve the fatherland is to serve the beloved leader. The zealots of the leader automatically become zealots of the national idea, and conversely zealots of the national idea become zealots of the leader. When finally power is won, the laws of the state will become personal orders of the Duce or Fuehrer.

In Italy

"Fascism is the religion of the fatherland," writes the Italian Gorgolini.[31] On the eve of the March on Rome, Mussolini himself declared: "Our myth is the nation. Our myth is the greatness of the nation!"[32] "A new religion," writes Gentizon, "is born in Italy . . . The divinity is the fatherland . . . The veneration displayed for it requires a whole sacred terminology. Read the fascist papers. On every page appear the expressions: *Holy Italy, Divine Italy!*"[33] The militiaman cries out in his daily prayer, "Lord, thou who lightest every flame and stoppest every heart, renew in me each day my passion for Italy!"

And the two cults now are but one. The prayer of the Italian militiaman ends with this supplication: "Lord, save Italy *in the person of the Duce.*"

In Germany

The word *Deutschland* has become a fetish before which a whole people kneels. When Hitler utters it, he goes into ecstasy and his speeches become veritable sermons. "I cannot separate myself from the faith of my people and the conviction that this nation will arise again; I cannot separate myself from the love of this people, which is my own, and the conviction that the hour will come when the millions of men behind us will see the new German Reich, the Reich of glory, honor, strength and justice. Amen!"[34] "The divine reality," exclaims Professor Hauer, "is the people and the national history!"[35] And Baldur von Schirach, leader of the Hitler youth, in celebrating the pagan festival of the Solstice, delivers this sermon: "Before the burning flame we all swear to devote ourselves to the service of the fatherland, for the greatness and purity of the eternal German empire."[36]

The mysticisms are now but one: "Adolf Hitler is Germany, and Germany is Adolf Hitler!" This will be the *leitmotiv* of National Socialism in power.[37]

4

Around this central mysticism, fascism maintains a certain number of collateral mysticisms, for instance the cult of the dead. Fascists fallen in the civil war are the object of constantly nourished veneration.

In Italy

"A tradition," writes the historian Volpe, "henceforth exists, *founded and strengthened by the dead.*"[38] Gentizon notes in one of his dispatches, "Those who died for the fatherland or the black-shirt revolution are *martyrs* for an ideal of which they were the *apostles.* In their memory, altars are raised, votive flames lighted, and rites celebrated."[39] "I believe," we read in the *Credo of the Balilla*, "in the communion of martyrs of fascism." A special room in the Exposition of the Fascist Revolution is dedicated to them. "From a circular gallery rises very soft singing, exalting the memory of those who have disappeared."[40]

In Germany

The first stanza of the *Horst Wessel Lied*, the official anthem of National Socialism, evokes the memory of the dead:

> Comrades, the victims of the Red Front and Reaction,
> March in spirit in our ranks.

Rosenberg wrote that "the sacrifice of all the dead for National Socialism makes it a religion."[41] This cult has, as in Italy, its grandiose ceremonies. Thus in 1935, the anniversary of the Munich putsch of 1923 was dedicated not only to the victims of the putsch but to all those who died for the party, to the number of 225. "In the street each has his special pillar with his name in golden letters. When the procession passes, a flame will be lighted in the urn at the top of each of these black-draped pylons."[42]

5

Another mysticism is that of the "youth." Fascism has skilfully taken over in Italy the heritage of Futurism, and in Germany that of the *Jugendbewegung* (Chapter 2); it exalts youth in itself, recognizes it as an "autonomous factor in the social community," and promises its support in the struggle against the adults, the "has-beens," and the old world.

In Italy

"There was in the early days of fascism," writes Volpe, "something higher than politics and its problems, and that was above all the youth, the Italian youth, the postwar youth, a youth overflowing as if the nation were being rejuvenated. The fascist revolution is in good part its work. Thus the myth of youth grew up, by virtue of which a man of forty almost has to beg pardon for existing."[43] Gentizon stresses that "fascism considered adolescence not only a transition period between childhood and manhood but a phase in itself, with special characteristics, requirements and necessities. Before fascism, Italian youth was, so to speak, an intermediary zone between the unconsciousness of the child and the career of the man. Fascism, however, *by giving it its own laws, has made it of value in itself.*"[44]

In Germany

As early as 1921, Spengler's essay, *Prussianism and Socialism*, started the vogue for appeals to the youth. They are found in all

Hitler's harangues from 1921 to 1923: "We appeal above all to the powerful army of our German youth . . . The young Germans will some day be the architects of a new racist state."[45] Later, Goebbels lyrically exclaimed: "The revolution we have made . . . has been almost entirely the work of the German youth."[46] "In Germany, it is the youth that governs. . . ."[47]

6

And finally, there is the mysticism of the "war veteran" (Chapter 2).

In Italy the first groups founded by Mussolini in 1915 were *soldiers' Fasci*, and the *Fasci* of 1919 were formed under the sign of the "spirit of the trenches."

"Only unknown men can save the German people," Hitler declared, "but these unknown must come from the front . . . they must come from the ranks of those who did their duty during the war."[48] And Rudolf Hess asserted: "The Third Reich was founded on an idea that came from the trenches."[49]

The Duce and the Fuehrer are pictured as "anonymous" soldiers of the great war. Mussolini published his *War Diary*, and Hitler related his war exploits in *Mein Kampf*.

7

It is not enough to create a mysticism; it must be spread everywhere. So fascism forges itself an instrument of prodigious resources, *propaganda*. Before taking power, propaganda is its principal weapon; and after the victory, it plays such an important role that a special ministry is devoted to it, entrusted to a high dignitary in the government—to the Duce's son-in-law in Italy, to Goebbels in Germany.

In *Mein Kampf*, that amazing handbook of a political agitator, which might have the subtitle, "Or the Art of Taming the Masses," Hitler explains: "I was always extraordinarily interested in propaganda, an art that remained almost unknown to the bourgeois parties. Propaganda should considerably precede organization, and first win the human material to be kneaded by the latter." Goebbels stated later that "propaganda is an essential function of the modern state. No one else has brought to such a degree of virtuosity the art of dominating the masses. The feeble attempts of other countries to imitate us are those of mere amateurs."[50]

Fascist propaganda rests on a fundamental principle, *scorn of the masses.* "Propaganda must be kept on the level of the masses, and its value should be measured only by the results obtained,"[51] Hitler advises. And his pupil Goebbels cynically repeats: "Propaganda has only one aim, to win the masses. And any means that serve this end are good."[52]

In order not to go beyond the limits of this work, we shall be content to give a brief summary of these means:

Employment of modern technical methods (made possible by the big subsidies of the industrialists). After taking power, Hitler explained: "Without automobiles, airplanes, and loud speakers, we could not have conquered Germany. These three technical means enabled National Socialism to carry on an amazing campaign. Its adversaries were finally crushed because they underestimated the importance of these three means of propaganda . . ."[53]

Intensive utilization of symbols—Visual—the fasces of the lictor, or the swastika; vocal—"Eia Eia Alala," or "Heil Hitler"; physical—Roman salute, etc.

Repetition—Fascism hammers its slogans into skulls by repeating them tirelessly: "The great masses' faculty of assimilation," Hitler writes, "is very limited, their understanding small, and their memory poor. Therefore all effective propaganda must be confined to a very few points, set forth in stereotyped formulas as long as is necessary to make the last person in the audience comprehend the idea."[54] This procedure, however crude it may be, succeeds. When a person has heard these platitudes a number of times, he comes in the end to take them for the expression of his own thought, and rejoices at finding it on the lips of the speaker.[55]

The power of the word—Spoken propaganda is much more effective than written propaganda. Hitler constantly boasts of the "magic power of the word," the mysterious bond that in a public meeting unites listeners and orator. He has a predilection for the "mass meeting," the only way, because it is personal and direct, to exert a real influence on large crowds and to win them over.[56] Thanks to the radio, the human word is transmitted everywhere, even to the most distant village.

Suggestion—Mussolini learned from Doctor Le Bon that the crowd was extremely impressionable, and that its leaders exercise over it a "fascination truly magnetic."[57] Hitler exalts this "miraculous influence which we call mass suggestion."[58] The whole art of fascist propaganda is to create a circuit for this mysterious current. "Mussolini's manner of speaking," Volpe relates, "amounted to action, so well did he succeed in taking hold of his listeners' souls, so well did he know how to arouse them to an emotional state . . . He evoked visions."[59] "The medium of the German crowds," is the way a journalist described Hitler. "His arms rise, his hands clench, his hair falls down over his brow with its swollen veins, his voice strangles, a sort of ecstasy seizes him, which he communicates to the crowd."[60]

Assembling of vast crowds, and spectacular settings—When great masses of human beings are gathered in one place and an appropriate background sets them off, the current does not even need to be spread by orators; it flows from the crowd itself, drunk with its own power. Fascism excels in this sort of spectacle. Are we not assured that in Germany "the great leader does not disdain to concern himself with them. He is interested in the rehearsals, and is no stranger to the arrangement of masses, lines and colors, and the rhythm of movement."[61]

Hitler had a sort of speaker's stand and microphone built, which serves to broadcast his addresses. Likewise, from this stand, by manipulating a series of electric buttons, he himself can increase or reduce the strength of the floodlights. He can also get into direct communication with the motion picture cameramen and give them the signal to start their cameras rolling.[62]

"Marching together" and the uniform-fetish—a similar impression is produced by the parades of fascist troops. *Zusammen-*

marschieren, to march together! Here again the current does not need to be created; it is generated spontaneously by this wave of men whom the uniform renders identical to the point of forming a single body. And this current is communicated to the crowd that watches them pass. The crowd is acclaiming itself—idealized, sublimated, transformed into an army on the march.

8

At the conclusion of this analysis, a question comes to mind: *What has the labor movement done to combat fascist "mysticism"?* In Italy as in Germany, socialism in this field was manifestly inferior. Let us try to analyze the reasons.

Some are legitimate and derive from the very nature of socialism. 1) Socialism is less a religion than a scientific conception. Therefore it appeals more to intelligence and reason than to the senses and the imagination. Socialism does not impose a faith to be accepted without discussion; it presents a rational criticism of the capitalist system and requires of everybody, before his adherence, a personal effort of reason and judgment. It appeals more to the brain than to the eye or the nerves; it seeks to convince the reader or listener calmly, not to seize him, move him, and hypnotize him.

Doubtless its propaganda methods need to be rejuvenated and modernized. Socialism should place itself more within the reach of the masses, and speak to them in clear and direct language that they will understand. It is even to its interest to utilize symbols and slogans, but it cannot, *on pain of self-betrayal,* appeal like fascism to the lower instincts of crowds. Unlike fascism, *it does not despise the masses,* but respects them. It wants them to be better than they are, to be the image of the conscious proletariat from which socialism emanates. It strives, not to lower, but to raise their intellectual and moral level.

2) Socialism, seeking above all else the improvement of the *material* condition of the workers, cannot, like the Church and fascism, preach scorn of the goods of this world in the name of so-called "religion."

Besides these reasons inherent in its very nature, there are others which arise from the degeneration of socialism.

1) Socialism is an old movement which has lost its original flame. Although in the beginning it put immediate material improvement of the workers' lot in the foreground, and promised, at a more distant date, "happiness on earth," it did not conceal the fact that winning these improvements in the present, and this "earthly paradise" in the future, demanded an unceasing struggle, struggle made up of suffering and sacrifice.

And in fact, early socialism, *more than any other movement*, required of its pioneers and militants an unheard of amount of unselfishness and devotion. It had, more than any other movement, its heroes and martyrs. Although *materialists*, the proletarian revolutionists were, in the words of Marcel Martinet, "the only idealists in the modern world."[63]

But little by little socialism degenerated. It came to believe that immediate advantages, as well as the "paradise on earth," could be achieved without struggle and sacrifice, by the vulgar practice of "class collaboration." In order to follow the curve of this degeneration, it would be necessary to retrace the whole history of the labor movement in Italy and Germany from its beginning to the war, which would exceed the scope of this study. It would be necessary to recall the golden age of Italian socialism, going back to the years 1890–1900, the years of heroic struggle against the bourgeoisie. "In the golden age of socialism," the fascist Gorgolini concedes, "it is a fact that young people rushed to it, moved by a generous impulse."[64] Then it would be necessary to show socialism sinking gradually into the swamp of "social peace" and parliamentarism and follow the growth of that bureaucracy of the trade unions and the cooperatives—well paid and increasingly conservative—whose whole ambition was to do business and to get new subsidies for themselves, even government orders during the war.

In Germany, too, it would be necessary to start with the heroic years 1880–1890, years of bitter class struggle, and evoke with Gregor Strasser "that faith, that violent aspiration, that enthusiasm of millions of men . . . this party which a fiery temperament like Bebel's had made great, and for which thousands of ardent hearts, devoted to the point of renunciation, sacrificed themselves."[65] Then we should see the Social Democracy gradually degenerate, sinking likewise into class collaboration, and transform itself into a vulgar party of "democratic reform." "Marxist Germany," writes the National Socialist Rosenberg, "lacked a mythology; it no longer had an ideal in which it believed and for which it was ready to fight. It had given no heroes to the militant army of workers."[66] It would be necessary to describe that labor bureaucracy, conservative and routine-minded, implanted in the existing order, well fed and complacent high priests, who ruled in buildings paid for by the workers' pennies and called "peoples' houses." To win a legislative seat or find a soft berth in a union office had become the rule of life for the leaders of this degenerate socialism. They no longer believed, they enjoyed. And they wanted troops in their own image, troops without ideals, attracted only by material advantages.

2) At the same time, in the field of doctrine, socialism has distorted one of its essential conceptions, "historical materialism." The first Marxian socialists were *materialists* in the sense that, according to them, "the means of production in economic life condition in general the processes of social, political, and intellectual life."[67] Unlike the "idealists," for whom the profoundest motive force of history is an already existing *idea* of justice and right which humanity bears in itself and which it achieves gradually through centuries,[68] those early socialists thought that the relations of production, the economic relations of men with each other, play a preponderant role in history. But if they stressed the economic base, too often neglected before them, they in no way disdained the juridical, political, religious, artistic, and philosophical "superstructure." That was conditioned, they believed, by the base; but the superstructure had its own value none the less, and was an integral part of history and life.[69]

The degenerated Marxists, however, believe it is very "Marxist" and "materialist" to disdain the human factors. They accumulate figures, statistics and percentages; they study with great accuracy the profound causes of social phenomena. But by failing to study with the same care the way in which these causes *are reflected in the consciousness of men*, and failing to penetrate the soul of man, they miss the *living reality* of these phenomena.

Hence, being interested only in the material factors, they understand absolutely nothing of the way in which the privations suffered by the masses are transmuted into a religious aspiration. Why do not these petty bourgeois, these peasants, these young intellectuals, these unemployed youths, come to those who possess the Marxist truth, who denounce with such clarity the faults of the capitalist system, and who have so brilliantly analyzed the economic causes of fascism?

Without a doubt, the socialist movement does not aim to maintain and exploit the mystical tendencies of the masses, but, on the contrary, to destroy the material roots of religious sentiment by abolishing the capitalist system, the source of suffering and chaos. The surest way to stamp out the forms of reactionary mysticism (traditional religion and fascist "religion") is to hasten the end of capitalism and the advent of socialism. But while waiting for success, socialists face a concrete fact that they must take into account: the survival of religious sentiment.

This religiosity can be turned to account by transforming it, counterposing a superior substitute to fascist mysticism: an "idealism" which would not be fallacious, because it would be based on reality, with both feet on the ground, guided by a scientific concept of history and by its highly "spiritual" purpose of ending man's alienation.

But the socialists are incapable of this demystification, since they are bogged down in the swamp of class collaboration and they also have a "materialist disdain for the human factor." Thousands and thousands of men, women, and adolescents who are burning to give themselves, will never be attracted by a socialism reduced to the most opportunistic parliamentarism and vulgar trade unionism. Socialism can regain its attractive force only by saying to the masses that to win the "paradise on earth," its supreme goal, requires great struggles and sacrifices.

4

Fascist demagogy:
"Anti-capitalist" capitalism

"Mysticism" is not enough; it fills no bellies. The individuals composing the fascist troops are not all equally fanatic, and even the most fanatic do not forget their material interests. Concern for these interests continues to dwell in their subconscious. In order to win them and keep up their enthusiasm, fascism must *also* hold forth to them a practical solution for the ills from which they suffer. Although in the service and hire of capitalism, it must—and this is what radically distinguishes it from the traditional bourgeois parties—make a show of demagogic *anti-capitalism*.

But this anti-capitalism, if closely examined, is quite different from socialist anti-capitalism; in fact it is *essentially petty bourgeois*. Fascism thus kills two birds with one stone: on the one hand it flatters the middle classes by becoming the faithful interpreter of their most reactionary aspirations; on the other, it feeds the working masses, and particularly those categories of workers lacking class consciousness (Chapter 2), with a utopian and harmless anti-capitalism that turns them away from genuine socialism.

But this "pass-key" demagogy will not satisfy everybody. Fascism is obliged therefore to speak, not without understandable embarrassment, to the conscious workers, and to the small peasants hungry for land, in a more radical language.

We shall see that they will push this self-styled "socialism" very far—in words. Is it really useful, the reader will ask, to go to such pains to dissect this lying phrasemongering? The undertaking is indeed necessary, both to understand what slogans the fascist demagogues have used to dazzle their followers, and to point up the gulf between promises and fulfillment.

1

Fascism's game is to call itself anti-capitalist without seriously attacking capitalism. It first endeavors to transmute the anti-capitalism of the masses into *nationalism*. An easy task! In all periods, as we have seen, the hostility of the middle classes towards big capital is accompanied by a tenacious attachment to the idea of the nation. In Italy and Germany particularly, the masses as well are disposed to believe that the enemy is less their own capitalism than foreign capitalism (Chapter 2). Hence fascism has no difficulty in shielding its financial backers from popular anger by diverting the anti-capitalism of the masses to the "international plutocracy."

In Italy

Long before the war, the syndicalists of the school of Sorel—who were later to become fascists—coupled their revolutionary syndicalism to an increasingly pronounced nationalism. Rossoni discovered that "the fate of the Italian workers is indissolubly linked to that of the Italian nation." Labriola demanded the right of Italy to try its fortune by leading the crusade against plutocratic Europe.[1] Syndicalists and nationalists joined in proclaiming Italy *the great proletarian*.[2] Mussolini had only to delve into their writings. From 1915 to 1918 he incessantly repeated that "the war must be given a social content."[3] Later he declared that the League of Nations "is only a sort of insurance policy of the successful nations against the proletarian nations."[4] The minister Rocco recalled that "there is not only an internal but an international problem of the distribution of wealth," and counterposed the poor nations to the rich nations: "The Italian proletariat suffers from the inferior position of the Italian nation with respect to rival nations far more than from the avarice or greed of its employers." Therefore, in order to improve the condition of the Italian masses, it would be necessary first to improve the international position of the "proletarian nation."[5]

In Germany

As early as 1919, the founder of the National Socialist Party, Drexler, asserted that "Toiling Germany is the victim of the greedy Western powers."[6] Moeller van den Bruck took up the formula of the proletarian nation: "Socialism," he wrote, "cannot give justice to men if there is no previous justice for nations. The German workers should realize that never before have they been enslaved as they are today by foreign capitalism. . . . The struggle for liberation that the proletariat is carrying on as the most oppressed section of an oppressed nation is a civil war that we are no longer waging against ourselves but against the world bourgeoisie."[7]

However, it was Gregor Strasser who became the brilliant and tireless propagandist of this synthesis: "German industry and economy in the hands of international finance capital means the end of all possibility of social liberation; it means the end of all dreams of a socialist Germany. . . . We young Germans of the war generation, we National Socialist revolutionists, we ardent socialists, are waging the fight against capitalism and imperialism incarnated in the Versailles treaty. . . . We National Socialists have recognized that there is a connection, designed by providence, between the national liberty of our people and the economic liberation of the German working class. German socialism will be possible and lasting only when Germany is freed!"[8] Goebbels summed this up in a particularly striking formula: "What is the aim of the German socialist? He wants the future Germany to have no proletariat. What is the aim of the German nationalist? He wants the future Germany no longer to be the proletarian of the universe. National Socialism is nothing but the synthesis of these two conceptions."[9]

2

Would it be possible to transmute the anti-capitalism of the masses into still something else? Fascism found in the Jews—under favorable circumstances—a second scapegoat.

Anti-Semitism exists in a latent state in the subconscious of the middle classes. Throughout the entire nineteenth century, the petty bourgeoisie, victim of capitalist development, had a tendency to concentrate its animosity on the Jewish usurer or banker and the little Jewish merchant. Toussenel, the Frenchman, gave his *Financial Feudalism* the subtitle, "The Jews, kings of the epoch," and wrote: "I advise all makers of revolution to take the banks from the Jews." By exploiting the theme of racism, the fascists were sure to please the middle classes; at the same time it protected its own financial backers from popular anger, and it diverted the anti-capitalism of the masses to the Jews.

In Italy

In Italy, where the Jews were only a small minority of the population (fifty or sixty thousand out of forty-four million), this demagogy had little chance of success, though fascism did not completely neglect it. The newspaper, *Il Tevere,* stated after the publication of the Labor Charter that *the time of domination by Jewish bankers is now past.*[10] The fascist "extremists" readily attributed the economic miscalculations of their regime to *the Jewish action of international banking.*[11]

It was not until July 1938 that Italian fascism, in imitation of its ally Hitler, and to distract attention from its current difficulties, officially added anti-Semitism to its demagogic arsenal.

In Germany

Anti-Semitism found a much more favorable field in Germany. Numerically the Jews constituted only one per cent of the population, but following the war a sudden influx of more than 100,000 Jewish immigrants from Poland, the Ukraine, and Lithuania, revived the "Jewish question." The role played by the Jews in the economic, political, and intellectual life was considerable. There were enough Jews at the head of banks for the identification of high finance with Judaism to be readily accepted by the masses; at the head of the big department and one-price stores there were enough Jews for the anger of the small shopkeepers to be transferred to the Jews. There were enough Jews prominent in Anglo-Saxon finance for its debtor, Germany, to seem to be the slave of "world Jewry," and among the speculators carrying on profitable operations on the Stock Exchange there were enough Jews for the small investors to consider them responsible for their ruin. The Marxist parties also had at their head enough stirring and brilliant Jewish leaders to make it possible to denounce the collusion of capitalism and Marxism, and to represent Jewish bankers and Jewish workers as working hand in hand for universal domination by the Jewish race, according to the plan revealed by the so-called *Protocols of the Elders of Zion*—a legend already invented in the nineteenth century. Finally and most important, there were enough Jews belonging to the middle classes and the liberal professions—enough small Jewish shopkeepers, doctors, lawyers, journalists, writers and artists, hated by their "Aryan" rivals—to make it possible when the time came to unleash popular fury against them, and thereby protect not only the "Aryan" industrial magnates and bankers but even the big Jewish financiers![12]

National Socialism's trick is to transmute the anti-capitalism of its followers into anti-Semitism. "Socialism," Goebbels wrote, "can be achieved only in opposition to the Jews, and it is because we want socialism that we are anti-Semitic."[13]

Subsequently the sorcerer's apprentice, as in Goethe's famous ballad, became a prisoner of the evil spirits which he had invoked. Besieged by a fearsome coalition of great powers which he caused to unite against him, face to face with the dilemma "to be or not to be," his delirious imagination saw in the Jews, by the very fact that he persecuted them, not only a scapegoat, but a servant of the Devil: at home invincible adversaries, and abroad directors of a global encirclement. He imagined they were some foreign body that he must "kill or be killed by."

In the madness of a persecutor himself persecuted, he massacred an entire people, like Herod not even sparing the infants who, though innocent, were threatening because they might perpetuate this race of bogeymen. The slaughter was heaviest in Eastern Europe with its heavy Jewish population; the German conquest made this area the eastern rampart of the Third Reich. Thus anti-Semitism, which began as a racial prejudice exploited as a demagogic trick, ended in the most abominable genocide of all time.

3

Although fascism arouses the popular masses especially against the "international plutocracy" and the Jews, it cannot avoid—without unmasking itself—an attack on its own big bourgeoisie. However, the fascist declamations against the big bourgeoisie, if examined closely, are in no way *socialist*.

The middle classes' opposition to the big bourgeoisie differs sharply from that of the working class. The middle classes do not desire the elimination of the big bourgeoisie as a class. On the contrary, they would like to become big bourgeois themselves. When fascism proclaims itself anti-bourgeois, and when it denounces the "degeneration" of the big bourgeoisie, it has no intention of attacking the existing social order; rather, it wants to rejuvenate that order by injecting fresh blood, *plebeian* blood. Thus it flatters the middle classes, while at the same time diverting the masses from the class struggle and proletarian socialism.

In Italy

Gorgolini sneers when he describes this "bourgeoisie inhibited by the timidity which frequently attacks those who are too refined and made sluggish by digestive difficulties."[14] Lanzillo, at the time of the occupation of the factories, also ridiculed the "humiliated, clumsy, rotten, and corrupting bourgeoisie."[15] But here the cloven hoof appears. To restore to the big bourgeoisie "some of its energy,"[16] *new talents* must come on the scene: "The dynamic law of social history," declares a motion voted on October 5, 1924, by a fascist "trade union" congress, "consists less in an irreconcilable struggle between the classes . . . than a struggle of ability, that is to say, the struggle led by professionally skilled groups who are acquiring the ability to assume the functions of management, against groups who are losing their ability to fulfill these functions of command. . . ." To translate this gibberish into clear language: the big bourgeoisie must gradually give way to the "competent"—that is, to the fascist plebeians.

In Germany
  The Nazis make the big bourgeois their whipping boy. Hitler has not enough epithets at his command with which to flay the big bourgeoisie. He denounces its "proverbial cowardice," its "senility," its "intellectual rottenness," its "cretinism." But later his real meaning appears: it is necessary, he writes, "to take care that the cultivated classes are continually renewed by an influx of fresh blood coming from the lower classes."[17] August Winnig devotes an entire book to the theme that the mission of the popular masses is to rejuvenate an aged social order and regenerate an exhausted ruling class: "The raw material that is the proletariat has the vocation of creating its own new values, its own ideas, and introducing these forces into the old community, not in order to destroy it, but to rejuvenate it."[18]

4

Fascism cannot, however, unless it is to unmask itself, avoid taking issue with the capitalist system itself, though here again its anti-capitalism is very far removed from proletarian socialism.
  The anti-capitalism of the middle classes has as its chief target the organization of credit. Throughout the nineteenth century, the petty-bourgeois theoreticians attacked not *producing* capitalism but

idle capitalism—the lender, the banker. Toussenel, in his *Financial Feudalism*, denounced the usury which "burdens the national labor of France with a tax of two billion a year," and demanded that banking should become a state monopoly. After Saint-Simon, Proudhon, believing that "interest on money . . . is the heaviest fetter on labor and the most unjustified levy on consumption," launched his idea of "credit mutualized to the point of being without interest charges," thanks to which "every worker might become an independent entrepreneur."

Fascism, in its turn, concentrates its attacks on "loan capital," and thereby expresses the aspirations of the middle classes while diverting the working masses from the struggle against capitalism as a whole.

In Italy

Most of the radical demands of the fascist program of 1919 were directed against the banks and loan capital: "The dissolution of corporations; suppression of all sorts of banking and stock market speculation; state credit through the creation of a national organization for credit distribution; confiscation of idle income; a special graduated surtax on capital. . . . " In the *Popolo d'Italia* for June 19, 1919, Mussolini wrote: "This is what we propose now to the Treasury: either the property owners expropriate themselves, or we summon the masses of war veterans to march against these obstacles and overthrow them."

In Germany

In National Socialist demagogy, the struggle against capitalist organization of credit plays an important part. The various programs of the National Socialist Party propose control, and even nationalization of the banks. Thus in October, 1930, the National Socialist parliamentary group in the Reichstag presented a motion demanding "that the big banks should pass without delay into the hands of the state." In the Nazi program, too, are featured the closing of the banks, transformation of negotiable bonds into non-negotiable securities, and finally into partnerships. But the chief attraction was Gottfried Feder's idea of *abolishing interest slavery.* Feder dreamed of suppressing interest without suppressing capitalism. "Our vision is clouded by the fraud of sacrosanct interest," he writes. "Interest has as little connection with money as goiter has with the circulation of the blood. . . . Abolition of slavery to interest which, in the gigantic struggle waged throughout the universe is . . . the solution of the social question and the means by which, in the gigantic struggle waged throughout the universe between Capital and Labor, will come the liberation of Labor, *but without injuring property and the production of wealth.*"[19] Thus he can leave aside industrial capital and attack only loan capital, for the *good* Krupp died in 1826 without wealth and the capital of his company today amounts only to the modest sum of 250 million marks, while the fortune of the *bad* Rothschild, who started with a few millions, today amounts to 40 billion marks.

"We recognize clearly," Feder concluded, "that the capitalist system—capital itself—is not the scourge of the human race; the insatiable thirst for interest of big loan capital is the curse of all toiling humanity." Hence there is no need for a revolution of the Marxist kind. "*Capital must exist, and Labor too.* . . . Bolshevism imagines it can cure the malady by a surgical operation, whereas the real cause is the poison that should be eliminated. . . . To overturn economy as in Russia is useless, but there should be a united front of the whole producing population—from the manual worker crushed by indirect taxes, to the functionaries and office employees, artisans, peasants, inventors, and managers of industrial enterprises, intellectuals, artists, and scholars—against the slavery of interest."

The promise to abolish interest slavery was aimed especially at the small peasants whose bit of earth was laden with mortgages. When National Socialism comes to power, it was asserted, it would no longer permit the mortgaging of land, which would be proclaimed exempt from seizure and inalienable.

But when Feder tries to explain *how* he will abolish the slavery of interest within the framework of the capitalist system, he gets into difficulty. He calls for the rapid amortization of the standing public debt and of all loans and mortgages, without however indicating how the operation would be financially practicable. And after having solemnly condemned interest, he reintroduces it by the back door: industrial dividends will be simply converted into a fixed revenue of 5 percent; and under state control "credit cooperatives," with a regional and corporative base, will be able to grant, at regulated rates, loans on commodities and "labor power."[20] "Nobody will consider the few marks interest coming from savings or government bonds as interest slavery,"[21] he writes in 1930.

5

Fascism cannot however, without giving itself away, escape attacking *industrial* capitalism itself. And here again its anti-capitalism remains far short of proletarian socialism.

We have seen that the middle classes are less anxious than the working class to destroy the motive force of capitalism—that is, the exploitation of labor power and the appropriation of surplus value (Chapter 2). Throughout the entire nineteenth century and up to the present, petty-bourgeois ideologists limited themselves to attacks on competition and industrial concentration, and to asking the public powers to render the great monopolies (cartels and trusts) less injurious. By taking over these reactionary aspirations, fascism flatters the middle classes, and at the same time turns the working masses away from proletarian socialism.

In Italy

Gorgolini in 1921 denounced in most vehement terms the "magnates of big industry and commerce who have starved Italy [read: ruined the middle classes]. . . ."[22] Later, Bottai wrote: "We should strive for the development and definite victory of the artisan, especially for the following reason: in order to oppose the growing concentration of capital . . . of forces resting on the opposite principle. . . . It is not excluded that the worker may become a factor strongly influencing the development of our industry."[23]

In Germany

In Germany, where capitalist concentration was much more developed, trust-busting demagogy played an even more important role. "A few individuals," Goebbels exclaimed, "should not have the right to use the national economy against the nation! But in reality a few monopolies dominate, a few individuals have amassed enormous fortunes. These individuals have unlimited means for taking away from the people its daily bread and robbing it of its labor. . . ."[24]

Therefore the 1920 program demanded the *nationalization of all enterprises already incorporated* (trusts). Here fascist anti-capitalism seems to be on the verge of socialist anti-capitalism. But the Nazis hastened to water down their formula: Feder carefully explained that this nationalization would have nothing in common with Marxist socialism; it would be a preliminary to dismemberment. "A hundred thousand independent cobblers," he asserted, "are worth more to the economy of the people and the state than five giant shoe factories."[25] The program of 1920 provided likewise that the big stores be "communalized," and then broken up and rented cheaply to little merchants.

A young Nazi student defined this reactionary "socialism" in particularly striking terms: "National Socialism wants to stop the automatic movement of the capitalist wheel, put a brake on it, *then make it turn back to its starting point*, and stabilize it there."[26]

6

This modified capitalism, brought back to its origin, presupposes a return to the autarky of former times. National Socialism exhumes the plan, typically petty bourgeois, of the *closed commercial state* drawn up in 1800 by the philosopher Fichte. From such a state, competition—the accursed—is banished; the prices of all commodities are fixed by public authority. There is no risk of overproduction or shortage; supply is assured of finding its complementary demand, and vice versa. Nobody can grow rich, but neither can anybody be impoverished; every individual is the servant of the community and receives his fair share of the community's wealth. But such an economy is possible only if the state in question is strictly isolated from the outside world and protected from international competition. Hence the state must assume the monopoly of foreign trade and issue a purely internal currency.

Gregor Strasser has read his Fichte; in his *Fourteen Theses of the German Revolution*,[27] he rejects the liberal capitalist system "whose destruction is the prelude to the success of the German revolution," and proposes in its place an economy aiming not at profit but supplying the needs of the nation, or in the words of his brother Otto: "the satisfaction of the need of every member of the community for food, clothing, and shelter."[28] The odious law of supply and demand must be abolished, fixed prices established by the state for all commodities, and a balance assured between the quantities available and the quantities required. Nevertheless, the National Socialists did not conceal the difficulties of putting such a system into effect. Hence they wished first to experiment in agriculture, as the first field to be withdrawn from the liberal capitalist economy. But they insisted that "sooner or later, the other economic groups should join the peasantry and adopt its principles."[29]*

Such an economy is possible only after international competition has been abolished; it requires *autarky*—that is to say, prohibitive tariffs. Trade balances and exports are "things belonging to an epoch that is finished." "Each people should produce its own living requirements on its own soil."[30] It is necessary first to feed German citizens and only then think of exportation.[31] German commodities formerly exported would find their market within the country. The industrial crisis, the Nazis asserted, was merely a result of the agricultural crisis. Thanks to prohibitive tariffs, the prices of agricultural commodities would be revised upward, and agriculture, regen-

---

* For the way victorious National Socialism put this idea into practice, see Chapter 10.

erated, would be capable of absorbing the industrial products.

But how does one achieve this "closed economy"? By entrusting the state with the monopoly of foreign trade, and creating a new currency reserved exclusively for domestic use and independent of gold: "Going off the gold standard," Feder wrote, "is the necessary condition for a healthy economy in the Third Reich, an economy in which Labor will again take precedence over Money."

7

Corporatism is one of the lures fascism offers to the petty bourgeoisie and to workers with a petty-bourgeois mentality. On close inspection, one finds three distinct ruses in the corporatist demagogy of the fascists:

1. The promise made to workers with a petty-bourgeois mentality that they will be "deproletarianized." To be sure, this will not be done by erasing the sharp division between capital and labor and between bosses and employees, but by reconciliation of the two groups involved in production. These workers are assured that within the joint "corporations" they will be able to live like petty bourgeois— guaranteed a position, a "fair salary," and security in their old age— and, above all, that the bosses will deal with them on an equal footing, like true "collaborators" in the task of production.

2. The promise made to the independent petty bourgeois (small manufacturers, small merchants, etc.), who are victims of big monopoly competition and are in the process of being proletarianized, that a social order will be revived for them, inspired by that of the Middle Ages, the precapitalist era, a regime not of competition and "might makes right," but one where the small producers will be organized and protected within their autonomous "corporations," once again finding stability and security there.

3. Finally, the promise that the parasitic and incompetent parliamentary regime will be replaced by a "corporate State" in which all producers, grouped in trade and professional bodies, will have a voice in their local chapters, and where all interests will be reconciled in the name of the common weal.

enteenth century, the journeyman was a veritable proletarian. The guild was only a caste monopoly, a "fortress for a jealous and greedy oligarchy."[34]

However, the reactionary parties and the Church proposed to revive these medieval guilds, so long outmoded by economic evolution.

Thus in France in the first half of the century, an elite group of Catholic writers (Sismondi, Buchez, Villeneuve-Bargemont, Buret, et al.) denounced the crimes of competition and demanded the reestablishment of occupational organizations. The Count of Chambord, in his *Letter on the Workers* (1865), recalled that "royalty has always been the patron of the working class," and demanded "the formation of free corporations." After 1870, the Church officially included "corporatism" in its doctrines. "The only way to return to the peaceful state society enjoyed before the Revolution," the Catholic Congress of Lille declared in 1871, "is to reestablish, through Catholic organization, the reign of solidarity in the field of labor."

In 1894, Pope Leo XIII issued the encyclical *Rerum Novarum* in which, after having ascertained that capitalism "has divided the body of society into two classes and has dug an immense abyss between them," he proposed to remedy the evil by returning to the past: "Our ancestors long experienced the beneficent influence of the guilds. . . . Thus it is with pleasure that we now see everywhere the formation of societies of this sort." Subsequently, La Tour du Pin, who is both Catholic and monarchist, expressed the hope that the guild will reconcile the worker and the employer and will "replace false ties with a natural fusion."[35]

The reactionaries accorded these corporations or guilds only a consultative role, strictly subordinate to the political state. Politics comes first! For the Count de Chambord the corporations must become "the basis for the electorate and the right to vote." For La Tour du Pin, they will be "the natural and historical electoral colleges of all political bodies." But above them there will be the monarchy or the omnipotent, authoritarian state, for which the corporations will be "simple collaborators in economic matters."[36]

Whereas the reactionaries want to go backwards and revive the past, the social reformers of the nineteenth century, without demanding the actual restoration of the medieval guilds, do dream of applying the basic principle of the guild to modern society and of "organizing" labor. But their aspirations are confused. Saint-Simon wanted to divide up the "producers" (i.e., workers and factory owners both) into industrial "corporations."[37] His disciples asserted that the "regenerating principle" of the future society was "no different from the principles underlying the organization of society in the Middle Ages." "Legislative provisions had the object of establishing order in industrial relations. There then existed an institution which has recently appealed to many minds, and which answered to the need for unity and organization . . . in so far as was permitted by the state of society at the time—we refer to the corporation. Without question this organization was defective in many respects. . . . However, a bad organization was abolished without anything being erected in its place. . . . Because there have been institutions called corporations which we dislike, we should not conclude that industrialists ought necessarily not to form associations. . . . Hence we find instinctive efforts being made with the manifest intention of restoring order through a new organization of labor."[38] Proudhon also wanted to "reestablish on a new basis the natural organizations of labor—the trade guilds."[39]

The social reformers of the nineteenth century had no clearer idea than the Catholics and royalists of the division brought about by capitalism between capital and labor, employer and wage earner; or if they were conscious of it, they dreamed of bringing this division to an end and keeping alive or artificially reviving the small independent producer.*

Their successors, the "reformist" trade unionists, have rejected, it is true, the corporations of independent producers. But they hope

---

* One must, however, point out that Proudhon made an exception for modern big industry, which he believed should be nationalized and managed by the organized workers.

to "deproletarianize" the workers in another way; they wish to return to the corporations by a different road, by the practice of "class collaboration" within the organized trade. They would like, through the parallel development of employers' associations and labor unions, and on the strength of each group's experience in the industry, to reconcile the two "indispensable" factors of production. They flatter themselves that they can share the management of industry equally well with the employers, first within each trade and then in the nation as a whole, by instituting an economic parliament.

Paul-Boncour was formerly the brilliant exponent of this utopia.[40] After the war it fascinated reformists in many countries, especially in Germany, but also in Italy, France, and others. Almost everywhere, the reformists thought the hour of "economic democracy, corporatism, and class collaboration" had come. And despite all the disappointments they have suffered, international reformism lives yet upon this utopia: in Switzerland for instance, the unions announced their acceptance of the principle of "professional communities" legally grouping workers and employers. In Austria, shortly before the defeat, the *Wiener Arbeiter Zeitung* wrote that the socialists "could very well consider the idea of corporatism."

In Belgium, De Man called for a "joint organization of production along corporatist lines"; and in the program of the POB [Belgian Labor Party] this joint organization "goes from union recognition and industry-wide contracts to the establishment of an Economic Council in place of the Senate."[41]

In France the crowning of the CGT's "plan" was the National Economic Council, "composed of qualified delegates designated by the most representative of the employers and workers organizations."[42] Even the International Trade Union Confederation dreamed of a "true corporate state, meaning, in effect, the collaboration of employers and wage earners in a single common organization or institution."[43]

And the reformists always accord these corporate institutions only a consultative role. In the CGT plan, for instance, the economic parliament "inspires the government in its decisions." But it does not replace the government. The political state remains the ruler.

Fascist demagogy draws simultaneously on the reactionaries and the reformists. From the former it borrows the idea of resurrecting the medieval artisans' and small merchants' guilds. From the reformists it takes the idea of the corporation based on "class collaboration," and the notion of a consultative economic parliament. But in two essential respects it aligns with the reactionaries against the reformists:

1. The reformists wanted to set up their form of corporatism in the framework of a democratic political state, and the fascists in the framework of an authoritarian political state.

2. The reformists want their "class collaboration" within each corporation to be accompanied by full trade union rights. The fascists, on the contrary, do not conceal their intention to base their corporate state not on free trade unions but on trade unions placed in receivership.

In Italy

Mussolini had a model before his eyes: the "corporative" constitution proclaimed by d'Annunzio in Fiume on September 8, 1920, but which never went into effect. In certain respects the inspiration for this constitution was clearly reactionary. It created in the little artisan town of Fiume ten obligatory corporations enjoying autonomy "such as was established and exercised during the four glorious centuries of our communal epoch." But its drafter, the former militant trade unionist de Ambris, also introduced the reformist idea of an economic parliament composed of sixty members elected by the corporations.[44]

Moreover, Mussolini borrowed directly from the reformists. At about the time when the Italian Federation of Labor was proposing that laws should be drawn up by "consultative trade union bodies," he wrote a friend: "The future will see many parliaments of competents substituted for the single parliament of incompetents."[45]

At the constituent assembly of the *fasci* on March 23, 1919, he declared: "Present political representation cannot suffice for us; we want direct representation of all interests. . . . *The objection can be made to this program that we are returning to the corporations. What of it?*" And in fact, the fascist program of 1919 demanded the "creation of national technical councils of labor, industry, transportation, etc., elected by the entire profession or trade."

In Germany

From Fichte to the present, numerous reactionary writers in Germany, particularly at the end of the war, have advocated the reestablishment of the medieval corporations. "It was logical," writes Moeller van den Bruck, "that the attack on parliamentarism, which was carried on by the revolutionaries with the slogan of 'councils,' should be carried on by the conservatives with that of corporations. . . . In restoring their rights to the corporations, it was a question not of looking at them historically or romantically, but of following modern ideas. . . ."[46] The Nazis drink deeply from this same spring: "the point of departure" of National Socialism, in the words of Gregor Strasser, "*is the spirit and content of the professional system of guilds and corporations in the Middle Ages.*"[47]

Feder borrows from the reformists the idea of "uniting employers and workers in the different branches of economy in occupational corporations . . . in order to direct them toward the common aim of national production in a feeling of confidence and reciprocal responsibility."[48] In these corporations, "employers and employees should sit together *with the same rights.*"[49] Following the reformists, the Nazis take over as their own the idea of a consultative economic parliament, consisting of elected regional economic councils with a supreme economic Chamber at the top charged with conciliating the various interests.[50]

What do the great capitalists, fascism's financial backers, think of its "corporatist" demagogy? So long as fascism has not conquered state power, they see the weight of advantage on the side of demagogy. It draws many petty bourgeois into the ranks of the fascists, diverts a certain number of workers from trade unionism and the class struggle, and disparages parliamentary democracy.

But, despite their tolerance, fascism's backers are privately utterly hostile to corporatism, to any form of class collaboration, to any "equal dealings" with their victims. In their businesses as well as within their class, they want to give all the orders and maintain no equal relationships with their personnel. They fear above all that their victims may demand the right to control and participate in economic management.

They have not forgotten their postwar terror, when in Italy the workers occupied the factories and claimed the right of management of production; when in Germany the workers' and soldiers' councils were the sole legal authority for several days. Therefore, they systematically sabotaged every trace of corporatism and workers control which they might have momentarily had to accept in principle. In Italy, the "workers control" promised the metal workers after the factory occupations (1920) was never put into practice. In Germany, the bosses were totally opposed to the "socialization" laws of 1919, and within such organizations as the Potash and Coal Councils they refused any effective collaboration with the workers' representatives.

The employers wanted no "corporations," and even if they accepted them in principle, it was only when the idea was made unrecognizable and emptied of all content. So, for instance, the French industrialist Mathon deplores the fact that "those who have heretofore dreamed of recreating the guild" have understood by this "a collaboration carried at times to the point of workers sharing in the management and profits of businesses." This domain must remain the bosses' private reserve. Mathon upholds the "principle that the employers rule alone in the economic corporation. . . . They own the firms which constitute it; they therefore have supreme command and all responsibility. . . . They are the most qualified for this position of leadership. . . . They alone can judge with sufficient discrimination and breadth of vision, with all the necessary competence and experience. . . . One person in charge is an absolute necessity."[51] It follows that the economic corporation should be composed exclusively of bosses. But, granted that private domain, Mathon sees no disadvantages in bosses and workers joining together in the *social* corporation and debating questions of wages and working conditions.

All French employers who have written about "corporations," whether it be Maurice Olivier[52] or Lucien Laine[53], have expressed the same opinion: no participation by workers in economic management: "This would be the road to anarchy." Hitler himself expressed a similar opinion in a moment of sincerity. When Otto Strasser asked him, in 1930, "Well then, economic self-management for coal miners?," he answered angrily, "The system is basically fair; there can be no other. Co-ownership and co-management by the workers is Marxism. . . ."[54]

The great capitalists are just as hostile to independent "corporations" for the independent petty bourgeoisie (small manufacturers, small merchants). They have no desire to see the small producers protected from competition in such "corporations." They are likewise opposed to a "corporate state" within which all interests would actually have a voice at the local level. They do not want to harmonize their interests with the interests of others, but rather seek hegemony for their interests by crushing and fleecing everyone else.

The German National Party, which unlike the Nazis did not address itself to the broad masses, expressed the inner thoughts of the big capitalists when it included in boldface in its 1932 program: "We reject the corporate state."

We shall see later how the fascists in power lay aside their corporatist plumage.

We shall see later how the fascists in power parade in corporate feathers but only keep a shadow of corporatism in practice lest they displease their backers.

8

Such are the essential components of fascist "anti-capitalism." In order to analyze them, a certain amount of schematization has been necessary. Unlike socialism, fascism does not have—and cannot have—a definite and coherent doctrine: "There is a fascist demagogy," as Pierre Gerome has said, "which varies according to the country, and within each country according to social classes and circumstances. It makes very little difference to fascism how many contradictions it piles up in its program . . ."[55] Hence its "anti--capitalism," of which only the main lines have been traced here, permits many variants. And this without taking account of the fact that fascism, as it approaches power, waters down its program before it betrays it.

Especially when it is striving (in vain) to win the conscious workers, the Socialists, Communists, or syndicalists, fascism is obliged to "stiffen" its program. To these conscious workers it not merely offers a vague "corporatism" (which would fail to dupe them) but adopts in their honor the class terminology; it not only claims it does not reject the principles of socialism but declares itself to be *more socialist* than the socialist parties.

In Italy

"Fascism is not opposed to socialism in itself," but to its "theoretical and practical degeneration," states the *Handbook of the Italian Fascist*. "Fascism," Gorgolini writes, "will never prevent socialism from following its course and keeping its promises, of which the essential, it must be confessed, cannot be rejected." Fascism "has more boldness in reform than pure socialism."[56]

In Germany

Gregor Strasser speaks of the "German labor movement, an entirely justified movement, which we recognize and affirm in its most fundamental content."[57] "We do not fight Marxism because it is a working class movement," exclaims Goebbels, "but because it is a distortion of one. . . ."[58] "The only real socialists in Germany, in all Europe, are ourselves!"[59]

9

To the conscious workers, fascism brazenly presents itself as the natural protector of labor unions.

In Italy

"Mussolini attaches the greatest importance to the labor union movement," writes Gorgolini. "He has sympathy for the trade groups [of the working masses], their unions and cooperatives, of which they have a right to be proud because they represent a continuous and lasting effort. He appreciates their strength when organized into solid national and international federations, which have existed for years, and which express not only the desire for a theoretical emancipation but real proletarian interests. Fascism does not dream of depriving the proletariat of its organizations."[60] What the workers have gained cannot be touched: "Nobody can dream of driving the working masses back to less favorable working and living conditions than those of today," writes Mussolini.[61] On the very eve of the March on Rome, fascism asserted in a proclamation: "Labor has nothing to fear from the fascist power. . . . Its just rights will be loyally guaranteed."[62]

In Germany

The same assurances, the same solemn promises, were made by National Socialism. "We believe absolutely necessary," Gregor Strasser declares, "the organization of workers into unions within the dominant capitalist system. . . . We have always recognized the unions as the necessary representatives of the workers, and we will always recognize them."[63] August Winnig asserts: "Today, less than ever, the existence of a healthy community is inconceivable without labor unions. This must be understood."[64]

10

Fascism claims to support, if not *political* strikes, at least *economic* strikes.

In Italy

"Fascism," we read in the *Handbook of the Italian Fascist*, "advises the proletariat to use all methods of struggle to insure the development of the community and the well-being of the producers." Rossoni declares: "We should not condemn *a priori* the strike as a weapon when its causes are economic. When a party such as fascism has made a revolution with 100,000 bayonets, we should not be astonished if, in certain circumstances, it resorts to energetic measures in order to impose the recognition of a just right."[65] In 1924, Mussolini warned the industrialists that if they did not raise wages, "the workers would have the right to act on their own account."

But the fascist strike must never become *political*. During its session of April 24–25, 1925, the Grand Council "considers the strike to be an act of war which can be resorted to when all peaceful methods have been tried and exhausted . . . [but] it clearly establishes the difference between the fascist strike, exceptional and with definite aims, and the socialist strike, which is a regular act of training for revolution with distant and unattainable ends. . . ."

And, in fact, so long as independent unions were not suppressed, fascism competed with them in regard to strikes. In 1924, the fascists supported the miners' strike of San Giovanni Val d'Arno, and that of 30,000 marble workers in Carrara, etc. In March, 1925, the fascist metal workers' "union" issued an order for a general strike to the workers of the Togni factory in Brescia, etc.

In Germany

Hitler likewise writes: "as long as there are employers devoid of social understanding or lacking a feeling for right and justice, their employees . . . have the right and duty to defend the interests of the community against the greed or unreasonableness of a single person. . . . When men are treated unworthily . . . thereby making resistance necessary . . . *force alone will decide conflicts.*"[66] The propaganda pamphlet issued by the National Socialist "industrial cells" states even more unblushingly: "As a workers' party, National Socialism *recognizes without restriction the right to strike. . . . It is a shameful lie to say that the National Socialists, when they have taken power . . . will deprive the workers of their supreme weapon: the right to strike.*"[67]

But the strike must preserve its economic character and not become political. "For the Nazi corporation," Hitler writes, "the strike is not a means of destroying or weakening national production, but a means of increasing it by overthrowing all obstacles of an anti-social nature that hamper the economic progress of the masses."[68]

And as a matter of fact, before taking power, National Socialism supported extensive movements for labor demands. For instance, in October, 1930, it supported the strike of the Berlin metal workers, in which 100,000 workers took part. In November, 1932, it, together with the communists, instigated the Berlin transport strike.

11

But fascism goes still farther. As a lure for the conscious worker it leaves a door *ajar* for the management of production by the workers.

Italian fascism did not absolutely reject the possibility that one day the workers themselves would control production. The 1919 program promised the labor unions control of public services and institutions with, however, this qualification: "provided they are worthy of it, morally and technically." In his speech to the constituent assembly of the *fasci* (March 23), Mussolini used this intentionally ambiguous language: "We wish gradually to make the working classes capable of directing industry, *were it only to convince them that it is not easy to run an industry or business. . . .*" During the occupation of the factories, he accepted not only the famous workers' control of the factories but also social, cooperative control of industry. However, he made this reservation: "I demand that the factories should be more productive. If this can be assured by the workers in place of the industrialists, I am ready to say that the former have the right to replace the latter."[69]

But after the taking of power, workers' management turned out to be nothing more than a distant hope: "Fascist unionism does not exclude that in the distant future the producers' unions may be the essential nuclei for a new type of economy. But it does deny that the proletariat today is in a position to create its own type of civilization."[70]

12

Finally, fascism dangles before the eyes of the conscious workers a fundamental transformation of property rights.

In Italy

"Fascism," we read in the *Handbook of the Italian Fascist*, "takes a realistic position which does not recognize only one possible type of political system but declares itself favorable to all forms, whether individualist, collectivist, or otherwise, that can assure the maximum production and well-being." Rossoni has also declared in an interview: "The fascist corporations have no prejudices regarding a system of production. As between capitalism and communism, they prefer whatever system guarantees the most abundant production, and they decide in accordance with the requirements of the historical moment."[71]

Professor Ugo Spirito wants the "corporations" some day to become proprietors of all the means of production. When capital and labor will have completed their fusion, when the corporations will control the means of production and exchange, when the members of the corporations will be the shareholders, then the idea of property, in the capitalist meaning of the word, will be "outmoded."[72]

In Germany

Gregor Strasser cleverly digs up "the old Germanic conception of the collective ownership by the tribe or the nation of the means of production and the soil, property of which each individual producer is only the *vassal*, in the service of the community." The Marxists, he explains, are right in demanding "ownership of the means of production"; but no single class—not even the working class—

should be the owner, but the whole nation.[73] We must therefore distinguish between *Eigentum* (property) and *Besitz* (ownership). Only the people should be the proprietor of the national wealth; individuals can be only its *depositaries,* responsible to the community. Hence the *ownership* of wealth is not in question at present, but the future is another matter: the nation being the sole proprietor, everybody can keep the hope that some day the "fiefs" will be redivided among the "vassals."[74]

Otto Strasser goes further than his brother. He proposes that each "comrade of the people" should become a co-possessor of the German economy. All that is necessary is for the state, the sole proprietor of the national wealth, to bestow as a "fief" on each employer his own business in return for an assessment to be paid in five or ten years. The business would be inalienable. Ownership, management, and profits of the business would be divided into thirds among the employer, the employees, and the state. The right of inheritance would be limited; if the owner of property dies without a male heir judged fit to succeed him, the fief would return to the people.[75]

13

Appealing to the small peasants, fascism is also obliged to "stiffen" its program a little. It affects to take as its own the slogan of the *division of the land.* It claims to be more *socialist* than the Socialists, who in Italy and Germany had not dared to touch the big estates.

In Italy

The fascist program of 1919 was categoric: "We wish to give the land directly to the peasants . . . to be cultivated by them jointly." "The land for those who till it," was the slogan the *fasci* used to reach the peasantry. In 1921, Gorgolini declared fascism was "irrevocably opposed to excessively large estates." He attacked "the *latifundium* with its unproductive absentee ownership, leaving vast tracts uncultivated. . . . The latifundists who fail to cultivate their estates . . . actually lose their property rights."[76] Mussolini, in an article dated March 23, 1921, wrote these flamboyant phrases: "In a few months, all of Italy will be in our power . . . and we shall be entrusted with the task of accomplishing the only revolution possible in Italy, the agrarian revolution, which must give the land to those who cultivate it."

In Germany

National Socialism likewise inscribed in its program the partition of the great estates, or "colonization." Walter Darre made innumerable demagogical attacks on the agrarian feudalism "squatting on its property and bank accounts like the decadent Roman nobility denounced by Ferrero."[77] Another specialist, Dr. Carl Hartwich, devoted an entire pamphlet to the question; he expected Hitler to solve the *problem of the East.* "Big estates in the East must for the most part disappear. . . . The East must be colonized. We cannot preserve the big estates out of respect for tradition."[78] Even after the taking of power, the Governor of East Prussia, Koch, proclaimed that a "great historical development has just begun" with the "socialization of the East." He announced the launching of a big "colonization" plan to be carried out within from five to eight years.[79] Kube, the Governor of Brandenburg, promised a similar plan, "more important than the peasant liberation achieved by von Stein."[80] "The real socialists," said the *Taegliche Rundschau,* "like Presidents Erich Koch and Helmuth Brueckner, have uttered words these last few days that give the signal for the agrarian revolution, which will make a clean sweep of agrarian capitalism and unbearable and outworn property relations. The reaction embodied in the great capitalists and agrarians will be carried away by the mounting wave, and soon they will be only a historical memory."[81]

5

Fascist strategy on the
march to power

We shall now see fascism go into action, first attacking the organized workers; then setting out to conquer power; and finally, once master of the government, using the machinery of the state to complete the destruction of democracy and the workers' organizations in order to set up an open dictatorship.

1

At first, the fascist gangs have the character of *anti-labor militia* entrusted by the capitalist magnates and country landlords with the mission of harassing the organized proletariat and destroying its power of resistance (Chapter 1). If the manner of using these bands varies somewhat from one country to another, the tactics are basically the same: *military* and *aggressive*. Fascism confronts the power of numbers with "audacious minorities," and the amorphous and generally unarmed working masses with disciplined, well-armed squadrons.

In Italy

Immediately after the war there was a veritable flowering of anti-labor leagues in Italy: Mussolini's *Combat Fasci,* the *Anti-*

Bolshevik League, Fasci for Social Education, Umus, Italy Redeemed, etc. At the same time, the members of the *Arditi,* the war volunteer corps, on being demobilized, formed a militant association of 20,000 members, which became the shock troops for the various anti-labor leagues and had headquarters in the principal cities.[1] Almost everywhere peaceful processions of workers, parading through the streets with women and children, were unexpectedly attacked by the *Arditi* in groups of twenty or thirty, armed with daggers and hand grenades. For instance, in Milan, on April 15, 1919, when an impressive parade, formed after a socialist meeting, had nearly reached the center of the city, a little troop of young men rushed into the crowd, and the paraders, surprised by the attack, stopped, hesitated and retreated. On the afternoon of the same day, another band sacked the offices of the paper *Avanti.* On December 1, 1919, when the new Chamber opened its session, the Socialist deputies were attacked and beaten as they left the parliament building. In July, 1920, the Rome edition of *Avanti* in its turn suffered the attack of the young desperados. Soon the *Arditi* and other anti-labor leagues merged with Mussolini's *fasci.*

During the same year, 1920, a colonel was sent out by the War Ministry as a sort of "military expert in civil war." After traveling through Italy and finishing his investigation, he made a report which contained, writes Rossi, "a detailed plan for an anti-socialist offensive."[2] But, for this task the 25,000 mercenaries it had been decided to recruit to insure internal order would not suffice: *"There must be added an idealistic [sic] militia organized by the most expert, courageous, strong, and aggressive among us. This militia must be capable both of military resistance and political action. . . . Local actions, with the view to subduing the insolence of the most subversive centers, will be an excellent school for our militia and will at the same time serve to demoralize and crush the enemy. . . ."* Already he was christening these "actions" "local punitive expeditions." The militia to be formed should have strict military organization and tactics. Only thus would they get the better of the enemy forces—"heterogeneous mobs," badly armed, passive, and incapable of planned and coordinated action.

There was nothing more for Mussolini to do but put the good advice of the colonel into effect. We know that in the autumn of 1920, after the blow dealt by the occupation of the factories, the subsidies of the industrialists and agrarians flowed into his coffers. From then on he could buy arms, pay his young recruits and the ex-officers who enrolled. "Revolutionary action squadrons" were formed. They first tried their hand in the country, where the workers could be more easily crushed because of their isolation. The offensive began with a provocation in Bologna, the center of Emilia's "Red Leagues." The municipal elections there in November, 1920, had brought a victory for the Socialist Party. On November 21, while the Municipal Council was in session, the Black Shirts attacked the town hall, and a reactionary municipal councilman, Pietro Giordani, who was a lawyer and war veteran, was killed. Who fired the shot, nobody knew, but his corpse served as a springboard for the reaction. The Bologna affair, according to one of Mussolini's own apologists, "opened the great fascist era. . . . The law of brutal retaliation, atavistic and savage, reigned in the peninsula. It was the will of the fascists." "A year and a half later, the body of a woman who had been murdered and cut to pieces was found in Bologna. The assassin was arrested and recognized as the same man the police had arrested at the door of the municipal council chamber the day the lawyer Giordani was killed. Since he was a fascist gunman and a police informer, he was immediately released. Everything pointed to his guilt. . . . Nobody in Bologna doubts that he was the murderer of the municipal councilman, or that he acted on orders."[3]

"Action squadrons" appeared on the scene in all the villages of the Po Valley. At their heads were the sons of the big landowners. Armed by the landowners, who also supplied automobiles, they undertook "punitive expeditions" against the red villages. Then, encouraged by their success in the country, they attacked the proletariat in the cities. From the beginning of 1921, in Trieste, Modena, Florence, etc., fascist gangs wrecked the labor exchanges and the offices of cooperatives and labor papers.

In the country and in the city their tactics were the same: to use the effect of surprise. The squadrons, subject to iron discipline, blindly obeyed their leaders and struck with lightning rapidity, concentrating at a given point, transported in trucks, and few in numbers, they burst into the midst of their much more numerous adversaries. As Malaparte related, "they are trained in the tactics of infiltration and surprise attacks, and armed with daggers, hand grenades, and incendiary material."[4] Generally, before the workers had time to recover, the bands had completed their work of destruction and death and had swiftly withdrawn. If the slightest resistance was shown, reinforcements, prepared in advance, entered into action. If the fascists were forced to retreat, they returned the next day in greater numbers and carried out terrible reprisals. Militant workers were purged with castor oil, tortured or assassinated.

An important fact is that the fascist squadrons had at their disposal, even in this period, not only the subsidies of their financial backers but the material and moral support of the repressive forces of the state: police, *carabinieri* and army. The police recruited for the squadrons, urging outlaws to enroll in them and promising them all sorts of benefits and immunity. The police loaned their cars to squadron members, and rejected applications for arms permits by workers and peasants while extending the permits granted to fascists.[5] The guardians of "law and order" had their orders to remain idle when the fascists attacked the "reds" and to intervene only if the latter resisted.[6] Often the police collaborated with the fascists in preparing attacks on labor organizations. The liberal, Gobetti, tells of a student who took part in punitive expeditions being summoned by the police and receiving, with the congratulations of the authorities, the fascist cap.[7] We also have the confessions of the fascists themselves. For instance, Umberto Bianchelli states in his *Memoirs of a Fascist:* "Fascism, it must be confessed, developed and had almost a free hand because we found among the functionaries [of the police] and officers Italian hearts who rejoiced to see us come to the rescue. [They] vied with each other in helping the *Fasci.*" A fascist student and squadron member, in a sort of public statement which he sent to a communist paper, wrote: *"We have the police disarm you* before we advance against you, not out of fear of you whom we despise, but because our blood is precious and should not be wasted against vile and base plebeians. . . ."[8]

The courts on their side, handed down "centuries in prison for the anti-fascists and centuries of absolution for the guilty fascists."[9] In 1921, the Minister of Justice, Fera, "sent a communication to the magistrates asking them to forget about the cases involving fascist criminal acts."[10]

But it was the army, above all, that favored the Black Shirts. We have seen the role played by the colonel whom the ministry of war charged with studying the technical problems of the anti-socialist struggle. Shortly afterwards, General Badoglio, Chief-of-Staff, sent a confidential circular to all commandants of military districts stating that the officers then being demobilized (there were about 60,000 of them) would be sent to the most important centers and required to join the *Fasci,* which they would staff and direct. They would continue to receive four-fifths of their pay. Munitions from the state arsenals came into the hands of the fascist bands, which were trained by officers on leave or even on active service. Many officers, knowing that the sympathies of their superiors had been won over to fascism, openly adhered to the movement. Cases of collusion between the army and the Black Shirts grew more and more frequent. For instance, the *Fascio* of Trent broke a strike with the help of an infantry company, and the Bolzano *Fascio* was founded by officers of the 232nd Infantry.

In November, 1921, with the aid of General Gandolfi, the "squadrons" were welded into a veritable military organization; the best fighters and surest elements, the *Principi,* were organized into sections, centuries, cohorts, and legions, and given a special uniform. In addition to this active army, there was set up a sort of reserve, the *Trairi,* who were given missions of secondary importance.

The *Principi,* numerically stronger, then proceeded to a systematic occupation of the regions they wished to subjugate. "Thousands of armed men," Malaparte relates, "sometimes fifteen or twenty thousand, poured into a city or the villages, borne rapidly in trucks from one province to another."[11] Everywhere, they attacked the labor exchanges and the headquarters of cooperatives and working class publications. In the beginning of August, 1922, they seized the city halls of Milan and Leghorn, which had Socialist administrations; they burned the offices of the newspapers *Avanti*, in Milan, and *Lavoro*, in Genoa; they occupied the port of Genoa, the stronghold of the dock workers' labor cooperatives. Such tactics gradually wore out and weakened the organized proletariat, depriving it of its means of action and support. The fascists only waited for the conquest of power to crush it once and for all.

In Germany

In Germany likewise there was, immediately after the war, a great flowering of anti-labor leagues composed of demobilized ex-officers, adventurers, and thugs. Such were the "volunteer corps" (*Freikorps*) which helped crush the Berlin Commune of January, 1919, and the Munich Commune of April, 1919, and which terrorized the agricultural workers of Pomerania in the summer of 1919 and the workers of the Ruhr in the spring of 1920. They were the ones who, between 1919 and 1923, were guilty of all the assassinations of leftist politicians.[12]

The National Socialist Party, which as we have seen was in its early days only one of the numerous "combat leagues," ended, as fascism did in Italy, by absorbing all the others. Its tactics were inspired by those of Italian fascism. In the summer of 1920, at almost the same time that Mussolini's Black Shirts began attacking the working masses, Hitler formed a little shock troop, which he called "Service For Order" (*Ordnertruppe*), and which he trained to disrupt the public meetings of his opponents. On January 4, 1921, he announced to the crowd assembled in the Kindl beer hall: "The National Socialist movement will in the future prevent, if need be by force, all meetings or lectures that are likely to exercise a depressing influence. . . ."[13]

His tactics, like those of the Black Shirts, were essentially aggressive: a handful of daring men, ready for anything, would burst into a crowd of workers and, thanks to their cohesion and swift and brutal action, emerge masters of the field. "It happened more than once," Hitler recalls, "that a handful of our comrades held out heroically against enormous masses of Reds who shouted and fought with their fists. It is true that these fifteen or twenty men could have been overcome in the end but their opponents realized that before that, at least two or three times as many of their own partisans would have had their heads broken. . . . And how our boys went into the fight! Like a swarm of wasps, they rushed upon the disturbers . . . without worrying about the enemy's numerical superiority, even if it was overwhelming, and without fear of being wounded or shedding their blood."[14]

It was about this time that the Munich Chief of Police, Poehner, when the existence of "veritable organizations of political assassination" was pointed out to him, replied: "Yes, yes, but too few!"[15]

At the meeting in the Hofbraeuhaus on November 4, 1921, the *Ordnertruppe* surpassed itself. Before the meeting began, Hitler got his men together, made them stand at attention, and informed them that they should not leave the room except as corpses. "My men rushed into the attack like wolves. They hurled themselves on their adversaries in packs of eight or ten and began to drive them out of the hall by showering them with blows. The hubbub lasted twenty minutes. By this time, our adversaries, of whom there were perhaps seven or eight hundred, had most of them been thrown out of the hall and driven down the stairs by my men, of whom there were less than fifty. . . . That evening we really learned many things."[16] The lesson was, in fact, to be useful. In October, 1922, Hitler, accompanied by eight hundred Nazis, went to a congress at Coburg. As they left the station, they were greeted by a huge crowd of workers, who shouted "Assassins! Bandits! Criminals!" and began to throw stones. But the Nazis, faithful to their aggressive tactic, launched an attack. "Then our patience," Hitler relates, "was at an end, and blows fell like hail on all sides. A quarter of an hour later, nothing red dared show the end of its nose in the streets."[17]

After the battle of the Hofbraeuhaus, the *Ordnertruppe* was given the more appropriate name of Storm Troops (*Sturm-Abteilung*), and soon came to be known by the initials alone, S.A. Later, in August, 1923, Hitler formed a personal guard, the "Hitler Shock Troops," the nucleus of the subsequent *Schutz-Staffel*, or Elite Guards (literally "Protective Columns"), known as the S.S.

After an eclipse of several years, the National Socialists in 1926 and 1927 revived successively the S.S. and the S.A. Like the Italian *Principi*, the S.S. were chosen troops recruited from the most reliable partisans. As for the S.A., they constituted a vast popular army entrusted with missions of secondary importance.

The Hitler bands resumed their disruption of working class public meetings. In 1927, one of Hitler's pupils, the young Goebbels, succeeded in installing himself in the Red districts of Berlin. He boasts of having "sought the enemy in its own fortress," and "forced it to fight." Having rented the Pharus hall for a meeting—a place customarily reserved for Communist meetings—he scattered his men throughout the room and, at a given signal, launched them against their revolutionary opponents. The latter made the mistake of remaining in groups and had to yield the field to adversaries much inferior in numbers.[18]

After 1930 the struggle was carried into the streets. The Brown militiamen provoked their working class enemies and assassinated them on the public highways. No Sunday passed without a bloody combat.

The repressive forces of the state supported and armed the fascist bands. At the end of 1930, General von Schleicher had a very friendly interview with Captain Roehm, leader of the S.A. Schleicher stated that he was entirely in favor of the Storm Troops, provided they did not infringe on the prerogatives of the Reichswehr.[19] The General Staff authorized the young militiamen to drill on military fields and assigned military instructors to train them.[20]

It is true that the fascist bands did not attack, as in Italy, the headquarters of labor organizations. But they demoralized their enemy by displaying their force, and by violence of all kinds weakened its capacity for resistance until the time should come for completely annihilating it, after power had been achieved.

2

How did the labor movement defend itself against the fascist gangs during this first phase? In the beginning, the bold military tactics of the Black Shirts or Brown Shirts took the workers by surprise, and their reply was feeble. But they would have quickly adapted themselves, spontaneously, to their adversary's tactics if their own leaders, afraid of direct action, had not systematically put a brake on their militancy.

Let us be careful not to reply to fascist violence, the reformist leaders said in both Italy and Germany; we should arouse "public opinion" against us. Above all, let us avoid forming combat groups and semi-military bodies, for we should risk antagonizing the public authorities, who, we are confident, will dissolve the semi-military groups of fascism! Let us not borrow the weapons of fascism, for on that ground we are beaten in advance.

These legalistic and defeatist tactics tended to profoundly demoralize the working class, at the same time as they increased the enemy's audacity, self-confidence, and feeling of invincibility. If from their first exploits the fascist bands had come up against organized proletarian resistance and suffered harsh reprisals, they would have thought twice before undertaking "punitive expeditions" or raids on proletarian meetings. They would also have gained fewer recruits. And the victories won by the proletariat in the anti-fascist struggle would have given it just that "dynamic force" which was lacking.

In Italy

The Socialist and union leaders obstinately refused to reply to fascism blow for blow, to arm and organize themselves in military fashion. "Fascism cannot in any case be conquered in an armed

struggle but only in a legal struggle," insisted the *Battaglia Sindacale.*
In the province of Rovigo, union leader Matteotti and the labor
exchanges gave the word: "Stay home: do not respond to provoca-
tions. Even silence, even cowardice, are sometimes heroic."[21] As they
possessed contacts in the state apparatus, the socialists on several
occasions were offered arms to protect themselves from the fascists.
But "they rejected these offers, saying that it was the duty of the
state to protect the citizen against the armed attacks of other citizens."[22]

They relied on the bourgeois state to defend them against the
fascist bands. Hence in the spring of 1921, they took seriously Prime
Minister Bonomi's attempt to "reconcile" the Socialists and fascists.
They imagined that the fascists would dissolve their semi-military
bodies on their own initiative. In the Chamber, Turati, turning toward Mussolini and his friends, exclaimed in a pathetic tone: "I shall
say to you only this: let us really disarm!"[23] The "peace pact" was
signed August 3.

But a few months later the fascists denounced the "pact," and
civil war was resumed. Then the Socialists looked to the public authorities to dissolve the fascist bands. On December 26, the government did send a circular to provincial governors calling for the occupation of the headquarters and confiscation of all arms of the
semi-military bodies, as well as for the prosecution of those who
organized them. But the carrying out of these measures was left to
the local authorities, and the governors and their assistants limited
themselves to a few raids directed, as might be expected, chiefly
against the People's Houses and workers' organizations "to confiscate," writes Rossi, "the few arms that might remain there, thus leaving the way clear for the fascist onslaught."[24]

To make up for the shortcomings of the Socialist and trade union
leaders, a number of militants of various tendencies—revolutionary syndicalists, left socialists, young socialists, Communists, Re-
publicans, etc.—together with several ex-officers, created in 1921,
at the instigation of a certain Mingrino, an anti-fascist militia, the
Arditi del Popolo. But this militia was recognized officially neither

by the Socialist Party nor by the Federation of Labor, and in fact received only their hostility. "The *Arditi del Popolo*," mocked the *Avanti* on July 7, 1921, "perhaps has the *illusion* that it can dam up the armed movement of the reaction. . . ." The Socialist Party, when it signed the "peace pact" with the fascists, was only too happy to seize the occasion to "repudiate the organization and acts of the *Arditi del Popolo*." The Communists in their turn ordered their members to leave the militia on the pretext that the *Arditi del Popolo* included "doubtful" elements, "without class consciousness." They organized separate "Communist Squadrons," which, except for a few actions undertaken in Milan, Trieste, etc., played a rather obscure role.[25] The *Arditi del Popolo*, with the proper leadership, could have become the rallying point for all the proletarian forces who were ready to reply to fascism with arms.[26] But left to themselves, repudiated by the two proletarian parties and the Federation of Labor, they became a real force only in a few isolated towns.

The result was that when the Black Shirts undertook a "punitive expedition" against a locality and attacked the headquarters of labor organizations or the "red" municipalities, the militant workers were either incapable of resisting or offered an improvised, anarchic resistance that was generally ineffective. For the most part, the aggressor remained master of the field. While the fascists moved their troops in trucks and quickly brought reinforcements to the scene of operations, their opponents lacked communications and had no organization or means of sending swift reinforcements from one town to another. "Fascism," Rossi writes, "has an immense advantage over the labor movement in its facilities for transportation and concentration. . . . The fascists are generally without ties. . . . They can live anywhere. . . . The workers, on the contrary, are bound to their homes. . . . This situation gives the enemy every advantage: that of the offensive over the defensive, and that of mobile warfare over a war of position."[27]

After a "punitive expedition," the anti-fascists abstained from reprisals, respected the fascists' residences, and launched no counterattacks. They were satisfied with proclaiming "general protest strikes." But these strikes, intended to force the authorities to protect labor organizations against the fascist terror, resulted only in ridiculous parleys with the authorities, who were in reality the accomplices of fascism.[28] As these strikes were not accompanied by direct action, they left the enemy's forces intact. On the other hand, the fascists profited by the strikes to redouble their violence. They protected "scabs," served as strikebreakers themselves, and "in that threatening vacuum a strike creates around itself, dealt swift and violent blows at the heart of the enemy organizations."[29] However, on the rare occasions when the anti-fascists offered an organized resistance to fascism, they temporarily got the upper hand. For instance, in Parma, in August, 1922, the working class population successfully checked a fascist attack in spite of the concentration of several thousand militiamen "because the defense was organized in accordance with *military* methods," under the direction of the *Arditi del Popolo*.[30]

In Germany

If in the beginning, when the Hitler bands were still weak, the workers' parties had answered them blow for blow, there is no doubt their development would have been hampered. On this point we have the testimony of the National Socialist leaders themselves. Hitler confessed in retrospect: "Only one thing could have broken our movement—if the adversary had understood its principle and from the first day had smashed, with the most extreme brutality, the nucleus of our new movement."[31] And Goebbels: "If the enemy had known how weak we were, it would probably have reduced us to jelly. . . . It would have crushed in blood the very beginning of our work."[32]

But National Socialism was not crushed in the egg; it became a force. And to resist that force, the German Socialists could conceive only one tactic: to trust the bourgeois state and ask for its aid and protection. Their *leitmotiv* was: *State, intervene!* They relied not on themselves and the militancy of the masses but on the Prussian police—which they thought they controlled since there was a Socialist cabinet in power in Prussia—the Reichswehr, and President Hindenburg. They expected the public authorities to dissolve the Storm Troops. In April, 1932, General Groener, minister in Bruening's cabinet, gave them an ephemeral satisfaction: he forbade the S.A. But he thereby signed his own death warrant, for he had to resign on May 13, to be followed shortly by the entire Bruening government on May 30. And the new Chancellor, von Papen, hastened to authorize the Storm Troops again and to remove the entire Socialist government of Prussia, thereby depriving it of control of the police.

It is true the socialists had had an anti-fascist militia since 1924, the *Reichsbanner,* numerically very important. They paraded this militia in uniform in impressive displays, but they refused to involve it in action. On every occasion when it could have been tested against the fascist bands, it was withdrawn from the battlefield. For instance, on January 22, 1933, when the Nazis paraded in front of the Karl Liebknecht House, headquarters of the Communist Party, the divisions of the *Reichsbanner* were ordered, as if by coincidence, to make a long training march outside of Berlin.[33] Not only did the leaders of the *Reichsbanner* flee the fight, but they let themselves be disarmed like sheep by von Papen's police.

Meanwhile, a number of union organizations had themselves formed defense groups, either in the shops where they had members or among the unemployed. But the Labor Federation considered "the situation not sufficiently grave to justify the workers preparing for a struggle to defend their rights." Far from "centralizing and generalizing these preventive measures," it considered them "superfluous."[34]

The Communists likewise had an anti-fascist militia: the "League of Red Front Fighters." From 1929 to 1931 their slogan was: *Strike the fascists wherever you find them.* And courageously the Red Front Fighters replied to the Brown militiamen, even attacking on many occasions the latters' headquarters and barracks. But after 1931, the party abruptly renounced physical struggle against the fascist bands. Torgler confessed later: "For a long time the Communists had ordered their members to renounce all terror. The formula, *strike the fascists*, was condemned." The physical struggle was abandoned for the "ideological struggle." Torgler boasts of having carried on discussions in public meetings with National Socialists and Storm Troopers without losing his composure.[35]

When the Storm Troops announced their intention of parading on January 22, 1933, in front of the Karl Liebknecht House, the party leaders begged the Ministry of the Interior to forbid the Nazi demonstration. "The Communist Party," they stated to the press, "holds the authorities responsible for what will happen in the Buelow Platz. . . ." *Send letters of protest to the Chief of Police:* such was the instruction given the workers.[36] Furthermore, combat groups which were ready to counterattack, received formal orders not to intervene and had to obey, rage in their hearts.

Not only did this tactic leave the workers disarmed before the armed bands of fascists, but it demoralized them. Not being permitted to fight, the Red Front Fighters, who were not all conscious militants, through need of action went over in large numbers to the Storm Troops.[37] So did some other Communists, with the idea of "boring from within" the S.A.

3

At a given moment the capitalist magnates no longer use the Black Shirts or Brown Shirts merely as anti-labor militia but launch fascism for the conquest of the state.

In order to understand fascist tactics during this second phase, it is important to dissipate a common error which poses the problem of taking power in the same way for proletarian socialism as for fascism.[38] There is, in reality, a *vital difference* between the taking of power by the one and the other. For proletarian socialism is the *class enemy* of the bourgeois state, even the democratic state, while fascism is *in the service of the class* represented by that state. Revolutionary socialism knows it will conquer power only through a real struggle, and that it will have to break down the bitter resistance of its opponents. Although socialism utilizes all legal methods supplied by the law or the constitution, it does so without the slightest illusion; it knows that the victory in the end is a question of force. Of course this does not apply to opportunist "socialism," which aims not at *conquering* power but at most at "holding" it and governing for the benefit of the bourgeoisie.

Fascism, on the contrary, from the instant it embarks on the conquest of power, already has the consent of the most powerful section of the capitalist class. It is assured, moreover, of the sympathy of heads of the army and the police, whose ties with its financial backers are close. As for those in control of the bourgeois democratic state, it knows that even if they represent interests somewhat different from those of its financial backers, they will not offer armed resistance; class solidarity will be stronger than divergencies of interests or methods. The Hitler putsch of November 9, 1923, in Munich, and the Paris riot of February 6, 1934, should not mislead us. In reality they were *premature* attempts. If the police opened fire on the fascists in these instances it was because the capitalist magnates had not yet decided to entrust the power to the fascist bands.

The fascists know, therefore, that in reality the conquest of power *for them is not a question of force*. They could take possession of the state immediately if they so wished. Why do they not do so? Because they do not have behind them a sufficiently large section of public opinion. It is impossible in our time to govern without the consent of large masses. Hence fascism must arm itself with patience and first win over these large masses. It must give the impression that it is swept into power by a vast popular movement and not simply because its financial backers, including heads of the army and the police, are ready to hand over the state to it. Thus its tactic is essentially *legalistic;* it wants to come into power through the normal action of the constitution and universal suffrage.

On the other hand, fascism must give its shock troops and militiamen the illusion that it is a *revolutionary* movement which, just as socialism, launches an assault on the state, and that only the valor and spirit of sacrifice of its Black Shirts or Brown Shirts can assure its victory. That is why it must play at war and pretend to conquer the state by force.

Nevertheless, as soon as its legalistic tactic has made it possible for fascism to gather around it the indispensable masses, or at least a large enough section of public opinion, then, without dealing a blow, and in the most legal way in the world, it installs itself in the government. The trick is turned.

In Italy

We have seen that in Italy the magnates of heavy industry, the leaders of light industry, and the great landowners were in agreement after the beginning of 1922 on bringing fascism to power (Chapter 1). The heads of the army and the police had been won over to fascism; eleven generals publicly joined the movement between July and September, 1922; two other generals, Fara and Ceccherini, were present at the staff meeting of October 18 when the March on Rome was prepared. Fascism enjoyed "much sympathy among the lower officers,"[39] and there were numerous fascist cells even among the rank and file of the army. As for the members of the Facta government, they were already secretly the accomplices of Mussolini, or were resigned to offering him no resistance when it should please him to demand the power.

But fascism still needed to win over large sections of public opinion. Therefore Mussolini decided on an essentially legalistic tactic. He looked toward "a legal conquest of power by means of a continually deeper penetration into all regions and communes, especially the most important; the establishment of an overwhelming majority throughout the country; reform of the electoral law; and new elections that would give the Fascist Party control in the Chamber and hence in the government. . . ."[40]

To the National Council of the Fascist Party, Mussolini declared in April, 1922, that no doubt it was necessary to preserve the armed organization, but the *possibility of the fascists participating in the government was not to be excluded.* He had the National Council vote a resolution pledging fascism to concentrate its activity on parliament and the administrative institutions. On August 11, in Naples, he declared that the March on Rome, which everyone was talking about, "is possible, but not strictly necessary and inevitable." On the 13th, in Milan, Michele Bianchi demanded immediate elections, which would give fascism "representation proportionate to its political importance in the country."[41] In October, Mussolini was still ready "to participate" in a Giolitti government if fascism were entrusted with certain "levers of control." Above all, he insisted on the government's adopting the new electoral law and proceeding immediately to hold elections.

But at the same time he had to bluff and appease the militiamen, who were impatient for action. There were many in the fascist ranks, in fact, who contemplated "extra-legal, insurrectionary and military" action, and who "dreamed of a greater, more revolutionary *coup d'etat* than a mere legal conquest of power."[42] For them, the drills and maneuvers of the *Principi* were intensified. At the end of May, 1922, ten thousand Black Shirts from Ferrara, Modena, Venice, etc., gathered in Bologna and, camping in the public squares, proceeded to occupy the city in military fashion. On May 28, all the *Fasci* of Tuscany—that is, several thousand men—were concentrated in Florence. At the end of May, Mussolini wrote in the *Popolo:* "Fascists of all Italy, consider yourselves from now on as mobilized, both materially and spiritually. If necessary, you will leap with the speed of lightning to concentrate in the places designated, and everything will fall before your onslaught." On July 29, he threatened the Chamber with a *fascist insurrection.*

This language and the show of force in the March on Rome have led some people to believe that Mussolini, unlike Hitler, conquered power by force. This is not correct. If Mussolini did not wait for new elections or until he had an absolute majority in the country before taking power, it was not at all because he believed in either the need or the virtue of a *coup d'etat.* He was as legalistic as Hitler, but he *did not have the time* to wait for new elections. *He was pressed by financial difficulties.* He lacked the immense resources Hitler had at his disposal. It required large sums to keep up the militia; fascism had tens of thousands of unemployed on its hands to feed; there was urgent need *"to find a regular source of income, which only the State budget could provide."*[43]

And Mussolini, though without abandoning his legalistic tactics, had to rush things a bit. So, on October 16, four "quadrumvirs" were delegated to carry out the so-called *coup d'etat:* Bianchi, de Vecchi, General de Bono, and Balbo. On the 18th, the "quadrumvirs" elaborated their "mobilization plan" and designated where the fascist columns should assemble for the March on Rome; and by the 24th, 30,000 Black Shirts, cavalry divisions, and cyclists, augmented by 20,000 workers from fascist "unions," had been gathered in Naples and were reviewed by Mussolini. On the 26th, the secret order for the mobilization of the fascist legions was issued, and executed on the 27th, after midnight.

But although Mussolini was bluffing, there were some he did not need to bluff, and he was very careful not to "break with the last vestige of legality."[44] The democratic state surrendered without a fight. A little comedy was enacted. Facta, to save face, proclaimed a state of siege, but the King refused to sign the decree. Throughout Northern Italy, the military authorities allowed the Black Shirts to occupy public buildings, enter barracks, take possession of arms, and fraternize with the troops and officers. On the 29th, Mussolini was summoned to Rome by the King; he went in a comfortable sleeping car and had entrusted to him, in accordance with parliamentary usages, the task of forming a cabinet. Only when all was over did there begin the spectacle which has been called the March on Rome. By special trains, the 50,000 Black Shirts were brought to the capital, where they paraded.

In Germany

After 1930 the financial backers of National Socialism—that is to say, the big industrialists and the land-owners—launched it for the conquest of power. As for the commanders of the Reichswehr, they were openly protecting the Brown militia. In May, 1932, the generals begged President Hindenburg not to rely on the Reichswehr to defend the Bruening cabinet in case of a fascist putsch.[45] After July 20, National Socialism had no longer to fear resistance from the Prussian police.

Hitler, like Mussolini, was certain of conquering power without coming into conflict with the repressive forces of the State. But before venturing to govern, he wanted to have the majority of public opinion with him. Therefore, between 1930 and 1933, he embarked on a practically uninterrupted electoral campaign, which was crowned with success: 12 seats in the Reichstag of 1928–1930; 107 seats in September, 1930; and 230 seats in July, 1932. He explained to the Supreme Court of Leipzig in 1930: "Two or three more general elections and the National Socialist movement will have the majority of the Reichstag; it can then prepare the National Socialist revolution. . . . We shall introduce ourselves into the legislative body in such a way as to give our party the preponderant influence there. Once in possession of the constitutional powers, we shall shape the State in the mold we consider good." And when the Chief Justice sceptically asked the specific question: "Then you intend to follow only legal methods?" Hitler answered without hesitation, "certainly."[46]

And, in fact, when Hindenburg on March 28, 1931, suspended by decree the constitutional guarantees, Hitler asked his party to respect to the letter the will of the President. As some of his partisans were astonished, and some impatient, he gave the order: "Any National Socialist who allows himself to infringe [the presidential decrees] will be immediately expelled."

So certain was Hitler of achieving his ends by legal means that he was willing, if need be, to arrive in power by the back door—by "participating" in the government of the Reich. In spite of the protests of his extremist followers, he authorized Dr. Frick in 1930 to enter the reactionary government of Thuringia, and in 1931 Dietrich Klagges was permitted to enter the Brunswick government. If he appeared hostile on several occasions to the participation of National Socialist ministers in the government, it was only because of the pressure of the extremists, and to save face. For instance, at the end of 1932, he was personally in favor of authorizing Gregor Strasser to enter the Schleicher government, but Goebbels and Goering hastily intervened and made him change his mind.[47]

National Socialism was, as a matter of fact, forced to keep up the appearance of being a "revolutionary movement" and had to bluff because there were so many in its ranks who had not given up the idea of an insurrectionary conquest of power. The Berlin Storm Troops, for example, who were under the command of Captain Stennes, mutinied in March, 1931, and accused the political leadership of the party of having "bourgeois and liberal tendencies" and of making "the National Socialist Party a party like all the others." To keep up the enthusiasm of his troops, Hitler had to play at war. Mysterious plots were hatched; in the party's "agrarian department," directed by Walter Darre,[48] plans were worked out for a putsch. The great idea of Darre and his friends was to conquer power by force under cover of a "communist uprising" manufactured out of the whole cloth; the Prussian police in March, 1932, while searching the headquarters of the Pomeranian Storm Troops, found a complete plan for a *coup d'etat* to be carried out in this manner. At the same time National Socialism publicly displayed its forces: a veritable army which it supported and fed, lodged in its own barracks, trained like regular troops, and exhibited in gigantic parades, while its airplane squadrons streaked across the sky.

But the Brown Shirt army was a show army; it did not conquer power. The state surrendered without a fight. Chancellor Schleicher did *not* mobilize Potsdam garrison, despite the rumor to that effect at the time. But on January 30, 1933, the Marshal-President, in most bourgeois style, invited Herr Adolf Hitler to form the new government of the Reich. And only after it was all over did the Brown Shirts parade triumphantly through the streets of Berlin.

4

During this second phase, how did the organized proletariat attempt to check fascism? To tell the truth, the question should not even be put in this way, *for the labor leaders did not for a moment try to bar fascism's road to power.* Up to the last minute, they refused to believe in even the possibility of a fascist victory.

In Italy

The Italian fascist, Giurati, was able to speak of the "stubborn and stupid underestimation of fascism and its men. For our opponents, Mussolini was only a demagogue like so many others. . . . Nobody was aware that under the stagnant and putrid water of the political pond the volcanic eruption was being prepared."[49] The Italian Socialists were suffering from "parliamentary cretinism": because fascism received only a limited number of votes in the elections and had only thirty-five representatives in parliament, they did not consider it dangerous and even periodically announced its decline and decay.[50] On the very eve of the March on Rome, the party leaders laughed when anybody spoke of possible danger.[51] As for the Communists, they forced themselves to deny the fascist danger by asserting that all forms of bourgeois domination were identical, whether wearing the democratic or fascist label. Thus in 1922, at the second congress of the Communist Party in Rome, Bordiga rejected the hypothesis of fascism's taking power and believed a compromise among all the bourgeois parties was inevitable. When the mobilization of the Black Shirts began on October 28, the party secretariat sent a communication to all the branches stating that "the march on Rome will never take place."[52]

In Germany

The German Socialists and Communists similarly refused to believe in the triumph of National Socialism. More than that, they periodically announced its rout. The Socialists uttered shouts of victory on every occasion: in August, 1932, because President Hindenburg refused Hitler's demands; and after the elections of November 6, because the votes for the Nazis showed a falling off. On that date *Vorwaerts* said: "Ten years ago we predicted the bankruptcy of National Socialism; it is written in black and white in our paper!"[53] And just before Hitler's accession to power, one of their leaders, Schiffrin, wrote: "We no longer perceive anything but the odor of a rotting corpse. Fascism is definitely dead; it will never arise again."[54]

The Communists were scarcely more perspicacious. After the election of September 14, 1930, the *Rote Fahne* stated: "September 14 was the culminating point of the National Socialist movement in Germany. It will be followed only by weakening and decline."[55] In 1932, Thaelmann was aroused against "opportunistic overestimation of Hitler fascism."[56] In all the Communists' literature of 1932, they speak of nothing but *retrogression, decay, break up,* and *retreat* in the fascist camp. After the elections of November 6, we read in the *Rote Fahne*: "Everywhere S.A.'s are deserting the ranks of Hitlerism and coming over to the Communist flag. They are beginning to repudiate Hitler in his own movement."[57] And on the eve of fascism's taking power, Thaelmann spoke of a "turn of the class forces toward the proletarian revolution."[58]

But what tactics could the organized proletariat have used against fascism on the way to power? Do not forget that fascism won power *legally.* Workers' militia, indispensable for fighting fascist bands while they played merely the role of "anti-labor militia," would no longer suffice to prevent fascism from gaining seats in parliament, winning public opinion, and entering the government through legal channels. Nor could a simple "general protest strike," even if effective throughout the country, block fascism's road to power—unless the strike was the point of departure for a revolutionary offensive. The Italian reformists tried it; at the end of July, 1922, they called a general strike throughout the pennisula. But they sought only to bring pressure on the government, on parliament and the Crown, to defend "civil liberties and the Constitution." But because the stoppage of work was not accompanied by aggressive action, it was child's play for the fascists to smash the movement. They insured the essential public services with "scabs" and made themselves masters of the streets. Far from blocking their road, this disastrous general strike was a moral victory for them—"the Caporetto* of the working-class movement."[59]

Then what could the organized proletariat have done? Once fascism embarks on the road to power, the labor movement has only one recourse left: outstrip the fascists and win power *first*. But the proletarian parties did not show themselves to be revolutionary; not for an instant did they dream of conquering power by force. The truth is that on the eve of fascism's victory, in both Italy and Germany, the labor movement was profoundly weakened and demoralized: not only because of unemployment; not only because of repeated defeats that came from want of bold tactics in the daily clashes with fascist bands; but chiefly *because the union organizations had been unable to defend the gains won by the working class*. In Italy, the Federation of Labor did not know how to resist the wage cuts during the crisis, or to force the employers in the metal industry to observe the law for workers' control. In Germany, the German General Federation of Labor prevented the workers from fighting against Bruening's decree-laws, which cut wages, on the pretext that to defend their livelihood would endanger the Bruening government, and Bruening was "better" than Hitler. This tactic, known as that of the "lesser evil," greatly demoralized the workers.

When fascism embarked on the conquest of power, the labor movement showed itself to be inert and absolutely incapable of outstripping it. In Italy, the Socialists posed as defenders of the established order and crawled at the feet of the rulers of the bourgeois state. They implored the royal *carabinieri* and the army not to yield power to Mussolini. At the end of July, their leader Turati went to the King to "remind him that he is the supreme defender of the Constitution."

In Germany, the reformist leaders begged Hindenburg and the Reichswehr to "do their duty" and not hand over power to Hitler.

---

* In this small town in Venetia, Italian troops were routed by the Germans and Austrians in 1917.

When Papen removed the Socialist government of Prussia on July 20, 1932, they limited themselves to protesting this "violation of the Constitution." They appealed to—the Supreme Court in Leipzig. Ten days before Hitler came to power, the executive committee of the Federation of Labor called on President Hindenburg. The union leaders "clung to faith in the state. They still hoped for help from the President of the Reich."[60] And on January 30, 1933, the day Hitler formed his government, *Vorwaerts* printed in a special edition: "In the face of a government that threatens a *coup d'etat*, the Social Democracy stands firm on the ground of the Constitution and legality." As for the Communists, in spite of their revolutionary verbiage, they took refuge behind the excuse that the reformists would do nothing—and so did nothing themselves.

5

Fascism is now in power; its leader has been entrusted by the head of the state with forming a government. But the last word has not been said, because the real adversary, the organized proletariat, is not yet conquered. The workers' parties and the unions still exist and are legal. We shall see how fascism utilizes the machinery of state to complete its victory, exterminate the workers' organizations, and install the dictatorship.

During the preceding period, when fascism was on the way to power, its tactics, as we have seen, were primarily legalistic. Its preparations for insurrection were only a bluff, intended to keep up the morale of its own troops. Now, just the reverse is true. Legalistic tactics are now only a war ruse intended to put the adversary to sleep, a mask under the cover of which fascism is already violating legality and methodically preparing a violent *coup*.

In Italy

When Mussolini was charged by the King with forming a cabinet, he realized that it would be dangerous to skip stages. The labor movement was not dead. The abrupt imposition of a dictatorship might provoke dangerous reactions, both on the part of the organized proletariat and the democratic and liberal parties. The former had to be put off their guard; the latter reassured. So the wolf disguised himself as a lamb, and in October, 1922, the new head of the government telegraphed to his lieutenants: "We must preserve discipline and respect others. In no case should we infringe on personal liberties." On November 9, he published a communique in which he declared he was determined to maintain liberty, reopen the labor exchanges, etc. At almost the same time he confided to Count Sforza, who had resigned as Ambassador from Italy in Paris, his intention to "preserve a democratic program."

This tactic achieved its end. Mussolini succeeded in taming the liberals. The wretches let themselves be persuaded that fascism was nothing more than a "strengthened liberalism," whose only purpose was to add a few touches to the democratic regime, strengthen the administration, and reconcile authority and liberty.[61] The old Giolitti smiled on the new Caesar; Amendola stated in an interview that for the first time there was a stable and lasting government in Italy capable of planning its work well into the future. Free Masonry, which had helped subsidize the March on Rome, rallied to the new regime in the person of its Grand Master, Torrigiani.

Mussolini was following a very definite plan, which was to obtain an absolute majority in parliament with the help of the liberals. In July, 1923, he was successful in getting the Chamber to pass a new electoral law; henceforth two-thirds of the seats were to be given to the party that obtained the majority of the vote, on condition that the latter represented at least 25 percent of the vote cast. The liberals not only accepted this law, but they went so far as to make a joint slate with the fascists in the elections of April 6, 1924. Fascism, which had had only 35 seats, won 286. From then on it had an absolute majority.

But while Mussolini was observing the rules of the constitutional game, behind the scenes he was already violating legality and preparing for a dictatorship. Throughout the peninsula, he permitted the local fascist leaders to take possession of the socialist, liberal, or *Popolari* (Catholic) municipal governments, and to behave like potentates. He secretly encouraged his bands to continue the bloody struggle against the organized proletariat. Publications, although legally authorized, were confiscated; printing plants were pillaged; labor exchanges and cooperatives were burned. The 1924 elections took place in an atmosphere of violence and fraud. And little by little, as the mask was lifted, the face of the dictatorship appeared. On June 6, 1924, Mussolini interrupted a Communist in the Chamber to exclaim: "We have admirable masters in Russia! We have only to imitate what has been done in Russia. . . . We are wrong not to follow their example completely. If we did so, you would be doing forced labor instead of being here. . . . You would get a load of lead in your back. We are not lacking in courage, and we will prove it sooner than you think."

Mussolini, in fact, could not temporize much longer. Water and fire, legality and illegality, cannot be wedded indefinitely. Once entered on the path of violence, it is necessary to go to the end. But constitutional guarantees had not been suspended and freedom of speech had not been abolished. The Socialist deputy Matteotti on June 10, 1924, denounced in the Chamber the violence committed during the electoral campaign. Mussolini's intimates replied by having him assassinated. This crime unloosed a wave of indignation throughout Italy. The press took hold of it. The liberals, finally disillusioned, suddenly perceived the real face of fascism. For six months the opposition, which was not yet gagged, used all the constitutional weapons at its disposal against the government.

Mussolini realized that it was high time to resort to dictatorship. On January 3, 1925, in the Chamber, he threw off the mask and cynically revealed his intentions. Following this, the police staged a series of attempts against his person, which he used as a pretext to promulgate emergency laws permitting him to exterminate his adversaries, dissolve the proletarian and democratic parties and union organizations, suppress all liberties, and confer on himself dictatorial powers (especially that of legislating by simple decree-law).

In Germany

When Hitler was appointed chancellor of the Reich by President Hindenburg, he likewise realized that it would be dangerous to go ahead too fast. The forces of the workers' parties and the Federation of Labor were intact. The sudden advent of a dictatorship might drive the proletariat to a general strike or an armed insurrection. It was better to lull the adversary by pretending to observe the Constitution. During the entire month of February, Hitler repeatedly asserted his respect for legality and called for calm.[62] Like Mussolini, he used this respite to assure himself an absolute majority in parliament. Having obtained from President Hindenburg, not without difficulty, the dissolution of the Reichstag, he scheduled new elections for March 5 and plunged his party into a new campaign.

But while Hitler was playing the role of a wolf in sheep's clothing, his friend Goering was feverishly preparing for a violent coup. He had learned from the Italian experience that it was impossible to play the two games at once—legality and illegality—for very long. So, what Mussolini took two years to do, he did in a few weeks. Master of the Prussian police, he began by purifying it; all the "republican" elements, from the Berlin Chief of Police to the pettiest inspector of the criminal force, were dismissed and replaced by reliable Nazis. A decree-law of February 4, practically gave the police the power to forbid all opposition publications or public meetings. Goering promised to protect personally all policemen who used their weapons against the "Reds." By another decree, he attached to the *Schupo's* (Berlin police) an "auxiliary police force" of 50,000 men recruited from the S.A. and S.S.

At the same time he secretly encouraged his bands to continue the bloody struggle against the proletariat. Everywhere the Nazis attacked their opponents, invaded their headquarters, and disrupted their public meetings. In Berlin they shadowed workers on their way home at night, beat them up, murdered them. According to the official figures, fifty-one anti-fascists were killed in political "riots" between January 30 and March 5.

It was impossible to postpone the violent coup until after the elections, for without it there would be no absolute majority. Before March 5, the date of the balloting, it was necessary at all costs to capture the imagination of the undecided, terrorize the recalcitrants by some extraordinary event, and—in case enough seats were not obtained—simply exclude the Communist deputies from the new Reichstag. Therefore Goering resorted to provocation. He took up the old idea of Darre and his friends of using an alleged Communist putsch as a pretext for violating legality and unleashing a crushing offensive against the proletariat. On February 24, the police staged a huge raid on the headquarters of the Communist Party. Goering claimed they found documents proving the imminence of a Bolshevik revolution (though the booty was so meager that the documents seized were never published). Then on the evening of the 26th, a small fire was discovered in the Berlin castle, but the attempt failed. Finally, on the night of the 27th to the 28th, Goering's men egged on a young terrorist to set fire to the Reichstag. At once the government pictured the fire as the signal for a Communist insurrection and, without losing an instant, got the President to sign a decree abolishing all constitutional rights and proclaiming a "state of emergency."

Within forty-eight hours, all power passed to the police. The Storm Troopers who had become "auxiliary policemen," beat, tortured, and assassinated the militant workers; the election meetings of the anti-fascist parties were forbidden, and the Communist deputies arrested. Thanks to this setting and terror, the Nazis won a striking victory in the March 5 elections, obtaining 288 seats. In order to have an absolute majority, they had only to outlaw the Communist Party and send a few Socialist deputies to concentration camps.

The dictatorship was still to be sanctioned. On March 24, the new Reichstag, in a room filled with armed Storm Troopers, passed by a vote of 441 to 94 a law granting full powers to Hitler to legislate "without following the procedure established by the Constitution"—that is to say, merely by decree-law. Two months later, all workers' parties and the unions were dissolved or "coordinated."[63]

6

What did the organized proletariat do during this last period? How did it try to resist? The labor leaders let themselves be put off guard by the apparently legalistic methods of the fascists. They issued no orders to take up arms. They did not call a general insurrectionary strike. No, they hoped to get the better of fascism, already installed in power, through winning an electoral victory.

In Italy

The Italian Socialists, as blind as ever, continued to cling to legality and the Constitution. In December, 1923, the Federation of Labor sent Mussolini a report of the atrocities committed by fascist bands and asked him to break with his own troops.[64] The Socialist Party took the electoral campaign of April, 1924, very seriously; Turati even had a debate at Turin with a fascist in a hall where Black Shirts guarded the entrance. And when, after Matteotti's assassination, a wave of revolt swept over the peninsula, the Socialists did not know how to exploit it. "At the unique moment," Nenni writes, "for calling the workers into the streets for insurrection, the tactic prevailed of a legal struggle on the judicial and parliamentary plane."[65] As a gesture of protest, the opposition was satisfied not to appear in parliament, and, like the ancient plebeians, they *retired to the Aventine.* "What are our opponents doing?" Mussolini mocked in the Chamber. "Are they calling general strikes, or even partial strikes? Are they organizing demonstrations in the streets? Are they trying to provoke revolts in the army? Nothing of the sort. They restrict themselves to press campaigns."[66] The Socialists launched the triple slogan: *Resignation of the government, dissolution of the militia, new elections.* They continued to display confidence in the King, whom they begged to break with Mussolini; they published, for his enlightenment, petition after petition. But the King disappointed them a second time.

In Germany

The German Socialists issued appeal after appeal for *calm*. On February 7, 1933, Kuenstler, head of the Berlin federation of the party, gave this instruction: "Above all, do not let yourselves be provoked. The life and health of the Berlin workers are too dear to be jeopardized lightly; they must be preserved for the day of struggle."[67] The party took the elections very seriously. "The people will have the opportunity on March 5th to take its destiny again into its own hands," exclaimed Otto Wels in a speech.[68] And when Hitler, having set fire to the Reichstag, unleashed the fascist violence, the executive committee of the German General Labor Federation sent President Hindenburg a tearful protest: "The unions have always opposed terrorism in all its forms. They have educated their members to struggle for a new social order without using violence."[69] Finally, on the night of March 5, the responsible leaders of the *Reichsbanner* divisions in the principle cities of Germany went to Berlin by motorcycle, begging to be given the order to fight. They received the reply: "Be calm! Above all, no bloodshed."[70]

Nor did the Communists organize any resistance. "The Communist Party," Torgler confessed in the Leipzig trial, "could expect nothing from an armed insurrection, and aspired for only one thing: to survive without accident until the elections, when it expected to win a marked success."[71] On February 26, one of the party leaders, Pieck, wrote: "Let the workers beware of giving the government any pretext for new measures against the Communist Party!" and Dimitrov himself exclaimed during the Leipzig trial: "Of all the National Socialist politicians, of all the police functionaries who appeared in this room to testify, I asked whether at the time of the Reichstag fire actual preparations for revolution could be observed. They all answered, with a few variations, 'No!'"[72]

As for the union leaders, their attitude was still more strange. They imagined that the union movement could come to an agreement with the fascist government as with previous governments, and that there was no absolute contradiction between union freedom and dictatorship. Imperceptibly, from one retreat to another, they *rallied to fascism.*

In Italy

The leaders of the Federation of Labor were ready to continue with the new state the same "collaboration" that had worked so well for them with the old. Mussolini understood their mentality, and immediately after the March on Rome he invited the general secretary of the Federation to enter his government. D'Aragona accepted. If Mussolini finally gave up this plan, it was only because his intimates objected. But the union leaders continued to offer themselves. The organ of the railway workers, the *Tribuna dei Ferrovieri,* published under the title, "Without Reservations," an editorial offering the fascist government the "collaboration" of the railway unions.[73] For a few months direct negotiations were carried on between the union leaders and Mussolini. In August, 1923, D'Aragona explained to the national committee of the Federation of Labor that the "collaboration" would not in any case be *political,* but only *technical* (sic). The Federation of Labor would participate in the advisory bodies of the state and in all bodies where problems of labor and production were to be discussed. "The Federation's policy cannot follow preconceived ideas. . . ." In the meantime, it broke with the Socialist Party.

But its servility did not save the Federation of Labor. At the end of 1926, it had to dissolve. Then its leaders substituted for it a Center for Cultural Association—intended to "assist by its advice and criticism the social action of the government." They published a manifesto in which they declared: *"The fascist regime is a reality, and any reality must be taken into consideration."* The union movement in the past, they explained, could not decide to declare itself either in favor of, or against, the state. However, it was necessary to choose and either wage a struggle for the destruction of the state or collaborate with, and integrate itself within it. They had decided on the second alternative—an alternative that "implies naturally the abandonment of the principle of class struggle."[74]

In Germany

The German union leaders were the twin brothers of their Italian colleagues. Therefore certain Nazi leaders, who were well acquainted with them, tried after 1932 to conciliate them. In one speech Gregor Strasser rejoiced that the discussions of the Federation of Labor had revealed opposition to the Socialist Party. "This is a development that makes it possible to foresee a united front of all German producers." In October, at a meeting in the Sportpalast, he issued a more specific invitation to the secretary of the Labor Federation, who had just made an outright nationalist speech: "If Leipart really thinks in this manner, we have the broadest perspectives before us. . . ."

When Hitler took power, the Federation's executive committee declared that it "will await the government's actions." First of all, the Federation broke with the Socialist Party, and on March 20th it published a manifesto: "The union organizations are the expression of an indisputable social necessity, an indispensable part of the very social order. . . . As a result of the natural order of things, they are increasingly integrated into the state. The social task of the unions must be carried out, *whatever the nature of the state regime.* . . . Union organizations make no claim to influence state power directly. *Their task here can be merely to put at the disposal of the government and parliament knowledge and experience acquired in this field.* . . ."

On April 7, Leipart raised his bid and declared that the unions *"are pursuing the same end as the government, namely to found freedom of the nation at home and abroad on the productive forces of the whole people."* On April 20, the national committee of the Federation invited unionists to take part in the May 1st celebration as a symbol of the incorporation of the working class into the National Socialist state.[75]

Painting of Italian fascist martyr slain by Socialists (in the Exposition of the Fascist Revolution).

The Hitler-Storm Troop, a predecessor of the S. A., in Munich in 1923.

Freikorps parades in Munich in 1923.

"Steelhelmets" parade in Coblenz in 1930.

Members of Social Democratic Reichsbanner League defend 1930 Berlin rally.

German Communist Party leader Thaelmann, in Red Front uniform, gives clenched-fist salute.

Nazi Storm Troopers march on Communist Party headquarters in Berlin on January 22, 1933.

Youth organizations of the Italian (left) and German (right) fascists rally.

Mussolini (with sash) participates in ceremony marking the tenth anniversary of the March on Rome, 1932.

Hitler and Von Papen on way to Reichstag after Reichstag fire, 1933.

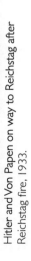

King of Italy and Mussolini ride through the streets of Milan in a carriage.

Mussolini addresses rally in Milan in 1936.

Swastika flag flies over Nazi-occupied trade union headquarters in Munich in 1933.

6

The rise and fall of the
fascist plebeians

1

Fascism has won power. Its financial backers have attained their objectives: the annihilation of parliamentary democracy, the extermination of the proletarian organizations, and the formation of an authoritarian state through which they can impose their will and raise their profits.

But there is a reverse side to the medal: the capitalist magnates are now at grips with the demands of the fascist *plebeians*. We are already familiar with the mentality of these plebeians (Chapter 2). They conquered power not only for the sake of their financial backers *but also for their own sake.* They constitute, in Mussolini's words, "a new political class."[1] They are determined to drive out ruthlessly, with the brutality of parvenues, the old political staff of the bourgeoisie. They demand all posts and functions for themselves.

The magnates are a little worried by these demands—not that they have entirely failed to foresee them. For some time they have realized there was a danger in abandoning the entire direction of the state to the fascist plebs. That is why they would have preferred, at least in the beginning, merely the participation of fascism in a

159

traditional bourgeois government. But the plebeians' impatience thwarted these plans.

Nevertheless the magnates obtain some safeguards: the fascist ministers are surrounded by reliable people belonging to the "old political class." But the plebeians have other intentions; they insist on having *all the power* and demand that the former political servants of the bourgeoisie be driven out to the last man. Should the magnates yield or not? They have very little choice because *they still need the plebeians.* The assistance of the latter is indispensable for the transformation of the democratic state into a dictatorship, for dealing the death blow to the organized proletariat. Nobody can beat up, nobody can torture the militant workers better than these men who have come from the people. Hence the magnates resign themselves, not without apprehension, to sacrificing their old political staff; they abandon *all power* to the fascist plebeians.

The phenomenon, to tell the truth, is not entirely new: there is an historical precedent. On December 2, 1851, the French bourgeoisie in the same way permitted the plebeian partisans of Louis Bonaparte "to suppress and annihilate" its old political staff, "its speaking and writing section, its politicians and its literati, its platform and its press." "At the court," Marx says, "in the ministries, at the head of the administration and the army, a crowd of fellows pushes forward, of the best of whom it can be said that no one knows whence he comes, a noisy, disreputable, rapacious crowd of Bohemians. . . ." The bourgeoisie put up with this invasion because, thanks to the plebeians' aid, it was assured of the "strong and absolute government" it needed to save its profits. And deceived by appearances, taking this replacement of one "political class" by another for a real revolution, the old fool Guizot wrote: "This is the complete and final triumph of socialism!"[2]

In Italy

Long before taking power, the Italian plebeians understood that the "tainted class [the political bourgeoisie] was giving up its hand, turning public affairs over to those who were worthier."[3] Hence the

The rise and fall of the plebeians 161

government formed by Mussolini after the March on Rome was far from satisfying them. More than half of the ministers belonged to the "old political class"; the fascist ministers were surrounded by gentlemen like General Diaz in the War Department, Admiral Thaon di Reval in the Navy, the liberal Gentile in Public Instruction, the Nationalist Federzoni in the Colonies, and the Radical Colonna di Cesaro in Posts and Telegraphs. The plebeians were annoyed by the duration of the "transitional regime" and brought pressure on Mussolini to get rid of his non-fascist collaborators and to found at last what they called the *totalitarian state*. During the summer of 1923, the tension was great between the temporizers and extremists in the party. Rocca was expelled for daring to declare that "the revolution has been made by the fascists for Italy and *not alone for the fascists*," and for having advocated the transformation of the fascist party into a great national party. Mussolini took up the defense of Rocca against Farinacci, the leader of the plebeians.[4] In 1924 he wrote, "Beside party fascism, there is the Italian nation."[5]

But in his heart, he had already chosen the *totalitarian state*. As early as August 11, 1922, he declared in Naples: "A process is under way through which fascism will embody the state." Later, he confessed to Emil Ludwig that he *intentionally* began "by 50 percent," with a coalition government, before proceeding to totalitarian fascism.[6] In April, 1923, an official notice from the Volta agency informed the public that "the fascist regime, properly speaking, has *not yet* begun, and the present period is only a *preparatory period*."[7]

But already the fascist state was being superimposed on the established state. On January 13, 1923, Mussolini duplicated the cabinet with a "Grand Council" that was 100 percent fascist, composed of the chief leaders of the party. The Grand Council decided, in one of its first sessions, to supplement the regular army with a "voluntary militia for national safety," to be personally directed by the head of the government. Functionaries were duplicated in all ranks of the administrative hierarchy by fascist supervisors. Finally, after Matteotti's assassination, Mussolini decided to give satisfaction to the plebeians, and he proclaimed the advent of the "totalitarian state." "Our motto," he exclaimed, "*is all power to fascism!*"[8]—a caricature of the slogan of the October Revolution, "*All power to the Soviets!*" Olivetti explained that the fascist party, being an army, "cannot admit the coexistence of other armies with different aims. It demands a unified command. . . . The other parties have no right to exist."[9] Fascism claimed to be identical with the state, and Sergio Pannunzio coined the expression, *Party-State.*[10]

Between 1925 and 1926 all parties except the fascist party were forcibly dissolved; fascism was implacable not only toward labor organizations and proletarian parties *but also toward the bourgeois parties and the former political staff of the bourgeoisie.* "The liberals," Volpe wrote, "either became fascists or left political life. Many irreconcilable adversaries went into exile abroad either voluntarily or by compulsion."[11] Malaparte says: "After having forcibly dissolved the republican and Catholic organizations, the Black Shirts went to work against the liberals, democrats, and Free Masons."[12] By a decree of November 26, 1925, Free Masonry was forbidden, the "Masonic lodges invaded and wrecked, their equipment and insignia destroyed or thrown into the streets."[13] The library of the liberal philosopher Benedetto Croce was sacked, and the liberal leaders, Amendola and Gobetti, as well as later the Grand Master of the Masons, Torrigiani, were subjected to such physical violence that they died from it. Any attempt to revive the old parties was punishable by twenty years imprisonment. Moreover the secret police *(Ovra),* and "Special Court" set up by the laws of November 26, 1926, undertook to make this extremely difficult, if not impossible.

After 1925 the government was "composed entirely and exclusively of fascists."[14] The members of the old political staff of the bourgeoisie, such as Federzoni and Gentile, found grace with fascism only by embracing the fascist faith. One of the "superfascist" laws of 1925, that of December 24, authorized the head of the government to "discharge from service all civil and military functionaries of the state whose conduct, whether in office or outside, does not fully demonstrate their ability to perform their duties faithfully, or is incompatible with the political principles of the government." The army staffs were renewed, officers being retired and replaced by reliable fascist elements. A "constant preoccupation" of the plebeians was "the attempt to concentrate in their own hands unconditional control of the army."[15] Aviation, the modern branch of the service par excellence, was entrusted to a plebeian, Italo Balbo.

The erection of the totalitarian state was completed by the law of December 19, 1928. The fascist Grand Council is now the "supreme body responsible for coordinating all the activities of the government." The Grand Council discusses all governmental problems *before* the Cabinet, which has only an administrative function, has acted on them. The sovereign himself is reduced to the role of a rubber stamp, for the Grand Council assumes the right of intervening in certain questions, such as the right to declare war or make peace, which had formerly been prerogatives of the Crown. The succession to the throne will henceforth be determined only by a constitutional law enacted after consultation with the Grand Council—without which consultation the law would be void. In the same way, the designation of a successor to the head of the government, in the event of a vacancy, belongs exclusively to the Grand Council, which will "respectfully propose" to the Crown the new head, as well as his collaborators. As for the fascist party, it is merged with the state, and transformed from a simple private association into a public institution. "It was the foundation of the state power,"[16] "the axis of the regime, without which the regime can no more be imagined than a man without a backbone."[17]

The party secretary is henceforth named by governmental decree. He is given the title and functions of a Cabinet minister. He is the most important person in the regime, after the head of the government, and in the latter's absence replaces him in presiding over the Cabinet. The interpenetration of the party and state is not limited to the upper ranks; all the party's regional secretaries are appointed, on the nomination of the party's secretary, by a governmental decree.[18]

With the completion of the totalitarian state "the aristocracy of scarcely civilized peasants who make up the fascist leadership"[19] had achieved its ends. It had *all the power,* all the posts, all the stipends. As Silvio Trentin has said: "There was a fantastic rush for bounties, offices, jobs, adventures. . . . The public administration was put up for auction."[20]

In Germany

The National Socialist plebeians also intended to substitute themselves for the entire former political staff of the bourgeoisie. "History has never seen," states the *Voelkischer Beobachter,* "a state regenerated by others than those who were the creators and promoters of the new idea. *Nobody but ourselves* has the will and ability necessary to institute the new order."[21] Goebbels said: "When we have conquered the state, that state will be *our* state. . . . If in our struggle against a corrupt system, we are today forced to be a 'party' . . . the instant the system crumbles, *we will become the state.*"[22] Hence the government formed by Hitler on January 30, 1933, was far from being satisfactory to the plebeians. Gentlemen who had been members of the old political staff surrounded the National Socialist ministers: von Papen as Vice Chancellor and Commissioner in Prussia; Hugenberg, Minister of National Economy and Agriculture; von Neurath, Minister of Foreign Affairs; Count Schwerin von Krosigk, Minister of Finance; Baron Eltz von Rubenach, Minister of Roads and Communications; Seldte (head of the Steel Helmets), Minister of Labor; Gerecke, Unemployment Commissioner; etc.

Drunk with victory, the Nazi plebeians demanded that the old political staff be evicted. Goering hastened to duplicate the Prussian police with an "auxiliary police" recruited from the Storm Troops. And after the Reichstag fire, all parties except the National Socialist party were condemned to perish; National Socialism persecuted not only the labor organizations and proletarian parties *but also the bourgeois parties and the former political staff of the bourgeoisie.* The very day Hitler obtained full powers from the Reichstag, March 23, 1933, the Unemployment Commissioner, Gerecke, Hindenburg's former electoral agent, was arrested on the charge of embezzlement. On April 11, Hitler took from Papen his title of Commissioner of the Reich in Prussia. On April 26, one of the leaders of the powerful Steel Helmet association, Duesterberg, was removed. Nevertheless, the German National Party (conservative), tried to resist, and when deprived of the support of the Steel Helmets, it improvised a new militia in green shirts, the *Kampfring*. But in the early part of June, the Storm Troop plebeians attacked the *Kampfring* and occupied its headquarters, while the police chiefs prohibited its local sections. Hugenberg, realizing the uselessness of further resistance, gave up his two cabinet portfolios, and his party dissolved. Likewise, on July 5, the Catholic Centrist party voted for its own dissolution.

The fascist brutes were not tender with the old political servants of the bourgeoisie. One instance, among others: Doctor Oberfohren, Hugenberg's associate at the head of the German National Party, was found to have "committed suicide" in his home on May 6. The law of July 15 provided penalties of from three years imprisonment to "more severe punishment" for anyone trying to reconstitute the prohibited parties or found a new one. Moreover, the secret police (Gestapo) and the "People's Court" undertook to make this impossible.

The Reich's government was now composed exclusively of Nazis. Ministers who were members of the old political staff had to join the National Socialist Party or go out of office. In the governmental councils, the plebeians acquired numerical preponderance; Goering, Goebbels, Darre, Hess, Roehm, Rust, Frank, Kerrl, etc. in turn became ministers of the Reich.

A law of April 7, 1933, empowered the Fuehrer-Chancellor to remove all functionaries "who do not offer guarantees of always putting themselves at the service of the national revolution,"[*] and officers suspected of coolness toward the new regime were retired.

---

[*] The legislation applying to functionaries, promulgated in January, 1937, provides that any functionaries "who cease to offer all guarantees toward the National Socialist regime" shall be officially retired.

This was the case of the Commander in Chief himself, General von Hammerstein, a personal friend of General von Schleicher. The plebeians were obsessed with the idea of controlling the army, and they succeeded in naming to the ministry of the Reichswehr two "sympathizers," General von Blomberg and his adviser, Colonel von Reichenau. Goering, like Balbo in Italy, took over aviation.

On July 10, the papers published a "governmental notice" printed in large type: "There are no more parties. The National Socialist movement has become the sole pillar of state. . . . There are reliable National Socialists in all the important posts." On July 15, a law was promulgated stating: "There is in Germany only one political party: the National Socialist Party." Less than a year after taking power, the party was definitely merged with the state, the law of December 2, 1933, proclaiming that after the victory of the National Socialist revolution, the party became "the ideological support of the state, and remains indissolubly attached to it." It became a public body, and it was in order to make the fusion more concrete that Hitler's assistant in the party leadership, Rudolf Hess, and the chief of staff of the Storm Troops, Roehm, were named ministers of the Reich. The last stone of the totalitarian state was laid when President Hindenburg died and Hitler, the party leader, added by decree on August 2, 1934, to his title of Chancellor that of head of the state. Finally, at the Nuremberg Congress of 1935, the red flag with the swastika became the only state flag, the old imperial flag of black, white and red being definitely thrown on the scrap heap. Hitler launched the formula: "The state is the party, and the party the state."

With the completion of the totalitarian state the Nazi plebeians had achieved their ends. They had *all the power,* all the posts, and all the stipends. A caste of parasites, greedy and corrupt, was installed in the government; an idea of its numerical size could be obtained from the fact that at the Nuremberg Congress every year the parade of *party leaders alone* included nearly a million participants. A fantastic view! Most of these leaders "ride in luxurious cars and live in palaces, which are rising like mushrooms."[23] "We are now delivered over to gang leaders," sighed a lady of the old aristocracy.[24]

Later, a spokesman of the old "respectable" bourgeoisie, Hermann Rauschning, indulged in all sorts of self-recrimination, admitting that out of hatred for the proletariat, he and his kind had handed Germany over to people who respected nothing. He wrote a whole book on the theme: *We Had Not Wanted That*. In his chagrin, he went so far as to forget that these "nihilists" (whom he really did too great an honor in treating as revolutionaries) saved his class and the system it lives by at a critical hour. All he saw was the price they had to pay for services rendered.[25]

2

The capitalist magnates rightly felt a little uneasy when they turned over all power to the plebeians. The latter doubtless do not wish to attack seriously the privileges of those on whom they live, and who have never ceased overwhelming them with generosity. The industrialists continue, in fact, after the taking of power, to fill the coffers of the party and its associated organizations. These subsidies in Germany were christened "Adolf Hitler Funds from German Industry." In addition, the magnates give the plebeian leaders direct "rake-offs" in the form of paid posts in the management of their businesses, etc. But, on the other hand, the plebeians must take into account the popular masses they have "set marching." To win these masses, they spoke an *anti-capitalist* language (Chapter 4), which the masses took seriously. And now that the fascists are in power, the masses insist on their keeping their word. Fascism proclaims in vain that it has abolished the class struggle; the petty bourgeois and proletarians who donned the black or brown shirts continue to obey an obscure class instinct, and their interests remain in conflict with those of the capitalist magnates. But since victorious fascism is careful not to touch capitalist privileges, the rank and file plebeians grow impatient and demand that the revolution be *continued*, or even that it be followed by a *second revolution*.

The plebeian leaders, big and small, cannot disregard these demands. In a fascist, as in a democratic regime—and in spite of the suppression of the right to vote—politicians acquire and preserve their influence and prestige only to the extent that they are supported by a "social base." Each has carved for himself a piece of cake, a private fief, and he wants not only to preserve this fief but to enlarge it. Without a social base, he would represent only himself and cease to be a person who is flattered and feared; he would be suspended in a vacuum, at the mercy of the dictator's whim or a conspiracy of his rivals. Hence he must, *to a certain extent,* be the interpreter of the demands and aspirations of his troops, and proclaim—with more or less conviction—*that the revolution has only begun, that a second revolution is necessary.*

Such language is exceedingly displeasing to the capitalist magnates. They did not change their political staff in order to entrust the defense of their interests to agitators and demagogues. The specter of the "second revolution" haunts them. They demand that the most unruly plebeians be eliminated ruthlessly.

We have seen the state being absorbed by the party; *now we see the party being tamed by the dictatorial state.* Of course the government posts continue to be occupied by fascists, *but a pitiless selection of these fascists is being carried out.* Those keep their jobs who consent to be silent, to be nothing more than "an oligarchy expressly renouncing freedom of thought,"[26] and to be only the docile servants of the Leader and the money powers who rule under cover of the Leader. The others, the demagogues, must either recant and put a muffler on their demagogy, or disappear. After this purification, the party tends to become a mere government machine, a bureaucratic organism without life of its own, while the fascist militia, also purged, is disarmed and reduced to impotence. The dictatorship leans less and less on the popular masses and *more and more on the traditional repressive forces, the army and the police.* "Fascism, become bureaucratic, approaches very closely to other forms of military and police dictatorship."[27]

For convenience in exposition, the two processes have been presented as *successive,* but in reality they overlap one another, the fusion of the state and the fascist party being not yet accomplished when the dictatorial state is already beginning to subjugate the party.

In Italy

After power was won, the disappointment of the fascist troops was so great that the plebeian leaders had to take it into account and speak a violently demagogic language. "We have made the revolution. . . . We are ready if necessary to begin it again," states the *Popolo di Lombardia* on January 13, 1923. The *Assalto* of Bologna for April 14 published these lines from the pen of a plebeian leader: "The landowners and industrialists think that fascism should moderate the demands of the workers but not the exploitation of capital. It was not for this that two thousand fascists died and two hundred thousand are ready to die. . . . I have thrashed revolutionary workers, and I am ready to thrash the landowners in the same way." Eduardo Frosini addressed an open letter to Mussolini: "You have so transformed the program of 1919 that you are now protecting those whom fascism promised to combat. You have thrown yourself into the arms of those you wanted to crush. And fascism is identifying itself with the reaction in the service of the monarchy and the bourgeoisie." Forni spoke of the *necessity of a new March on Rome*. And the conflict was not limited to words: in Rome, Mussolini's partisans and extremists several times fought with machine guns; in Leghorn, extremists took possession of the militia barracks and the party headquarters. Practically everywhere in the provinces the local fascist leaders, the *"Ras,"* rebelled against the policies of the Leader.[28]

The capitalist magnates grew worried. They demanded that Mussolini should pitilessly eliminate the more troublesome plebeians. "During the first year," Mussolini told Emil Ludwig, "I had to rid myself of a hundred and fifty thousand fascists in order to make the party a more concentrated force. Not until later could I begin to train an elite in order to transform crude force into orderly government."[29] Silone speaks of several tens of thousands of fascists who took part in the March on Rome and who were expelled during 1923. Mussolini, Aniante states, "has sent a good number abroad, has thrown others in prison, and still others have been 'confined' to their provinces with the order not to move. . . . Some he has established outside of politics."[30] The party underwent profound alterations. Many *Fasci* were dissolved. "They eliminate," according to Silone, "all who show their discontent, and replace them with functionaries and public service employees whose loyalty is known."[31]

A second time, in 1925–1926, the party was cleansed from base to summit. "We were obliged," Mussolini explained, "to rebuild the fascist party from top to bottom."[32] A new batch of "old fascists" was thrown out. Farinacci was driven out of the secretariat, and at the same time the party membership books were closed and not reopened until 1931.

In 1928 there was a new purge. The federation of fascist "unions" was dissolved and its general secretary, Rossoni, as well as all the "trade union" plebeians placed by him in various posts in the organization, dismissed (Chapter 8).

As a matter of fact, Mussolini did not decide definitely to bless the union of the party and state *until the party, rid of its most restless elements, had become nothing more than an administrative machine servile to his orders.* Although the law of December 9, 1928, marked the completion of the totalitarian state, it marked at the same time the domestication of the party by the state. In appearance, no doubt, the party had absorbed the state, but in fact, even in the terms of the law, it was only a "civil militia *in the service* of the state." Commenting on the decree that gave the secretary of the party the title and function of minister, the Rome correspondent of the *Temps* wrote: "*The supremacy of the state over the party has now been established. The party has been absorbed by the state.*"[33]

While the party was subordinated to the state, the militia, rid of its undesirable elements, was subordinated to the regular army. Even before coming to power, Mussolini had revealed his designs. In an article in the *Popolo d'Italia* on October 26, 1922, he states in fact: "What shall we do with the squadrons of action when we are in power? . . . The fascist militia will be transformed. The squadrons will cease to be the organs of a party and become the organs of the state; transformed into bodies for premilitary training, they will be the ideal of the nation in arms. . . ."[34] It only remained to put this program into practice. The "squadrons of action" were incorporated into the militia in 1923 only after a careful weeding out. In August 1924, Mussolini staffed the militia with army officers. Little by little the "old fascists" were replaced by young men who had gone through the mill in the youth organizations. Finally, and most important, the militia was *disarmed.* In military parlance, it became only a "reserve." The militiaman was a civilian called on, at more or less rare intervals, to wear a uniform, undergo military training, or figure in parades. Only one part of the militia was on permanent duty, and it played the innocuous role of auxiliary police charged with watching the mails, railways, ports, highways, forests, coast defense, etc. In time of war the militiamen individually joined their regular troops; although several militia units preserved their identity, they were integrated into various army corps, *under the orders of army officers.* Such was the case of the Black Shirt divisions taking part in the Abyssinian campaign.[35] After February 1, 1935, the militia was charged with organizing, *always under the orders and control of army officers,* premilitary and postmilitary training.

In short, the fascist militia was no longer, as in the days immediately after the "revolution," responsible for internal order and the defense of the government. That task fell more and more to the *carabinieri,* who are *part of the army under the command of a regular army general.* At the end of 1935, the *carabinieri* units were sharply reinforced.

As for the youth organization, the *Opera Balilla,* it lost its autonomy and became, under the name of the *Italian Youth of the Lictor* (GIL), an organization for military training, controlled by the army and under official army regulations.[36]

While this evolution was going on, the role of the army continually increased: "The army," said the *Giornale d'Italia,* "is becoming, through the will of fascism, the new aristocracy of the nation."[37] A symbolic fact is that on several occasions soldiers of the regular army, and not militiamen, mounted guard before the Exposition of the Fascist Revolution.[38] On the twelfth anniversary of the founding of the *militia,* February 1, 1935, detachments of all the *regular* troops garrisoned in Rome paraded in the capital.[39]

The victory won in Ethiopia by General (promoted to Marshal) Badoglio completely established the preponderant position of the army—and not only the army but the King, supreme commander of the army, who up to that time had played a rather obscure role in the fascist regime. "The royal house and the military high command received all the honors," a journalist observed in May, 1936.[40] The King was made a marshal of the Empire at the same time as the Duce.[41]

Because fascism today in no way resembles the fascism of yesterday, the army—though at first somewhat reluctantly—allowed itself to be "fascized." Beginning with the winter of 1934, courses in "fascist education" were given in all the officers' and noncommissioned officers' schools. Various measures facilitated the entrance of officers into the fascist party, and in Genoa the officers of a cavalry regiment paid a ceremonial visit to the local secretary of the fascist party.[42] At the same time, the House of Savoy and the regime became more friendly: in a decree the King used the expression, the "fascist fatherland."[43] He paid a visit to Mussolini's birthplace in Predappio.[44] His cousin, the Duke of Pistoia, wrote an article for Mussolini's paper, the *Popolo d'Italia,* and the Rome correspondent of the *Temps* pointed out: "This is the first time a member of the House of Savoy has officially taken a position on political matters since the advent of fascism."[45]

The fascist "revolution," resting on Black Shirt plebeians, had became a *military-police dictatorship.*

In Germany

After taking power, Hitler sought to master the plebeian forces which he had himself unleashed. But he was overwhelmed by a vast wave from below—far more powerful than its Italian counterpart ten years before. The thousands of petty bourgeois and unemployed who had believed in National Socialist demagogy, behaving as if in conquered territory, demanded that the *anti-capitalist* promises be kept. Hungry young men from the Storm Troops, the workers of the "National Socialist shop cells," hammered their fists on the employers' desks, demanding wage increases and the control, or even the nationalization of industry. In a hurry to enlarge their respective fiefs, the plebeian leaders opened wide the doors of the party, the Storm Troops, and the "shop cells." A number of former Marxists thus came to swell the ranks of the Brown army, and the masses, already effervescent, were worked on by that yeast. The wave broke with such violence that it seemed likely to sweep everything away.

The plebeian leaders, lest they be isolated from their troops, had to speak a radical language. In a popular meeting organized by the S.A., one of them exclaimed: "Our revolution . . . has only begun. We have not yet attained any of our goals. They talk about a national government, a national awakening. . . . What is all that? What matters is the *socialist* part of our program. . . . We have only one more enemy to conquer: the bourgeoisie!"[46]

But the reaction was not slow to move. The bourgeoisie had sacrificed its former political staff and let the Nazi plebeians have the *entire power* only on condition that the latter should obediently defend its interests; it had not entrusted them with the task of crushing Bolshevism only to have a new bolshevism arise from their midst, even a "national" bolshevism. As early as May, the first signs of a turn were apparent. Goering, on the 9th, severely forbade any Prussian policeman to belong to the S.A. or S.S., or to wear the swastika.[47] Goebbels announced in an article that "The National Socialist Party will soon undergo a cleansing; undesirable elements will be expelled. We shall carefully guard against the shop cells being invaded by Marxist elements."[48] But these first purges did not suffice. The patience of the capitalist magnates was exhausted: President Hindenburg in their behalf summoned the Chancellor to Neudeck and demanded an immediate right-about-face, and the generals of the Reichswehr let him know that "there would be serious danger in going further along the road he has entered."[49]

Hitler immediately obeyed his financial backers. At a meeting of the S.A. and S.S. leaders, held at Bad-Reichenhall, Bavaria, on July 1 and 2, he made this unexpected announcement: "I will oppose with my last strength a second revolutionary wave. . . . Whoever rises against the regular authority of the state, will be unceremoniously collared."[50] On the 10th, the papers published in large type a "governmental notice" confirming the "close of the German revolution." "To speak of continuing the revolution, to say nothing of making a second one . . . such words constitute sabotage of the national revolution and will be severely punished."[51] At the same time that certain passages of this notice proclaimed the definitive fusion of the state and the party (see above), other passages announced the domestication of the party by the dictatorial state: "The organizations and groups of the National Socialist Party must not assume governmental powers. . . . At all costs and in all fields, the authority of the state must be assured."

Naturally these shifts of the helm to the right met with resistance: many mutinies broke out in the Storm Troops, the shop cells, and the labor camps; everywhere the disappointed plebeians openly revolted. Then Goering abruptly interrupted his vacation on July 23 to decree that political crimes would be punished pitilessly, even by capital punishment. On the same date, the military law was amended to permit the *Statthalters* [provincial governors] *to call on the forces of the Reichswehr in case of political disturbances.*[52]

While the law of December 2, 1933, apparently signified the final absorption of the state by the party (see above), it actually meant the subjection of the party to the state. Henceforth members of the party and the Storm Troops were subject to civil authorities empowered to impose severe legal penalties (arrest and imprisonment) for breaches of discipline and order. In January, 1934, Goering ordered the police to apprehend, in case of necessity, Nazi Storm Troopers, even in uniform; any resistance to the police would be prosecuted as an attempt to resist state authority.[53]

The plebeian torrent raged too violently to be dammed up so quickly. A young Nazi confided his disappointment in these words:

"How could our comrades in the government believe that capitalism, interest slavery, and shameless exploitation were destroyed? They pass the Stock Exchange with its crowned pediments and read interminable balance sheets and dividend reports in the bourgeois papers. . . . They see the capitalists defending their last bastions with the strength of despair. That is why the movement cannot give itself a breathing spell. Let us continue the struggle in the old spirit, for many things are not yet accomplished. . . . We still hope that our National Socialist revolution will not change its guise until we have built the Third Reich."[54] The young leader of the Berlin Storm Troops, Ernst, who was executed on June 30, had written in a sort of testament which there is every reason to believe authentic: "I have served the Fuehrer ever since I was eleven years old. I will remain faithful to him until death. . . . But it is unbearable to think that the S.A. is betrayed by the very ones it has put in power."[55]

In order not to cut themselves off from their social base, the plebeian leaders had to continue to resort to demagogy. This was particularly true of the Chief-of-Staff of the Storm Troops, Roehm. Doubtless this uneducated hireling, caring most of all for a gay life, was a "fake socialist."[56] But among the three million poor devils in brown shirts the idea of the "second revolution" remained alive, and it was impossible for Roehm to keep his troops in hand without becoming their spokesman. "Whoever imagines," he exclaimed, "that the task of the S.A. is done must resign himself to the idea that we are here and here to stay."[57] "The revolutionary tendency must be maintained in the S.A. I do not wish to lead sheep for the bourgeoisie to laugh at, but *revolutionists!*"[58] "The revolution we have made is not a national revolution but a National Socialist revolution. We must even put the accent on the last word, *Socialist*. Our Storm Troops are the complete incarnation of the revolutionary idea."[59]

Roehm felt all the more need to base himself on his troops because his personal position was threatened. An old disagreement brought him into conflict with the generals of the Reichswehr. The regular army never tolerated the infringement of its prerogatives by the S.A. and clung jealously to its monopoly. True, it admitted that the Storm Troops rendered useful services as associations for military training, but their members ought not to "play soldier." The Reichswehr distrusted the plebeian mentality of these irregular bodies: "Ambitious and utterly unscrupulous young men have been promoted in a few months to the rank of army major and brigadier generals. At an age when they would be at most captains in the Reichswehr, they are placed, without having served any apprenticeship, at the head of 100,000 men."[60] The S.A. for its part heartily detested the regular army, the citadel of "reaction." The state would never be "totalitarian" so long as any force escaped "coordination," and the army was not National Socialist; it pursued its own aims. "There is no bond," Roehm declared, "between the Reichswehr and the Storm Troops *since the army took no part in the national revolution.*"[61]

In reality the leaders of the Reichswehr were not hostile to National Socialism. Quite the contrary; they were grateful to Hitler for seeking to re-establish the military might of Germany. They even accepted, in principle, the fusion of the army and the regime—*but on one condition: that this fusion should not be to the advantage of the plebeian extremists, and that Hitler should first reduce these hotheads to impotence.* During a brief cruise on the Baltic in the early spring, the Fuehrer yielded to these demands. Roehm was expelled from the officers' associations and sent on leave for several weeks at the beginning of June, 1934. As for the Storm Troops, they too were "given a vacation" of a month, dating from July 1, during which time the men were not to have the right to wear uniforms.

The result of these measures was to intensify, and not quiet, the ferment. The capitalist magnates grew more and more alarmed. On June 28, Hitler had to go in person to Krupp, in Essen, to get his orders. In the *Voelkischer Beobachter* for June 29, General von Blomberg assured the Chancellor of his unlimited support, at the same time ordering a "state of alarm" for the Reichswehr.

And on the 30th, Hitler had his oldest collaborators, Roehm, Gregor Strasser, Ernst, and others, shot down like dogs. Throughout Germany, partisans of the "second revolution" were executed in hundreds. The Reichswehr remained in the background but ready to intervene, as it did in Munich.[62] After the slaughter, General von Blomberg, on terminating the state of alarm, publicly congratulated the Fuehrer for having "attacked and crushed the traitors and rebels."

On June 30, a veritable *coup d'etat* had been carried out. *From now on, the principle support of the dictatorship was no longer the plebeian Storm Troops but the regular army.* Manifestations of this development became more frequent. Hitler ceased to appear in public except flanked by generals, and he promised the army that "it will always be able to have confidence in him."[63] At the party congress in Nuremberg, which the generals attended for the first time, he exalted the "marvelous and glorious army,"[64] and set aside a special day for it.

The essential demand of the Reichswehr was granted: hereafter "the army alone bears arms in the state." The liquidation of the Storm Troops began. The law conferring on their commander the title of minister of the Reich was abrogated, and the upper ranks were reformed with reliable men. In the ranks a huge purge was undertaken. All doubtful elements were dismissed, and the Storm Troopers who were not dismissed had the right to wear uniforms only while on duty, which was seldom. The drills that were formerly held every Sunday became less and less frequent. A new police force, the *Feldjaegerkorps,* was given the special responsibility of supervising the Storm Troopers and of wearing uniforms. As for arms, they were put in a safe place—in armories controlled by the Reichswehr. From armed militiamen, the S.A. members had been transformed into simple propagandists for the cause.

The Elite Guards, the S.S., were treated no better. Nursing an old grudge against the S.A., they played a decisive role in the June 30 events. They hoped to reap the benefit and to absorb a part of the liquidated Storm Troops. The army, however, not only rejected that plan but undertook to liquidate the S.S. in its turn. The latter tried to resist, and at the end of December, 1934, there came near being a repetition of June 30. But finally the will of the generals prevailed, and nothing was left of the S.S. but a few contingents, carefully selected, which were assigned police functions under the control of the Reichswehr.

Finally—and most important—the army, whose intervention had already been required on several occasions, *was made responsible,* by the decree of January 17, 1936, *for maintaining order by force of arms in case of political disturbances.*[65]

At the same time that the Storm Troopers were being reduced to impotence, the party itself was purged from top to bottom. At the Nuremberg Congress in September, 1934, Hitler announced *a most rigid weeding out of party members* and the expulsion of all who were unwilling to subject themselves to the party without reservations.[66] At the 1935 Congress, he confirmed this: "Our ranks have been submitted to a severe cleansing."[67] Inside this enormous mass of more than four million members, expulsions, arrests, and even secret executions, became more and more frequent. The dictatorship attacked the "petty Fuehrers," the "little Hitlers," who, like the Italian *"Ras"* of the years of 1923 and 1924, had succeeded in carving out fiefs for themselves and appropriating for their own advantage a share of the state authority. Many subordinate party functionaries were relieved of their duties. Nor did the purge spare plebeians in high places in the hierarchy.

The party was more and more brought under the strict guardianship of the state. In November, 1934, it was established by decree that "all party public meetings and demonstrations . . . must be approved by the competent [governmental] authority." In April, 1935, the Fuehrer's deputy in the party leadership, Hess, declared that henceforth the party must consider itself subordinate to the state and must defer to "reasons of state."[68]

The reestablishment of compulsory military service on March 16, 1935, completed this evolution. The new military laws deprived the Nazis of one of their last remaining social bases, the "labor service," which was de-politicized and made an obligatory service for preliminary military training—that is to say, simply an adjunct to the army. The Green police—the "Goering police"—was incorporated into the army. Moreover, the party was deprived of one of the fields on which it set the greatest store, the training of youth, when the *Hitlerjugend* (Hitler Youth) lost its autonomy. It was transformed from a National Socialist organization into a state organization, the *Reich Youth*. It became nothing more than a huge institution for military training, subject to strict control by the army, and staffed by commissioned and noncommissioned army officers.[69]

Since National Socialism today no longer resembles that of yesterday, the army consented to be "fascisized." In the words of the Reichswehr's spokesman, Major Foertsch, "No force in the world can destroy the union between the army, the party, and its various organizations."[70] "National Socialism, as the basis of the new state, *cannot be touched* by the army. The army can be only National Socialist."[71] Instruction in National Socialist doctrines was introduced into the army ranks. In February, 1934, it was decided that soldiers and sailors should wear the swastika on their uniforms. In March, the "Aryan clause" was introduced into the army and navy. When the old Hindenburg drew his last breath, on August 2, 1934, General von Blomberg did not hesitate to consecrate Hitler head of the state and supreme commander of the army, and to have all the troops take an oath of loyalty to the Fuehrer. Soldiers and officers received the order to give the military salute to leaders of all ranks in the National Socialist Party when the latter were in uniform.[72] In November, 1935, the Reichswehr even consented to having its old war flag of black, white and red replaced by a special flag bearing the swastika.[73]

The National Socialist "revolution" which rested on the Brown Shirt plebeians had become a *military-police dictatorship*.

3

There is one thing, however, that distinguishes the fascist dictatorial state at this stage of its development from military dictatorships of the ancient type: fascism cannot get along altogether without a "social base," for it is impossible to govern in our time without a certain amount of popular consent. In order to appease the masses, who have suffered so severely from the crisis, and to hide its own connections with capital, fascism itself has to do the very thing for which it damned the extremists: *to a certain extent,* it must continue to resort to demagogy.

Furthermore, it must keep enough points of support among the people to prevent the crystallization of independent forces. It is impossible to suppress completely the party organizations and the militia—"to dispense," as Gentizon says, "with a similar means of control and action which can penetrate into all social organisms, an instrument which neither the army nor the police can replace. . . . [For] among a people without supervision, the most diverse extremist currents [could be] generated without difficulty. . . ."[74]

There is still another reason: the fascist dictatorship must, *to a certain extent,* meet danger from the "right." The completion of the totalitarian state, the brutal eviction of the old political staff of the bourgeoisie, and the "fascisization" of the army do not prevent certain traditionally conservative forces from remaining hostile to the regime and offering it an underground resistance. Part of the old bourgeois politicians, part of the army, part of the court or the circles around the head of the state, have come over to fascism—even a modified and purged fascism—only half-heartedly. Some day, under certain circumstances, these conservative forces might reappear on the scene, particularly if they should get financial backers. This is a latent threat which the supreme plebeian, the dictator, can ward off only by continuing to lean, *to a certain extent,* on the plebeian "left." Nevertheless, the danger from the "left" is a greater menace for him than the danger from the "right," and he can risk playing a leftist game only within quite narrow limits.

In Italy

Mussolini felt, after 1932, "that the regime is corroding and sinking,"[75] and that he had lost all contact with the people. The party had become merely a vast administrative machine from which life was absent. The deepening of the economic crisis required the dictatorship to recreate artificially a certain social base and to resort again to a *certain amount* of demagogy.

Moreover, Mussolini had to protect himself from the right. The complete liquidation of the party, desired by the nationalist conservatives, would call upon him "to liquidate his personal power and make the fascist state similar to a traditional reactionary state."[76] The conservative forces, in fact, were not entirely assimilated. Although the army had let itself be fascisized, not all of its leaders accepted the totalitarian fascist regime without reservations. A traveler in Italy wrote in 1935: "The higher officers have never been very enthusiastic about fascism. . . . Today the old disagreements have come to the surface, and, at least on the part of the military men, there is little effort made to conceal them."[77] In high government circles and the Court, they were not all partisans of fascism.

In case of sharp conflict with the conservative forces, Mussolini and his clique could no longer rely on a militia, disarmed and controlled by the army, nor on the *carabinieri,* who belonged to the army. He had still, it is true, a formidable weapon in the secret police (*Ovra*), but it was perhaps insufficient. Both to rejuvenate the regime and to protect himself from the right, the Duce needed to support himself once more, *to a certain extent,* on the plebeian base of the fascist party.

"Up to the last few months," Gentizon wrote, "the tendency was evident in certain circles to consider the party as a negative element, a dead weight in the political field. But everything at present indicates that in high places they are intending to give the party a new value."[78] After the great purge of 1925 and 1926, the party ranks were completely closed. Only young people who had come up through the youth organizations could enter it. But after 1932–33, the party doors were again opened, and all who had not previously belonged to it were admitted on application, provided they had "served the regime wholeheartedly"—that is to say, after careful scrutiny. From October, 1933, to the end of 1934, the party almost doubled its membership and was increased by almost a million new members. At the beginning of the year XII (October 28, 1934), the general secretary, Starace, congratulated himself that party activity had "developed in the direction of ever greater and more active participation in the life of the country, with the result that, *far from remaining a closed organization,* the party is penetrating into all fields. . . ."[79] This sudden influx of new elements might have been a danger. But this was warded off by admitting mostly young men, from whom they did not have to fear the rebellious spirit of the old-line fascist plebeians, and also by subjecting the party to increasingly strict control. Therefore discipline was strengthened, inspections made more frequent, and closer relations established between the central leadership and the subsidiary organizations.[80]

At the same time, desperate efforts were made to breathe a little life into the party and give fascism a little of its former "revolutionary" aspect. Mussolini launched the slogan: "Go to the people." He advised the party functionaries "to frequent working class circles and be with the people, not only morally but physically, especially in these difficult hours." And he added this significant recommendation: "In official ceremonies, no high hat, but the simple black shirt of the Revolution." We shall see later (Chapter 8) that on the occasion of the inauguration of the so-called "corporative state," he disinterred the old "revolutionary" and "anti-capitalist" demagogy. He had another relapse on the occasion of the Ethiopian campaign: "This war is the war of the poor, the war of the proletarians."[81] "It will hasten, instead of delay, the social evolution taking place in Italy." The fascist revolution is a "social revolution."[82]

Feeling themselves encouraged by those in high places, the plebeians began to speak again in "leftist" language. But as soon as they exceeded permissible limits, they were pitilessly crushed, sent to the Lipari Islands, and their writings and press were suppressed. For instance, in July 1935 the fascist youth magazine *Cantiere* was suppressed. In November, the magazine *Problemi del Lavoro,* which advocated nationalizations, was suppressed.[83]

Even the last episode in the saga of fascism does not contradict our analysis. In 1943 Mussolini, abandoned by the army and the monarchy, was compelled to seek some support from the left flank. He founded his phony "social republic." But that demagogic concession to extremism was only a facade. The plebeians of yore did not get their revenge. The closing scenes of fascism are a police state supported by the bayonets of the army—the German army.

In Germany

Hitler too—and even more than Mussolini—had *to a certain extent* to keep on humoring his left wing and relying on a plebeian social base. In fact it was indispensable for him to throw dust in the eyes of the masses, who were hard hit by the crisis, and to preserve points of support among them. Finally, and above all, he was faced with danger from the right. As early as the winter of 1934, monarchist elements were dangerously active, working for the return of the Hohenzollerns, and the government of the Reich was forced to dissolve all monarchist organizations. Then, early in June, there was a new offensive, all the more formidable in that this time it came from the same conservative circles who had held the Third Reich over the baptismal font. On June 17, Vice Chancellor von Papen in person, in an address at Marburg, recalled that the Hitler government had issued, on January 30, 1933, from an "alliance between National Socialism *and the conservative forces,*" and he attacked the basic principle of the totalitarian state: "The system of a single party is justified only as long as it is necessary to insure the change of regime, or until the new elite enters on its functions. . . . To maintain that there can be in one country citizens enjoying full rights and citizens having only limited rights is to return to the distinction established in old Sparta between the Spartans and Helots, *and which led to the fall of Lacedaemon. . . .*"

The anger of the Nazi plebeians can be imagined. Was an important section of the bourgeoisie, after having yielded the political stage, threatening to take it back? Goebbels replied with rage: "These people who are criticizing us today . . . represent retreat and reaction. We shall pass over their bodies. We are the youth of a new Reich. *We alone have the right now to represent Germany.*"[84]

Were the capitalist magnates and the army demanding the radical elimination of the extremist plebeians? So be it. But the National Socialist top bureaucracy *would allow nobody but themselves the task of carrying out that elimination, or the possibility of profiting from it.* They themselves acted—and *on two fronts:* Hitler, Goering, and Goebbels, at the same time as they dealt blows to the *left* by executing their oldest partisans, dealt a blow to the *right*—to the traditional conservative forces and the adversaries of the totalitarian state. Thus von Papen's immediate collaborators, who dictated the Marburg speech, were assassinated or imprisoned. The Vice Chancellor himself had several teeth broken and owed his life only to the opportune intervention of President Hindenburg. Also shot down like dogs were a number of generals (von Bredow and von Lossow), big landowners and members of the *Herrenklub** (von Gleichen, von Alvensleben, von Wechmar), and others.

Schleicher was not spared either. Apparently he was tempted to play a lone hand (wherein he differed from Papen) and to recapture power with the aid of Roehm and Gregor Strasser [cf. *New Statesman,* July 8, 1934]. But he also was backed by *certain magnates of the chemical industry*—doubtless the same ones who had supported him at the end of 1932, in his conflict with heavy industry.[85]

But after June 30, the dictator, not satisfied with having dealt a blow to the right, himself revived, *to a certain extent,* the left wing he had just decimated. This because the increasing fermentation in the masses worried him. Brown Troopers who had been discharged were boasting openly of having voted "no" in the plebescite of August 19, and discontent was being expressed even in the party's public meetings. Ballast must be thrown out at all costs. He had to protect himself from the right as well as the left.

At the same time, his immediate collaborators felt that their personal positions were threatened: Goebbels, Rosenberg, Darre, Ley, von Schirach, Streicher, Rust, and Frank were in the hot seat for

---

* An aristocratic club noted for its reactionary opinions.

several months while the old political staff of the bourgeoisie made its reappearance. The new economic czar, Dr. Schacht, for instance, named Dr. Trendelenburg, a former minister of the Weimar Republic, as deputy chief of the Economic Bureau of the Reich. He named Dr. Goerdeler, a former colleague of Bruening, as price commissioner, and even had the insolence to choose a Jew, Dr. Goldschmid, as his personal adviser.

Within the Reichswehr, devoted partisans of National Socialism such as the minister, General von Blomberg, and his adviser, General von Reichenau, lost ground to the opposition tendency embodied in the Commander-in-Chief, General von Fritsch. In November, 1934, the regular political lectures given in the garrisons were replaced with military lectures by army officers;[86] and during the summer of 1935, General von Reichenau and Major Foertsch were removed from their posts in the general staff of the army for having shown a sympathy for National Socialism that was considered excessive.[87] The right wing of the Reichswehr was trying to bring about the union of all the traditionally conservative forces, and it was supported by certain high state functionaries belonging to the aristocratic caste who either had been spared up till then by the "fascisization" or had left the National Socialist Party.[88] This right wing openly protected the Steel Helmets, who had never been really assimilated by National Socialism, and in whose ranks were gathered the remains of the old German National Party. It was also in touch, more or less secretly, with monarchist groups, whose activities experienced such a revival during the winter of 1935 that Hitler, alarmed, sent for the former Crown Prince and gave him a severe scolding.[89]

The National Socialist leaders therefore felt that they were threatened, and Goering most of all. Between him and the right wing of the Reichswehr relations were strained. The generals had not forgiven him for his "blows on two fronts" of June 30 and for having executed three of their own. They would not agree to the air force and police being taken from their authority, and placed under Goering's command. Goering, on his side, feeling the danger, tried to get his hands on the army itself and demanded that he be appointed Minister of War and that General von Fritsch be disgraced. But the latter won the first round. Goering not only failed to become Minister of War, but as commander of the air force he was placed *under the orders* of the Minister of War. Later, on April 20, 1936, the Minister of War, General von Blomberg, was named *Feldmarschall* with the three commanders of the army, navy, and air force (General von Fritsch, Admiral Raeder, and General Goering)—all likewise ministers—under his orders.[90]

In case of a real struggle with the conservative forces, the National Socialist top bureaucracy, Hitler, Goering, and Goebbels, could no longer count on the disarmed S.A. and S.S., or on the Green police incorporated in the army. They still had, it is true, a formidable weapon in the secret police (Gestapo), but perhaps it was not enough. Therefore they felt the need of again supporting themselves, *to a certain extent,* on their plebeian base. Shortly after June 30, therefore, they began again showering flattery on the S.A. At the Nuremberg Congress, on September 9, 1934, Hitler had the cynicism to state, in the face of all truth, that the S.A. more than ever constituted the force on which the regime rested and was the most powerful organization in German history—"so powerful that nobody would dare to oppose it." For those who wanted to damage the totalitarian state and weaken the position of his clique, he uttered the threat: "We have the power; nobody can take it from us, and we shall not give it up voluntarily."[91] In November, Goebbels exhorted two thousand veterans of the "old guard" to take stock of how much still remained to be done. Alluding to the danger of the return of the old bourgeois political staff, he cried: "Close ranks, prevent any foreign element from finding its way in."[92] On January 1, 1935, in a message to the party, Hitler insisted that it was "more than ever the only real support for the will of the Nation."

On June 29, 1935, Goebbels organized a great "day of the National Socialist Party of Berlin." While taking the precaution of paying tribute to the army, he violently attacked the detractors of the totalitarian state, as well as the state bureaucracy in which so many reactionary elements survived, or into which they infiltrated. "On all sides they demand the suppression of the party . . . They try to tell us: now everybody is National Socialist. We hope so but we don't believe it . . . The party upholds the faith in our country."[93] On July 18, the Berlin Nazis, under Goebbels' leadership, obtained the resignation of the Chief of Police, Rear Admiral von Levetzow, who sympathized with the "reactionaries" and appointed in his place a notorious extremist, Count Helldorf, who escaped the June 30 purge. The *Angriff* announced triumphantly "the inglorious end of that reaction . . . which gathers in certain circles and drawing rooms, and which believes it has found a way to block the present development."[94]

The Nuremberg Congress in September 1935 was devoted entirely to giving formal satisfaction to the plebeians. "We shall not deviate an inch from the fundamental principles of National Socialism . . . The conquest of power is a process which will never, never be completed," cried Hitler.[95] Hitler insisted it was neither the *economic leaders* nor the *soldiers* who were leading Germany from the abyss, but *exclusively the political soldiers of the party.* "Everything could crumble, but never our party." He paid vibrant homage to the Brown and Black troopers: "I salute you, my old S.A.! I salute you, my old S.S.! You are for me the old guard of the National Socialist revolution!"[96]

At the same time, he decided to make the swastika banner the only flag of the Third Reich, winning out against the traditional conservative forces, "these elements of a stupid, reactionary bourgeoisie who will never learn anything."[97] Shortly afterwards, on November 7, the *Stahlhelm* (Steel Helmet) organization was dissolved for once and for all, as well as the old student dueling societies, "hotbeds of aristocratic and reactionary opposition."

But these concessions to the plebeians were purely formal. The Storm Troops remained disarmed, on permanent leave, powerless; more than ever, the army and the Nazi top bureaucracy shared power.

An attempt has been made to interpret February 4, 1938, when

General von Fritsch and Marshal von Blomberg were both retired, as a return to the offensive by the Nazi left wing and as a victory for it. Such an interpretation, as far as can be judged, does not seem correct.

In the first place, it should be noted that February 4 was merely a "palace revolution"; the Nazi plebeians in the ranks, reduced to silence, had no share in it. The conflict brought to grips once more certain elements in the National Socialist top bureaucracy (Goering and his circle) with certain elements in the right wing of the Reichswehr (Fritsch and his circle). It ended with a victory for neither side, but with a compromise.

Although General von Fritsch and fourteen other generals sympathetic, it is said,[98] to the monarchy, were retired, Marshal von Blomberg, National Socialism's man in the Reichswehr, met the same fate. Although a little later the top bureaucracy won an old demand long refused by the Generals—the introduction of the Hitler salute into the army[99]—the facts remain: that the army preserves its complete independence in the framework of the state; that its new heads, Generals Keitel and von Brauchitsch, are old military men completely in the spirit and tradition of the Reichswehr; that Goering still has not succeeded in becoming Minister of the Reichswehr; that General von Reichenau (a Nazi tool) has not become Chief-of-Staff, and Himmler is even farther from being Minister of the Interior.

A significant fact, which seems to bear out the theory that there was a compromise, is that in the private council which Hitler has set up to assist him in foreign policy, the army and the Nazi top bureaucracy are equally represented. His anxious generals have bent to Hitler's will on only one point: he will drag them willy-nilly into war.

A regime which is simultaneously a police and a military dictatorship entails a certain duality. There is not a complete fusion between the top bureaucracy of the party and the Gestapo, on the one hand, and the army on the other. From time to time we hear the gears grinding in the mechanism of this supposedly "totalitarian" state. During the Second World War, these clashes steadily worsened. In the course of the regime's disintegration, the rivalry between the Wehrmacht and the Gestapo grew ever more open. The top bureaucracy of the party moved into battle against the army. Himmler's S.S. units, rearmed within the framework of the army, played a more and more leading role as the heads of the Wehrmacht deserted Hitler. But this process was in no way the plebeians' vengeance. The Brown Shirts of 1933 and 1934, searching for their "second revolution," never regained the upper hand. When the military conspiracy of July 20, 1944, was foiled, it was the sinister Himmler who climbed to the top of the heap, not the rank-and-file Nazi militants.

7

The real fascist "doctrine"

1

Fascism no longer needs to hide its real face, and in fact it finds it useful to legitimize its rule with a "doctrine." This doctrine, to be sure, was not elaborated for the first time after the conquest of power. Long before that, it could be found in the writings and speeches of the leaders, though submerged in "anti-capitalist" phraseology. Now demagogy retires to the background, yielding the spotlight to ideological justification of the dictatorship. And at last we see clearly that fascist doctrine is an old acquaintance; it is a twin of *reactionary* philosophy, the philosophy of feudalism, of absolutism.

This was precisely the philosophy that the bourgeoisie had to combat so bitterly at the dawn of its rule in order to achieve its own liberation. To the pessimistic dogma of the fall of man, the bourgeoisie opposed the idea of unlimited progress; to the "aristocratic principle" and the "Moloch-State," government by the masses and democracy; to brute force, human "rights."

But the day came when the bourgeoisie perceived "that all the weapons which it had forged against feudalism turned their points against itself, that all the means of education which it had produced

190

rebelled against its own civilization, that all the gods which it had created had fallen away from it"—when it understood that "all the so-called bourgeois liberties and organs of progress attacked and menaced its class rule. . . ."[1] Shaken to its foundations by the crisis of capitalism, able to save its threatened profits only by destroying democratic institutions and brutally exterminating the proletarian organizations, the bourgeoisie rejects the ideology that once helped it triumph over absolutism. Indeed, it dresses itself up in the ideology of that self-same absolutism—it denies progress, attacks reason, refuses the masses the right of self-government, tramples on democracy, invokes the "aristocratic principle" and "reasons of State," rehabilitates violence. There is nothing astonishing about finding *reactionary* thinkers who attacked with hatred the ideas of the French Revolution, democracy and liberalism, suddenly becoming great men. From these "masters of counterrevolution"[2] fascism borrows its doctrines. "We represent the antithesis . . . of all that world of the 'immoral principles' of 1789,"[3] a reaction against the "movement of the eighteenth-century visionaries and Encyclopedists,"[4] exclaim the Italian fascists. And the National Socialists say: "The year 1789 will be erased from history. . . ."[5] "We wish to destroy the immoral ideology of the French Revolution."[6]

2

The bourgeoisie used the idea of progress to batter down the bastilles of absolutism. Antiquity and the Middle Ages lived on the idea of the corruption and decadence of the human race, on the dogma of the fall of man: humanity, come perfect from the hands of God, was through original sin plunged into evil. Man is born wicked and is not perfectible—and similarly his political, economic, and social system. Man must accept it as imposed by God, without discussion and without hope of improvement. To this pessimistic doctrine, so convenient for the justification of tyranny and the legitimization of poverty, the bourgeoisie, eager to be freed, opposed the idea of infinite progress at the beginning of its domination. The golden age is not in the past but before us; humanity is perfectible and is continually rising from poverty to material well-being, from ignorance to knowledge, from barbarism to civilization. The great discoveries of the second half of the eighteenth century, the birth of the machine age and modern industry, gave new confirmation to the idea of progress. The young industrial bourgeoisie was sure the new means of production invented by it were capable of infinitely improving the lot of humanity. From this came the blissful optimism of the Saint-Simonian businessmen like Michel Chevalier.

But a day comes when the idea of progress is turned against the bourgeoisie. The productive forces, as they develop at a dizzy rate of speed, come into conflict with the social system. Capitalist society ceases to be progressive, and, far from holding out to humanity a prospect of well-being, it offers only poverty and unemployment. Then suddenly the bourgeoisie stops believing in progress. The opponents of progress become its ideological masters.

Italian fascism vulgarizes the anti-progressive diatribes of Georges Sorel, a combination syndicalist theoretician and reactionary philosopher. That original and ambivalent essayist wrote a whole book to denounce the *Illusions of Progress*. To be sure, what he hated in the idea of progress was above all its "facility"; he wanted man to fight and not passively wait, in *dolce far niente,* for happiness on earth. But, at bottom, he denied progress itself. In 1913 he confided to a friend: "Progress is only an illusion. . . . The idea of progress is a naive idea, belied by the history of humanity. . . ."[7]

Mussolini, who proclaims himself a disciple of Sorel, similarly rejects the idea of progress: "Fascism rejects the myth of happiness and infinite progress. . . . It does not believe in the possibility of 'happiness on earth,' advanced in the literature of the eighteenth-century economists." Hence he condemns 'teleological conceptions' according to which, at a certain moment of history, the human race will achieve a final stage of organization."[8]

3

Another weapon of the conquering bourgeoisie was reason. For revealed knowledge, it substituted the free exercise of intelligence, the supremacy of common sense. But today that weapon is being turned against it. The employment of reason and scientific analysis can no longer serve except to undermine the foundations of its rule and condemn the capitalist system of production; only a resorting to the "irrational" can permit it to prolong its reign. Let man renounce domination of the world and subject himself to it as to a "mystic phenomenon" (the expression is from Edouard Berth, another of Sorel's disciples);[9] let his intelligence be ready to abdicate before all the instinctive forces and be carried away by any "movement" whatever; let him be ready to follow the first charlatan who comes along, the first maker of miracles or myths; let him be ready to trust, not to reasoned actions but to blind faith in a Duce or a Fuehrer in seeking a way out from his sufferings.

In Italy

Here fascism utilizes—again vulgarized—the theories of Sorel. Sorel detests modern rationalism. He calls Descartes "charlatanesque" and against him champions the pious Pascal.[10] "Pascal," he asserts, "has defeated Descartes."[11] And his disciple, Edouard Berth, develops this: "The defeat of Descartes is the defeat of rationalism, that modern intellectualism . . . which was invented only to batter down Christian beliefs and to substitute for religion a scientific conception of the world that is the most stupid and foolish thing it has been possible to invent throughout the centuries."[12] To reason, Sorel opposes—following Bergson—"intuition." He wishes to captivate popular imagination by *myths,* "appeal to combinations of images capable of evoking *in a block and through intuition alone,* prior to any reflective analysis, the mass of emotions. . . ." As for these myths, it matters little whether they can become a reality: "It can even happen that nothing they embody will come to pass."[13]

As the enemy of reason, fascism proclaims itself a "movement," an "intuition summed up in a vision and a faith";[14] "a myth," Mussolini again asserts, and adds, in the purest Sorelian jargon " . . . it is not necessary for it to be a reality."[15]

"Mussolini," Volpe confesses, "propagated among those around him a sort of intolerance, almost contempt, for intellectuals. . . . It was only too easy for this turn of mind to degenerate in his followers into contempt for culture. Manifestations of coarse irony, full of scorn for culture and its representatives, were not lacking."[16] In an address Mussolini exclaims: "The century of fascism will see the end of intellectualizing and of those sterile intellectuals who are a threat to the nation."[17]

In Germany

National Socialism imbibes from Oswald Spengler a philosophy of the same brew. Like Sorel, the author of the *Decline of the West* overwhelms with mockery the rationalism, the "irreligious natural knowledge," the "critical science," a product of decadence, which dares to rival and even supersede religion. Like Sorel, in place of reason he sets up *intuition,* the *mythical power of the soul,* "the ability of a soul to fill its world with symbols."

Instead of reason, National Socialism offers a vague *mysticism of life* and a *dynamic force* that it would have a great deal of difficulty in defining.[18] "Hitler is the conductor of the German dynamic force," a professor solemnly declares.[19] To the twentieth century, Rosenberg offers nebulous myths, myths of Blood and Soil.[20]

They reject with rage "rationalism, the lesson of reason which is willing to recognize only intelligence and the brain . . . as guides for the destiny of the people."[21] Goering asserts that "the real leaders have no need for culture and science."[22] Hitler compares the intellectuals to queen bees who live off the worker bees.[23] A character in the drama *Schlageter* utters this line: "When I hear the word 'culture,' I load my revolver."[24]

4

Once absolutism was conquered, the bourgeoisie instituted the form of government that best corresponded to its historic mission. Free competition, *"laisser-faire,"* and free trade were the very conditions for capitalist expansion. Economic liberalism was extended to political liberalism, to parliamentary democracy. But a day comes when liberty and democracy are incompatible with bourgeois rule. The era of free competition is succeeded by that of monopoly capitalism. We have seen that in order to save their profits, threatened by crisis, the capitalist magnates need the support of the state. They have to substitute for the democratic state the authoritarian state (Chapter 1). Then the bourgeoisie tramples with rage on its old idols, and the reactionary theoreticians of *anti-democracy* become its ideological masters.

In Italy

Italian fascism draws on the work of both Sorel and Maurras. A ferocious hatred of democracy runs throughout Sorel's entire work. As early as his *Socialist Future of the Unions,* in 1898, he wrote: "Government by the totality of citizens has never been anything but a fiction. But this fiction [is] the last word of democratic science. . . ." Moreover, this bookish man has a strange passion for *heroism.* He demands struggles that can supply him with intense emotions. Alas! The filthy "democratic swamp" and the practice of "social peace" deprive him of the desired sensations. In this swamp, the two antagonists, bourgeoisie and proletariat, are both sinking. They must *both* be drawn out of their lethargy. So Sorel plays on them both. On the one hand, to be sure, he correctly warns the proletariat against the shortcomings of "social peace," *but on the other, he turns to the bourgeoisie and incites it to gather itself together and strike hard, in order to strengthen its domination.* "When the employers realize they have nothing to gain . . . from working for social peace or from democracy, *then there is some chance of their recovering their old energy.* . . . Everything can be saved if [the proletariat] succeeds in *restoring to the bourgeoisie some of its energy.*" He advises "thrashing" the orators of democracy; he goes so far as to call for dictatorship, and to wish for "a great foreign war which shall bring to power men with the will to rule."[25]

This odd theory—as might be expected—was to find more echoes among the bourgeoisie than among the proletariat. The proletariat, although not the dupe of bourgeois democracy, does not scorn democratic liberties, which are indispensable for its emancipation.

The bourgeoisie, on the other hand, willingly listens to Sorel's advice. As early as 1910, Paul Bourget produced a vile anti-labor play, *The Barricade,* for the idea of which he asserted he was indebted to Sorel. The latter, far from rejecting this compromising paternity, declared in an interview: "I would be happy if his great talent [Bourget's] *could persuade the bourgeoisie to arm and defend itself* and to abandon at last, in the face of the courageous ardor of its adversaries, its criminal and inglorious resignation."[26]

And very shortly Sorel, not having succeeded in convincing the proletariat, was placing his bets on one side only: hatred of democracy carried him to the extreme right. Sorelians and royalists joined in founding the *Cahiers du Cercle Proudhon* and adopted this common platform: "It is absolutely necessary to destroy democratic institutions."[27] Valois thus explained his adherence to the *Action Francaise:* "I owe to Sorel my final direction. It was he who definitively tore us away from democracy."[28] The Italian disciples of Sorel followed exactly the same development: hatred of democracy led them directly from revolutionary syndicalism—or socialism—to fascism. "It is to Georges Sorel," Mussolini has said, "that I owe the most. . . . He strengthened the anti-democratic tendencies of my nature."[29]

Hatred of democracy is also the ruling passion of Maurras. "We call on heaven as a witness," writes the author of the *Inquiry into Monarchy,* "to the ardor of our hatred for democracy and the absolutely false principle of the sovereignty of numbers."[30] "There is not one example in history of a fortunate undertaking being initiated by majorities."[31] For Maurras, the masses are truly incapable of governing themselves.

The two currents—that of the former Italian syndicalist disciples of Sorel, and that of the nationalists of the *Idea Nazionale,* who were disciples of Maurras—join and merge in fascism. Fascism is the supreme "anti-democracy."[32] Mussolini mocks in Sorelian tones that "democratic habit which makes everything grey and mediocre."[33] He "refuses to adore the new divinity, the masses."[34] "In the eighteenth century, they claimed that the government was an emanation of the free will of the people; but 'the people' is an abstraction. . . ."[35] "Fascism denies that numbers, through the mere fact of being numbers, can direct human society."[36] "The masses are not capable of having spontaneously a will of their own."[37]

In Germany

As for National Socialism, it here borrows again from Oswald Spengler. The author of the *Decline of the West* is also the mortal enemy of democracy. He hates it as the rule of the masses. The masses are for him only vile plebs, and he has no concern for their well-being or their moral or material progress.[38] Fortunately, democracy is celebrating its last victories. Soon, he announces, it will be crushed by the advent of *Caesarism* and replaced by a "wholly personal power, which is approaching gradually and irresistibly."[39]

His pupil, Goebbels, writes: "The masses were for me a dark monster (*ein dunkles Ungeheuer*). National Socialism does not, like the democratic-Marxist parties, blindly adore the masses and numbers."[40] "Many values," Roehm declares, "which are sacred to democracies . . . have been devalued in the new Germany . . . the absolute equality of all those who wear a human face, the deification of the will of the majority and of numbers."[41] And according to Moeller van den Bruck, "The masses realize very well that they cannot direct themselves."[42]

5

If the masses cannot govern themselves, they should be governed by a minority of men on whom nature has conferred exceptional ability—by a minority of *leaders*. In order to justify the fascist dictatorship, the bourgeoisie disinters the old "aristocratic principle" formerly put to rout by its ancestors.

In Italy

Here again Italian fascism utilizes Sorel and Maurras. Sorel is, at bottom, infected with aristocratic snobbery; he concedes virtues only to minorities. Although he was interested for a time in revolutionary syndicalism, it was because he believed he found in it a *new mode of selection*,[43] or, as Maurras says, "an essentially aristocratic doctrine in spite of its temporary ties with democracy,"[44] and because he tried to see in the syndicalist elite the embryo of a new aristocracy. There is scarcely need to stress in passing how this conception differs from that of workers' syndicalism. The syndicalist is *democratic* (in the real meaning of the word) and not *aristocratic*; he does not seek to differentiate himself from the masses. He knows, however, that the latter are subject to a certain inertia, and he therefore believes their best elements must act as a ferment in the masses while always remaining, in the words of Marcel Martinet, "the direct expression of the masses, constantly and fraternally controlled by them."[45] Like Sorel, Maurras wishes aristocratic minorities to impose their rule on "inert, indifferent and torpid" majorities. "Virtue, audacity, power, and ideas belong to minorities."[46]

Mussolini exploits to the utmost this essentially reactionary concept. He in his turn exalts *audacious minorities*: he claims that "in the labor movement it has never been a question of anything but minorities."[47] "You must feel in your blood the aristocracy of minorities," we read in the *Handbook of the Italian Fascist*—which means that an aristocratic minority should impose its will on the masses, even if it is necessary "to make them yield by force."[48] The masses, Rocco writes, "tend to do what a few dominating elements desire."[49] Malaparte carries the idea to its ultimate conclusion: "The people need tyrants."[50]

In Germany

National Socialism draws on Nietzsche for similar formulas. The author of the *Genealogy of Morals* exalts the "terrible and enchanting counter-warcry of the prerogative of the few." All the better if, in the course of history, a minority of masters, issued from aristocratic and conquering races, have enslaved the vile plebs! Hitler, after him, asserts that "everything extraordinary accomplished since the world was a world has been accomplished by minorities."[51] To govern, it is necessary for the masses to have over them an elite, a natural aristocracy, which derives its right to command from its alleged racial superiority.[52]

6

But above these leaders there is the state, the omnipotent state, the Moloch-State. Here we find again an old acquaintance. "The King-State, the God-State," as Gentizon says, "is the most fundamental characteristic of any Caesarian State, of any dictatorship."[53] At the dawn of its rule, the capitalist bourgeoisie demanded that the state call as little attention to its existence as possible, and it victoriously refuted the "barbarous" concept of the Moloch-State. But today, it needs the *strong state*. Hence it adopts the philosophers of absolutism and takes as its own, Hobbes' State, "a real mortal god"; Hegel's State, which is its own end, and for which the individual is nothing; and Treitschke's State, which "does not need to ask the people to consent but only to obey."[54]

In Italy

Italian fascism professes a veritable *statolatry*—the term is that of Pope Pius XI.[55] "For fascism," Mussolini writes, "the state is the absolute before which individuals and groups are only relative. . . . Individuals and groups are conceivable only within the state. . . . The state has become the true reality of the individual. . . . For the fascist, everything is in the state, and nothing human or spiritual exists or has value outside of the state."[56] For Rocco, "individual liberty is only a concession granted by the state to the individual."[57]

In Germany

National Socialism is in no way behind Italian fascism. "What is primordial for us," Goering declares, "is not the individual. . . . There is only one thing that counts: the National Socialist State must be placed above everything else."[58] Nazi law is based on "Reasons of State." The individual must efface himself before the state, whose "existence, growth, and perpetuity are declared supreme."[59] Cardinal Faulhaber has reason to denounce the concept that "the individual is reduced to the status of zero and the rank of a slave without rights." He has reason to warn against that "absolute state in which the individual is lost like a drop of water in the immense ocean."[60]

7

In the early days of its power, the bourgeoisie denied the legitimacy of violence and the "right of the strongest" as old barbaric notions deriving from the first ages of man upon which feudal and absolutist society still rested. Instead of force, the eighteenth-century philosophers championed human "rights." Relations between men should be no longer settled by force but determined by contracts; Rousseau refuted the "alleged" right of the strongest and declared that "might does not make right."[61] In fact, with the appearance of "right," the bourgeoisie, once it was the dominant class, ruled by force. But, not needing to display force too openly, it preferred to rule through the fiction of "law."

But a time comes when the bourgeoisie can save its threatened profits only by exterminating the proletarian organizations and governing through terror. Then it digs up the old notions of barbaric epochs; it rehabilitates violence and adopts reactionary apologists of violence as its authorities.

These apologists transfer the discoveries of Darwin from the domain of biology to the field of sociology, distorting them in the process. The great naturalist posed the theory of the development of the species according to the law of selection and the survival of the *fittest*; the reactionary apologists simply replace the *fittest* by the *strongest*.[62] And they decree that man, like the animal, must wage a ferocious "struggle for life"; that the strongest must exterminate the weak; and that this bloody struggle is the condition for the development of the world. Thus Nietzsche glorifies the "will to power," "the paramount superiority enjoyed by those plastic forces of spontaneity, aggression, and encroachment with their new interpretations and tendencies." He derides Rousseau's dream of a *contract* being the origin of the state: the state was created by a race of conquerors and masters who clutched an inferior people in their formidable claws. In magnificent language, this decadent sophisticate extols the brute.[63]

For Trietschke, "force is the very principle of the state; the state is force."[64] And Georges Sorel in his turn, just as his master Proudhon tried to rehabilitate war, undertakes to rehabilitate violence. He loves violence in itself and proclaims that "violence is moral." He laments that the introduction of the principles of 1789 into legislation has "debased right" by civilizing it; he curses democratic education "designed to attenuate our tendencies to violence to such an extent that we are led instinctively to think every act of violence is a retrogression towards barbarism."[65] After having brought violence back into good repute, he advises its employment, not alone by the proletariat *but also by the bourgeoisie.* But the proletariat has nothing to do with such a theory; it does not love violence for violence's sake. *From the ideal point of view, it is opposed to all violence* (Lenin).[66] It does not make violence a question of "morality" or believe that the struggle in itself is "regenerating," nor does it want a society built on the "right of the strongest." If it resorts to violence, it is only because there is no other way to overcome the violence of the enemy, to deliver humanity from the principle of violence, and to institute a classless society—a society of producers and not of warriors, and one from which every trace of barbarism and form of oppression will be banished.

But on the other hand, the Sorelian theory of violence has to be exploited by the bourgeoisie because this theory makes it possible to justify the increasingly brutal forms assumed by bourgeois domination and to legitimize its crimes at the same time as it rehabilitates war.

In Italy
Mussolini, in Sorelian style, proclaims the "value of the violent deed."[67] "Violence," he states, "is perfectly moral."[68] "Almost all my life I have been the apologist of violence."[69] "Struggle is at the origin

of everything. . . . Struggle will always be in the depths of human nature like a supreme fatality. Moreover, it is good that this should be so. The day when struggle ceases will be a day of melancholy, end, and ruin."[70] Man reveals his true self only "in bloody effort." "War makes all human energy sublime and sets the seal of nobility on the peoples who have the courage to accept it. . . ."[71]

In Germany

Hitler likewise hails the "victorious efficacy of violence": "Humanity has grown up in eternal combat; in eternal peace, humanity would waste away. . . . Nature annihilates the weak to give their place to the strong." He glorifies the right of the strongest as the "right which in nature is the only one possible, the only one reasonable." He boasts of "utilizing all weapons, even the most brutal."[72]

Thus a cultivated social class, proud of its "respectability," personified by an elderly gentleman honored by an entire nation, arrives at the point of entrusting state power to the most sinister gangsters known to all history.

8

Fascism in power:
Taming the proletariat

1

The industrialists have attained their ends: at last they have at their command the "strong state" they wanted. Through a series of economic and social measures, the fascist state will try to check the decline of their profits and make their businesses pay once more.

This action is directed *first and essentially against the working class.* The fascist state begins by creating conditions that will permit the slashing of wages. This means the destruction of labor unions, the end of their representation inside the factories, the abolition of the right to strike, the nullification of union contracts, and the reestablishment of the absolute rule of the employers in their businesses.

But this is only the first part of the program. In addition, it must prevent any future independent groupings in the working masses. Hence the fascist state puts all its authority at the service of the employers. It herds the workers into organizations where they can be policed, with leaders appointed from above—organizations which the members have no way of controlling, and which only by the sheerest imposture style themselves the workers' "representatives." The state severely punishes every attempt to strike; henceforth to fight the boss is to rebel against the state. To forestall all labor conflicts, it exercises compulsory "arbitration"—that is to say, it disguises the employers' wishes as arbitrative decisions, and anyone contesting these decisions is considered an enemy of the state. Finally, it sanctions with its authority whatever wages the industrialists are pleased to pay those they exploit. Not to accept these wages is to disobey the state.

In Italy

The destruction of the labor unions in Italy began considerably before the taking of power, which makes it necessary to retrace some of our steps. Fascism first attacked the agricultural unions, as the most vulnerable. It wrecked the offices of the "Red Leagues" and cooperatives of the agricultural workers and assassinated the labor leaders responsible for these organizations. At the same time, fascist "unions" were founded under the patronage of the big landowners. "How were these fascist unions born?" Mussolini asked later, and replied: "Birth date: 1921. Place: the Po valley. Circumstances: the conquest and destruction of the revolutionary fortresses."[1] Every means of pressure was brought to force workers to enroll in the fascist "unions." The landowners gave work only to laborers who belonged to the fascist unions and made contracts only with tenant farmers who belonged to them; the banks gave credit only to farmers who were members of the fascist organizations.[2] "Fascist" unemployed were brought from great distances, escorted by "squadra." As soon as they arrived in the district, "the local landowners ignored the union employment offices and tore up the union contracts with no fear of strikes, for the immigrant unemployed . . . were there to replace local labor. In this way the 'Red' unions were smashed."[3] In certain centers, where the socialist and cooperative ideas were firmly rooted, the resistance was stubborn and lasted for years.[4] But gradually the farm workers, condemned to die of hunger if they did not yield to the demands of their employers, resigned themselves to entering the fascist "unions," either individually or in groups. "They bundled up cards, membership lists, and flags,"

Gorgolini has related, "and went in a troop to deposit them at the headquarters of the nearest *Fascio*."[5]

It was chiefly after the conquest of power, however, that fascism dared attack the unions of industrial workers. After the March on Rome, the local *Fasci* almost everywhere succeeded in getting hold of the lists of union members, whom they gathered together and advised, under threats of violence, to join the fascist "unions." Those who were found to carry "Red" union cards were beaten up, persecuted, and boycotted. Bosses hired, and employment offices accepted, only the workers who had fascist "union" cards. Frequently the industrialists themselves enrolled their employees in the fascist "unions" and deducted the membership dues from their wages. Rossi, in his book on the *Birth of Fascism*, tells how the management of the great Terni steel plants helped fascism destroy the "Red" union. After July, 1922, the mills were closed down for lack of orders. The "Red" union had received assurances that they would reopen September 1. But on that date they were still shut down. Then the fascists invaded the city, called the Socialists "liars" and "cowards" and set fire to the two labor exchanges. This operation completed, the management reopened the steel mills. Thereafter it would deal only with the fascist "unions."

In August, 1923, the fascist Grand Council began negotiations with the General Federation of Industry (employers' association), which it invited to establish permanent relations with the fascist "unions." In December, the so-called "Chigi Palace" agreement was concluded, giving official recognition to the fascist "unions" by the employers. The General Federation of Industry and the Federation of fascist "unions" appointed a permanent mixed commission "to harmonize" the policy of the two associations. Strengthened with this recognition, the fascist "unions" legally took over the property of the labor unions. A decree-law of January 24, 1924, authorized the provincial governors to remove the heads of labor unions and to appoint "commissioners" to liquidate their property after the unions had been dissolved. When a certain number of deserters from a labor union had been gotten together in any city, the rival fascist "union" claimed and obtained the property of the original union, its office equipment, treasury, etc.[6]

But this tactic was far from being crowned with success. *So long as the unions had the right to exist,* so long as the Federation of Labor was legal, the fascist "unions," in spite of all the means of pressure they employed, made little progress among the industrial workers. In all elections for "factory shop committees," the fascist slates were "literally buried under an avalanche of Red votes."[7] In March, 1925, when the fascist union of metal workers in Brescia called a strike, only 20 percent of the workers responded; all the others answered the call issued two days later by the federation of metal workers (FIOM).

It was necessary to resort to force. When the totalitarian dictatorship began in 1925, the surviving labor unions were suppressed once and for all. By an agreement on October 2, known as the "Vidoni Palace" agreement, the General Federation of Industry granted the fascist "unions" an exclusive monopoly; henceforth they alone had the right to make union contracts. At the same time, the right to strike was abolished, and "factory committees" were suppressed. In November, the remaining labor exchanges, unions, and labor organizations were dissolved and their property confiscated. At the end of 1926, the Federation of Labor, which had only a nominal existence by that time, disappeared as well.

Precautions for the future remain to be taken. "How can working class resistance be paralyzed without unionization?" asks Kerillis in his *Inquiry into Italian Fascism.*[8] *To paralyze working class resistance* will henceforth be the role of the fascist "unions," which have become organs for "political discipline."[9] The workers are pigeonholed into a certain number of "trade departments,"[10] within which their activity can more easily be supervised and kept under control.

By the law of April 3, 1926,[11] the fascist "unions" had their monopoly of "union representation" confirmed. But they are *unions* only in name. The fascist "trade unionist" has no rights; he is deprived of the elementary right of freely choosing his own representatives.[12] Thus when the Roman typographers elected old leaders of the prefascist epoch to the executive committee, the "union" executive committee was immediately dissolved and a "government commissioner" with full powers appointed. These so-called "unions" are actually only administrative organs of the state. Mussolini could say in a speech on March 11, 1926: "Fascist unionism is an imposing force, a powerful mass movement, *completely controlled* by fascism and the government, *a mass movement that obeys.*" The union leaders are, according to Rossoni himself, "Black Shirts named by the government to direct the unions."[13] When from time to time unions and federations, or provincial unions, hold meetings or congresses, no discussion is allowed. A worker wrote to the newspaper *Universale,* of Florence: "As a matter of fact, I who am regularly enrolled in the union for my industry have never had an opportunity to get in contact with the organization, to discuss in meetings, or express myself freely."[14]

Membership in these "unions" is alleged to be *voluntary.* But in reality the workers who do not belong nevertheless have "compulsory contributions" deducted from their wages by the employers and are *forced to accept the working conditions and wages fixed by the "unions" in agreement with the employers.* Furthermore, every means of pressure is used to force the workers to join. The unemployed, for instance, have no chance of receiving relief or finding work at the unemployment offices unless they can show "union" cards.

Conversely, the fascist state can refuse to admit to the "unions"— that is to say, deprive of his livelihood—anyone it wishes. The law, in fact, provides that the constitution of each "union" must indicate the body entrusted with disciplinary power over members convicted of moral or *political* unworthiness.

The fascist state does not limit itself to enrolling the workers in "scab" organizations; it severely punishes every impulse towards independence displayed by the workers. Strikes, in particular, are considered crimes against the state, crimes "against the social community," and hence punishable by a whole graduated scale of penalties. Fines can be as high as 1,000 lire, and prison sentences range from one to three years. The "instigators" are subject to sentences of from two to seven years.

In the so-called "union contracts" made by the fascist unions under the protection of the state, the workers' duties figure much more prominently than their rights. No less than twelve provisions in the building construction contract, for instance, are devoted to discipline. The contract is drawn up like a military regulation: "All workers are subject to their immediate superior in the order established by the hierarchy."[15]

The law of August 16, 1935, places employees of factories *directly or indirectly* connected with war industries under military discipline and law. Anyone absent from the factory for more than five days is considered a deserter and punishable by from two to nine years in prison. Any infraction of discipline, "insubordination," or violence towards the technical managers of the factory is punishable by penalties of from six months to nine years in prison. In 1938, 580,000 militarized workers were employed in industries working for national defense and consequently came under the provisions of this law![16]

The fascist state has revived the "labor passport." In this the authorities note whether the conduct of the bearer has been "satisfactory from the national point of view," and the employer sets down, when a worker is dismissed, whether the discharged is competent or incompetent, reliable or untrustworthy.

In January, 1936, this passport was replaced by another that includes all forms of activity for every citizen from the age of eleven, a document indispensable for obtaining any kind of employment.[17]

To prevent all labor conflicts, the fascist state makes its "arbitration" obligatory. Whether the arbitrators are the "provincial interunion committees" (between 1927 and 1931), the "provincial committees of corporative economy" (after 1931), the "conciliation committees" of the "corporations" (after 1934), or, at the very top, the Labor Court (after 1926), the story is the same. Fascist state functionaries pretend to mediate impartially between the employers' representatives and the "workers' representatives," but in reality they pass off the bosses' wishes as arbitrated decisions. In a moment of sincerity, Mussolini told the president of the Federation of Industry, "I assure Mr. Benni that so long as I am in power, the employers will have nothing to fear from the Labor Courts."[18]

To resist the bosses' wishes is to disobey the state. Workers who refuse to abide by the decisions of the Labor Court are punishable by from one month to a year in prison and a fine of from 100 to 10,000 lire.

Finally, the fascist state lends the sanction of its authority to any wages the employers are willing to pay their employees. The Minister of Corporations in Rome drafts so-called "union contracts" in accordance with the employers' directions and then merely sends them to the "union" functionaries, who have nothing further to do but sign the name of their organization. As Professor Pic has said, they "are not contracts resulting from free bargaining but veritable *administrative regulations.*"[19]

To refuse to accept the wages and working conditions dictated by the bosses is to act as an enemy of the state. Any protest, any attempt to violate these so-called "contracts," can be punished by a fine of from 100 to 5,000 lire.

The industrialists have thus gained their objectives:

1) *Wages formerly fixed by union contracts have been replaced by wages fixed by the company*—The so-called "union contracts" that they have imposed on their workers through the intermediary of the fascist state are not, in fact, national or regional contracts; rather, all the provisions apply on a nationwide or regional scale *except those concerning wages.* The contracts formerly agreed to by the independent unions tended to reduce the discrepancy between wages in various regions and to give workers in backward regions certain of the advantages won by workers in the more economically developed ones. The wages in the fascist "contracts" vary from region to region, *from company to company.* The employer is free, in fact, to fix the wages of his employees as his fancy dictates.

2) *Wages can be cut without the slightest opposition*—Unlike the old contracts made by the independent unions, the fascist "contracts" do not fix wage rates for a certain period specified in advance; *rates are subject to change at any moment.* The law provides in fact that "Action to establish new working conditions is permissible . . . even before the expiration of the specified period, provided there has been a perceptible change in the situation since the date of the agreement."[20] At any time, whenever there is a labor conflict, the Labor Courts can make a decision changing the conditions specified in the contract, and apply it to all the workers in the industry in question.[21]

But frequently the employers do not even need to abrogate the "contracts" in force or get them amended by the Labor Courts; all they have to do is evade or violate the provisions openly, with the complicity of the state. They transfer workers from higher to lower classifications, or consider *minimum* provisions as *maximum,* and cut all wages above the minimum as soon as the contract is signed. Fascist "unions" sometimes even advise their members to accept conditions inferior to those specified in the contracts in order not to risk losing work.[22]

In Germany

Long before coming to power, National Socialism began, not to destroy the unions as in Italy, but to nibble at them. In 1928, a Berlin Nazi of working class origin, Reinhold Muchow, founded the "National Socialist shop cells" (NSBO). Their purpose was to compete with the unions in the factories and to get a majority in the "shop committee" elections. The NSBO began by establishing itself in the small and moderate-sized shops. In 1931, it was reorganized and set out to win the big factories.[23] But during that year, in spite of persistent propaganda, it obtained in the shop committee elections only 5 percent of the votes against 83.6 percent for the independent unions. Again in March, 1933, with Hitler in power, despite all its efforts, in the partial elections for factory committees it received only 3 percent of the votes. According to one estimate—

doubtless optimistic—it had scarcely 500,000 members on March 1, 1933, and these members were civil service employees enrolled by force, or unemployed who hoped to get work on the strength of NSBO cards.[24]

The National Socialists understood that *so long as union freedom existed,* they had no chance of attracting the industrial proletariat into their organizations. Force was still to be tried. Immediately after the Reichstag fire, the right to strike was practically suppressed; any instigation of a strike was subject to punishment by a prison term of from one month to three years. Several People's Houses (union headquarters) were occupied spontaneously by Brown Shirts. At the beginning of April, the National Socialist government took preliminary measures which left no doubt as to its intentions: the monopoly of labor representation in the Economic Council of the Reich and the Labor Courts was withdrawn from the unions; privileges and rights of shop committees, representing the unions in the factories, were limited; elections were postponed, and those in office could be recalled "for economic or political reasons" and replaced by appointed officers (appointed by the Nazis, of course). The committees themselves could be dissolved for "reasons of state." Employers were authorized to dismiss any worker suspected of being "hostile to the state," without his being able to invoke the defense procedure provided by the social legislation of the Reich. At the same time, the NSBO propagandized actively on the jobs and began to conscript by force the members of the independent unions.

After May First, which was decreed a "national holiday" and celebrated by great spectacles throughout Germany, all labor unions were "coordinated," their buildings occupied by Storm Troops, and their leaders imprisoned. A "Committee of Action for the Protection of German Labor," headed by Dr. Ley, the administrative chief of the National Socialist Party, took over the property of the defunct organizations. Everywhere the People's Houses were occupied without resistance and turned into "Houses of German Labor." A proclamation by Dr. Ley stated: "We are not dreaming—quite the contrary—of destroying the unions. No, Worker, your institutions are sacred and inviolable for us National Socialists!" On May 10, the "German Labor Front" was set up. It included the members of all the "coordinated" organizations, grouped into fourteen trade federations.

But at the constituent congress of the Labor Front, Hitler contradicted Dr. Ley's assurances; the National Socialists, he declared, took over the unions "*not at all to preserve them integrally in the future. . . .*"[25] On June 8, writing in *Soziale Praxis*, Schneider-Landmann, the head of the National Socialist federation of office employees, corroborated this: "It is clear from now on that the trade organizations will be deprived of the functions that have given them the character of trade unions up to the present." And, in fact, on May 16, the right to strike was abolished. On May 19, the "coordinated" unions were deprived by law of the right to make union contracts. On November 29, the admission of new members into the fourteen trade federations was suspended, and between January 1 and October 1, 1934, they were dissolved one after the other.

It now remains to take precautions for the future. "Nothing is more dangerous to a state," Dr. Ley very clearly explains, "than uprooted men deprived of their defense organizations. . . . Such men undoubtedly become victims of unscrupulous agitators and a constant source of disturbance. . . . The Labor Front was created to isolate these unscrupulous agitators."[26] *To paralyze working class resistance* is henceforth to be the role of the Labor Front. It becomes an enormous state apparatus, responsible for filling the workers with propaganda and policing them. Its propaganda chief, Selzner, has declared that its purpose is not economic defense of the workers, but that it is a *purely political* organization "giving an opportunity to enlarge" the scope of National Socialist propaganda. Its essential task, is "the preparation, through education, of all its members for National Socialism."[27] The basic organization of the Labor Front from this time on is the "shop community," which includes all the workers in the same shop whatever their trade. The workers are indoctrinated and supervised both by the employer—an ex-officio member of the "shop community"—and by the "National Socialist shop cell."

The connections of the Labor Front with the police are close. For instance, on February 13, 1936, the head of the secret police, Himmler, visited the headquarters of the Labor Front and stated: "The S.S. and the police can assure internal safety only if people are won over to the idea of National Socialism, and this is a task which falls particularly on the Labor Front."

Membership in the Labor Front is not compulsory, but as a matter of fact the pressure of the employers makes it very difficult for the workers to remain outside the organization. With increasing frequency the employers introduce into their contracts a provision that only members of the Labor Front can be employed.[28]

Conversely, the National Socialist state can keep out of the Labor Front—that is to say, deprive of a livelihood—anybody it wishes. The *Angriff* for January 14, 1936, stated: "The Labor Front is not obliged to accept all who wish to be admitted. It reserves the right to reject applications for membership and to expel members already admitted."

The National Socialist state is not satisfied merely to conscript the workers into "scab" organizations, but inflicts severe punishment on all expressions of independence from the workers. Workers who threaten "social peace in a business by malicious agitation among the employees" are brought before the labor "Courts of Honor" for "breach of social honor" and are subject not only to dismissal but to heavy fines and prison terms, in accordance with the law of January 20, 1934. Attempts to strike are suppressed with special severity; they are, in the words of the official commentator on the law, "an offense against the community."[29]

In the "internal shop regulations" posted by the employers with the consent and protection of the state, all sorts of disciplinary penalties are provided for slandering and inciting "comrades in work," spreading rumors about improvements in the shop, divulging trade secrets or even the wages received by the workers in the plant.[30] The *Angriff*, the Labor Front daily paper, for October 1, 1936, had to admit that "some shop regulations are reminiscent of penal codes. It is scarcely believable what juridical ingenuity has been able to accumulate in the way of fines, revocations with warning, prohibitions, etc." It should be added that the new German penal code makes "industrial espionage" (for instance, "to reveal the accounting of production costs") a crime of high treason punishable by the death penalty.[31]

The law of February 26, 1935, introduced, as in Italy, a "labor passport" in which the employer sets down his estimate of the worker when the latter leaves his employment, and which has to be presented on applying for a new job. One of Goering's ordinances provides that if a worker, "breaking his contract," leaves his employment before his time is up, the employer has the right to keep his labor passport until the expiration of the contract. Since a worker can work nowhere without his passport, he is thus bound to his job.

Although the workers themselves do not have the right to change employers, the authorities assume the right to shift them from one job to another regardless of their wishes. Goering's ordinance at the end of June, 1938, permits the conscription of any worker, his transfer and employment in any work "recognized as useful to the nation," without any guarantee that he will receive a wage equal to that earned on his previous job.[32]

In order to prevent labor conflicts, the National Socialist state exercises compulsory "arbitration." Disagreements, after coming up for mediation before the Labor Front's "shop community," the local "labor committee," and the district "labor commission" (in these last two bodies both sides supposedly have equal representation), are settled in each district by the official representative of the state, the "labor curator," assisted by a "council of experts" (also supposed to represent both sides equally). Of the thirteen labor curators appointed May 19, 1933, nine were former employees of employers' associations. If the curator believes penalties should be imposed, he takes the case to the "Court of Honor" in his district—a court composed of a presiding magistrate who is a state functionary subject to recall, an employer, and a "representative" of the workers, acting as associate judges. Finally, the decision of the "Court of Honor" can be appealed to a supreme court, the "Reich Court of Honor" in Berlin, which is also composed of magistrates, employers and "representatives" of the workers.

At every stage, the story of this "arbitration" is the same. National Socialist state functionaries, under the pretext of mediating between the employers' representatives and the workers' "representatives," force on the workers whatever the employers wish, and anybody who disputes this decision is considered an "enemy of the state" and punished accordingly.

Finally, the National Socialist state uses its authority to sanction whatever wage the employers wish to pay those they exploit. With the protection and consent of the labor curators, the employers fix in the "internal shop regulations" wages, hours, and working conditions for their employees. The Labor Curator for Westphalia admitted: "Owing to the large number of contracts submitted to me, it is absolutely impossible for me to verify them in every detail."[33] Not to accept the wage specified in the "internal regulations" is a "breach of social honor," and the culprit, brought before the labor courts, is subject to severe punishment.

The industrialists have thus reached their objectives:

1) *Union wages have been replaced by company wages*—The national union contracts (which were more often *regional*) are replaced by wage rates varying from company to company. "The center of gravity (*Schwergewicht*) shall henceforth be in each company," wrote the official commentator on the law.

2) *Wage differentials are secured*—The employers criticized the old union contracts for tending to equalize wages and thus suppress all reward for initiative or skill. Henceforth wages are greatly differentiated. "The minimum rates," the law specifies "must be established in such a way as to leave a margin for rewarding each employee *in accordance with his production.* Moreover, everything possible must be done to recompense suitably all exceptional services."

3) *Wages can be cut without encountering the slightest opposition—*

Since wages are no longer established by contracts extending over a certain period of time, but by "internal shop regulations"—which the employer himself draws up and can change with the complicity of the labor curator to suit his own wishes—there is no longer anything to prevent slashing of wages.

It must be said that a few precautions had to be taken in order to get the working class to swallow these innovations. The law of January 20, 1934, was to have come into effect on May 1, but the government, fearing too strong a reaction from the workers, extended the old union contracts for another period. It was only after the June 30 purge that the employers were authorized to rid themselves of their obligations under the old contracts and to put into effect their "shop regulations."

2

But this ingenious system for paralyzing working class resistance does not, at first, work smoothly. There is a worm in the apple, which must be eliminated.

The *plebeians* have got into the Italian fascist "unions" and into the German Labor Front. The reader is already acquainted with these plebeians (Chapter 6). They do not seriously dream of attacking capitalist privileges, but they feel the need of relying on a "social base" in order to preserve and increase their personal influence in the regime. Those especially who have staked out their claims in the fascist "labor" organizations and made them their fiefs understand that they can attract and hold the workers only by *disguising these organizations as class organizations.* Hence they have to speak a demagogic language and make themselves, with more or less conviction, the spokesmen of their supporters.

But this demagogy is displeasing to the industrialists, who fear that the fascist "labor" organizations, instead of playing their part of restraining and supervising the workers, will be overwhelmed by their members. They have not subsidized fascism for the purpose of having class-conscious unions come to birth under another form. Hence they demand that war be waged ruthlessly against the plebeians, that the bureaucracy of the fascist "labor" organizations be cleansed from top to bottom, and that the last vestige of class struggle in them be stamped out.

In Italy

Before the taking of power, when it was still a question of fighting the labor unions for control of the working masses, it was necessary to entrust the leadership of the fascist "unions" to plebeian demagogues. Therefore Italian fascism made use of a number of former revolutionary syndicalists. Disciples of Georges Sorel who had been converted to nationalism on the eve of the war, these "syndicalists" were to be found from 1918 to 1920 in the "Italian Workers Union" (UIT), a dissident syndicalist organization whose program was a curious mixture of revolutionary syndicalism and nationalism. When fascism created its own organization in 1921, Rossoni and his friends left the UIT and took over the leadership of the fascist "unions." The appointment of all "union" functionaries from above made it possible for Rossoni to place his creatures everywhere. He staffed the secretariats of local and regional organizations with plebeians.

Once power was won, the leaders of the fascist "unions" realized that they could attach the working masses to their organizations only in so far as they were successful in passing off these "unions" as class organizations. Therefore they persisted in their demagogy. "We say," Rossoni wrote, "that the class struggle in its various aspects can very well continue to develop and may even be inevitable."[34] At the end of 1927, immediately after the stabilization of the lira at a very high rate, the industrialists ruthlessly cut wages. There was profound discontent in the masses, and Rossoni and the plebeian leaders felt they were being overwhelmed. To keep their rank and file in hand, they themselves were forced, on many occasions, to preach resistance and to pretend to oppose wage cuts.

They were half sincere in their opposition to the industrialists, whom they did not forgive for placing them, by their untimely demands, in an impossible situation and for making the fascist "unions" appear in their true colors as *scab* organizations. Therefore the congress of fascist "unions" in Rome in 1928 took place in a stormy atmosphere. The delegates did not hesitate to observe that the bosses alone had greatly profited from the "class collaboration."[35] Rossoni went rather far with his demagogy: "We fascists," he explained, "burned the indictment of the suit which communism tried to bring against property. But if those who own property do not understand what their duty is, they will become our enemies, and perhaps we may have to reopen the case." He went too far. The industrialists were indignant. They had not subsidized fascism merely to have the class struggle, which they had thrown out the door, come back in through the window—merely to have the organs for policing the workers take the lead in working class resistance, or to have the federation of fascist "unions" bring to life in another form the defunct Federation of Labor.

Consequently they forced Mussolini to dissolve the federation (decree of November 22, 1928) and disgrace Rossoni. The central organization having been destroyed, there remained only industrial associations, thirteen in number. Henceforth the "union" leaders could not rely, in the smallest labor conflict, on a "labor bloc" of more than two million members.[36] In the various industries the employers had to deal no longer with the federation but only with an industrial association, or rather, with "union" leaders whose social base was greatly reduced. At the same time, the bureaucracy of the "unions," in the local and regional organizations, was radically purged. All the plebeians placed in office by Rossoni were dismissed and replaced by servile functionaries—the bosses' tools or young intellectuals fresh from the universities who knew nothing whatever of the working masses.

But despite these successive purges, impulses from below, weakened as they were, from time to time forced the bureaucrats of the fascist "unions" to affect a will to resistance and the display of a certain amount of demagogy. For instance, at the congress of the fascist federation of industrial workers held on June 30 and July 1, 1936, twenty-nine out of thirty-three speakers came out for increased wages. In this case, to be sure, they were satisfied at the end of the congress to vote a resolution of thanks to the Duce "for all he has done for the Italian workers." But when such demagogy went too far, then the dictatorship struck and purged.[37]

In Germany

In order to get control of the working masses away from the independent unions, the plebeian leaders of the "shop cells" before the taking of power had to carry their demagogy very far. Once in power, they continued to do so. Between March and July, 1933, they literally ran wild. In every shop, the members of the "cells" spoke loud and strong. They wanted to have their say about hiring and firing and intervened increasingly in the technical and commercial ends of the business. As most of the "cell" members were also Storm Troopers, they went so far as to put a number of "anti-social" employers under arrest.

But finally the industrialists grew angry. The most turbulent NSBO leaders were fired from their jobs, expelled from the "cells," and thrown into concentration camps. In a communication to the police, Goering recommended "energetic action against members of shop cells who have not yet understood the real character of the Third Reich."

To the great disappointment of the plebeians in the cells, the "coordinated" unions were not inherited by the NSBO but went to a new organization, the Labor Front. The NSBO was relegated to a subsidiary position. Its members, who had believed they were the elite soldiers of the National Socialist "revolution," had to return to the ranks. In the Labor Front they enjoyed no more privileges than the other members, and they were specifically forbidden to interfere in the internal life of the organization. The NSBO lost its financial independence, its budget being henceforth fixed by the treasurer of the Labor Front. It no longer had the right to intervene in economic or social questions or in the relations between employers and employees without the specific authorization of the Labor Front. In December, 1933, when the party merged with the state, NSBO members were automatically subjected to the special legislation, which was extremely severe, designed for party members. In February, 1934, employers were authorized to dismiss presidents of "cells" for any "irresponsible" criticism. On June 22 and 25, the NSBO was forbidden to make collections, under any form whatever, or to hold public meetings. Finally, June 30 signalized the final defeat not only of the S.A. but of the NSBO, whose national president was executed.[38]

Rid of the extremist virus, the "shop cells" were completely changed in character. Composed of unquestionably reliable elements, and under the supreme command of the heads of the companies, who were *ex-officio members,* the shop cells became the National Socialist nucleus in the new "shop community." In the factory, they went in for espionage and stool pigeon work.

But the plebeians had not yet completely surrendered. The struggle was now carried into the upper bureaucratic spheres of the Labor Front. Some of the founders and leaders of the NSBO had consoled themselves for the subjugation of the "cells" by accepting important posts in the Labor Front. And there the same causes produced, though to a lesser degree, the same effects. These plebeian leaders could not maintain themselves in their new functions and preserve or increase their influence except to the extent that they were supported by a social base. They felt the pressure of the masses, attenuated as it was. And they had to become, with more or less conviction, the masses' spokesmen.

In the spring of 1934, the approaching application of the law of January 20, "for the regulation of national labor," loosed a wave of anger among the masses. The plebeian leaders of the Labor Front feared they would be swamped. To keep their rank and file in hand, they had to resort to new demagogy and pose as defenders of the workers' living conditions. But this made the employers indignant, and after June 30 the plebeians were brutally silenced by a veritable slaughter of big and little leaders. Dr. Ley personally found his position compromised, and at Wiesbaden he let himself go so far as to say, "the bosses' arrogance secretly persists in spite of appearances."[39] This animosity had a basis of sincerity. He could not forgive the employers for placing him, through their unreasonable demands, in an impossible position, and for making the Labor Front show its real face as a *scab* organization.

The patience of the industrialists was exhausted. As early as July, 1934, some of them asked Hitler to dismiss Dr. Ley "whose demagogic agitation continues to disturb business."[40] By August, the position of the head of the Labor Front was so shaky that rumors spread through Berlin of his flight and even of his suicide; but, strengthened by Hitler's personal support, he succeeded in reestablishing his position. In December, however, he was again threatened. An open struggle burst out between him and Dr. Schacht. Dr. Schacht did not conceal his hostility for the "socializing tendencies of the Labor Front" or his intention to get rid of Dr. Ley.[41] The Labor Front was deprived of its daily paper, *Der Deutsche*,[42] and its Leipzig congress of March 26 to 30, 1935, sounded the knell of the plebeians. Dr. Schacht spoke there as master and announced that henceforth the Labor Front would be under the direct control of the employers: "An employer will be appointed as associate to the head of each Labor Front body, *whenever the head of that body is not himself an employer.*" The Labor Front could no longer inspect a plant without the consent of the head of the company. Dr. Ley succeeded in keeping his post only by humbly abjuring his errors: "Certainly," he agreed, "there might have arisen from the existence of the two organizations [one of the employers and one of labor] something like the class struggle of past times. . . ."

3

When the fascist state has destroyed the unions, paralyzed proletarian resistance, and rooted out every vestige of class struggle from its own "labor" organizations, the necessary conditions have been fulfilled for slashing wages.

In Italy

According to the figures supplied by the Italian press itself,[43] between 1927 and 1932 nominal wages were *reduced by half,* and as the cuts have continued since 1932, it would be no exaggeration to say that wages have been reduced from the 1927 level by from 60 to 75 percent. Wages in 1935 were rarely as high as those before the First World War. Although they have been twice raised by 10 percent since 1935, the cost of living in the meantime has risen 30 percent.[44]

And from these meager wages all sorts of deductions have to be subtracted: wage tax (reintroduced by a decree-law of November, 1922), compulsory "union" dues, "voluntary contributions" for winter unemployment relief, and assessments for social insurance, the party, *Dopolavoro* [recreation organization], etc.

The effect on wage levels of the so-called "campaign against unemployment" must also be taken into account. The fascist state, in fact, economizes on unemployment relief by making *workers with jobs*, who are transformed into partially unemployed, pay for the assistance to the jobless. For instance, in November, 1934, the forty hour week was introduced into industry *without maintaining weekly wages*. *Lavoro Fascista* confessed that "reduction of work will mean a considerable sacrifice for the workers already employed."[45] Compensation is provided only for workers who are heads of large families, but this supplement is taken from other workers who, in addition to the cut in their weekly wages, are deprived of another 1 percent of their pay for the "family allowances." In certain industries, work is rotated, the employees working one week out of two, for instance, which further reduces their weekly income by half.[46]

Another expedient was adopted in November, 1934, when an agreement was signed between the employers' association and the "unions" providing that women and young men can be dismissed from their jobs and replaced by adult unemployed men. But the employers pay the newly hired workers only the starvation wages previously paid the young men and women, and the measure helps to lower wage standards.

Finally, the unemployed who are given jobs on public works are paid at lower rates on the pretext that these works have "an emergency character as unemployment relief," and this too serves to depress wage levels.

So far only *nominal* wages have been taken into consideration. *Real* wages, however, have suffered a much more acute reduction as a result of the uninterrupted rise in the cost of living (Chapter 9). We must also take into account the speedup and longer hours, especially in the war industries, without any corresponding increase in pay for the extra hours worked. The Italians will overcome all difficulties, Mussolini declared, "even if they have to work twenty-five hours a day."[47]

In Germany

It has been estimated that between the advent of National Socialism (January 30, 1933) and the summer of 1935, wages were lowered from 25 to 40 percent. More than half of the German workers make less than 30 marks a week.[48] The *Angriff* admits that the monthly wage of the worker varies between 80 and 150 marks.[49] If the official figures are to be believed, 80 percent of the workers earn less than 150 marks a month.[50] Hitler himself has to concede that "the living standard of countless Germans is utterly insufficient,"[51] and the Bavarian Minister Wagner that "many German workers suffer from hunger."[52]

Furthermore, all sorts of deductions have to be subtracted from these wretched earnings: wage taxes (increased from 25 to 35 percent), municipal "poll" taxes (more than doubled), bachelors' taxes, contributions for unemployment insurance, disability insurance, health insurance, contributions for the Labor Front, the *Strength Through Joy* association [recreation organization], *Winter Relief,* anti-aircraft defense, victims of industrial accidents, the party or the Hitler Youth, etc. These various deductions lower the gross wage by from 20 to 30 percent. On the other hand, social insurance benefits (illness, disability, accidents, old age, unemployment) have been greatly diminished. The labor mutual assistance and insurance associations have been dissolved and their funds turned over to private insurance companies that pay smaller benefits.[53]

The effect of the so-called "fight against unemployment" on wage levels must also be taken into consideration. The National Socialist state, finding itself faced with widespread unemployment, succeeds in economizing on unemployment relief by making *the workers with jobs,* transformed into partially unemployed, pay for the relief of the jobless. The employers are forced by the public authorities or the party to hire more labor than they really need, but the latter make up for this additional burden either by reducing all wages or by shortening the working hours of each worker.

Another expedient is to dismiss women and young men from their jobs and replace them by adult unemployed men. A decree of August 28, 1934, gave the "labor offices" full power to deprive women and unmarried men less than twenty-five years old of their employment. But the employers pay the older workers hired in their place only the starvation wages previously paid the women and youngsters. By virtue of this decree, 130,000 workers under twenty-five were discharged. (Later the decree lost its importance due to the scarcity of labor as a result of the intensified rearmament program. In 1937, 370,000 women went back to work.)

Finally, the general level of wages is lowered because the unemployed put to work on various public work projects receive ridiculously low pay. The workers assigned to *auxiliary works* (about 400,000 in 1934) receive as their entire compensation the unemployment allowance plus some relief in the form of commodities. Workers assigned to motor highway construction (nearly half a million in March, 1936)—although this is "independent work" and not emergency work undertaken to combat unemployment—are paid, with the complicity of the labor curators, at a rate lower than the prevailing wage for laborers. The workers conscripted in 1938 for work on fortifications are not paid the wages they received on their former jobs. The young men conscripted in the *labor service* (about 250,000) and doing heavy work, receive merely the soldier's pay—that is, 50 pfennigs a day. Young girls forced to serve a *domestic apprenticeship* of a year in a family or on a farm[54] have to toil as "maids of all work" without their masters being compelled to pay them a fixed wage.

In the beginning of May, 1936, Hitler put "cheap labor" at the disposal of the Ruhr industrialists in the form of unemployed, paid from 1.50 marks to 2 marks a day. "This labor," the *Petit Parisien* stated on May 4, "would make it possible . . . to bring pressure on the wage levels of other categories of workers."

So far only *nominal* wages have been considered, but *real* wages declined much more sharply as a result of the uninterrupted rise in the cost of living (Chapter 9).

Finally, the speedup in production and longer hours to which the workers are subjected must be taken into account. When the *Strength Through Joy* association was formed, Dr. Ley announced: "We shall have to greatly increase the speed of production."[55] An employers' report rejoices because the new labor laws have had a fortunate effect "at the present time, precisely, which requires increased intensification of production. . . ."[56] Goering states in a speech: "We must work doubly hard today to lead the Reich out of decadence, impotence, shame, and poverty. Eight hours a day is not enough. We must work!"[57] One of his ordinances authorizes labor curators and inspectors to allow extra hours. This does not mean extra hours with pay for overtime but simply a *lengthening of the work day* to ten hours or more.[58] As early as 1934 and 1935, the number of cases of illness resulting in inability to work was 20.7 percent greater than in 1933.[59]

4

After having paralyzed proletarian resistance, destroyed the independent unions, stamped out every germ of the class struggle from its own "labor" organizations, and cut wages below the subsistence level, fascism must still try to conceal from the workers its real face as the dictatorship of big business.

Then it resorts to the bluff of the "corporative state." We have seen that long before taking power it held out to the workers the bait of "corporations" (Chapter 4). Victorious now, it must make a pretense of keeping its promises, don the mask of "class collaboration," and make the workers believe that their masters are dealing with them henceforth "on an equal footing" and allowing them to share in the management of the economy.

But here again the fascist plebeians make serious trouble for the dictatorship. With untimely ardor they bestride the war horse of "corporatism." They carry "corporatist" demagogy much too far. Why? As always, for reasons of prestige. Wishing to enlarge to the utmost their social base, to encroach if possible on other fiefs, and to acquire additional influence and power in the regime, they cannot permit any sphere of national activity to escape their control. They are annoyed because only the labor unions have been "fascisized" *and the employers' associations have remained outside their grasp.* Not that they are dreaming of seriously attacking capitalist privileges, but they are thirsting to force themselves and their services on these gentlemen of industry; they want to be important and to have something to say about the economy. Hence they dream of absorbing into a single organization—a huge corporative machine of which they will be the appointed leaders—both capital and labor, both the employers' associations and the labor "unions."

But the industrialists rebel against this demand. They will not permit "fascisization" to cross the boundaries of their private preserves. They want to remain masters in their own houses, in their businesses, cartels and trusts, and trade associations. They fear that in a *mixed* organization they would quickly be swamped by the plebeians. They are still haunted by the specter of workers' control. It was to drive these phantoms away forever, and not to see them again, that they subsidized fascism. So they veto all corporatist experiments *insofar as there is danger of the plebeians utilizing them to the detriment of the capitalists.* They consent to an absolutely inoffensive caricature of a corporative state—necessary for a smokescreen—only when the plebeians have been radically eliminated and deprived of all influence.

Something dishonest is not always easy to decipher. An outright lie is always difficult to counter. One must appeal to the patience and discernment of the reader, who must allow himself to be drawn into a labyrinth full of artificial creations. But we cannot avoid making a refined analysis if we are to raze these houses of cards erected by mendacious demagogy, if we are to dig through its byzantine face and uncover fascism's real plan on the one hand, and the persistence of the class struggle—that is, the workers' unwavering aspiration towards self-management and control over production—and the bosses' unshakable hostility towards any attempt, even a caricature, to challenge their absolute power—on the other hand.

In Italy

As far back as 1921, Rossoni and his friends christened the fascist "unions" with the name of *corporations,* thus indicating their desire to make them into *mixed* organizations that would include *under their aegis* employers and workers. "National unionism," said the first number of *Lavoro d'Italia,* "is reorganizing on a grandiose scale Italians from all walks of life, animated with a single conviction."[60] *Italians from all walks of life* meant employers and employees. The industrialists let them talk, but they took care not to enter the fascist "unions."

After the March on Rome, the plebeians demanded that the corporative principle be put into effect, and the fascist "unions" be transformed into mixed organizations. But, as Rosenstock-Franck said of these mixed organizations, "the industrialists will not hear of them at any price, for in them they are sure they would be overwhelmed at once."[61] The resistance of the industrialists and landowners was so strong that Mussolini had to have the fascist Grand Council pass a resolution on March 15, 1923, formally condemning the principle of mixed unions. "He allowed the General Federation of Industry and that of Agriculture," Hautecour relates, "to freely exist. The corporations had to give up the dream of mixed unions. . . . The General Federation of Industry, in a session that Mussolini described as historic, declared it was willing to work in collaboration with the corporations but insisted on remaining independent."[62]

But the plebeians would not admit they were beaten. They had not given up the idea of imposing themselves and their authority on the industrialists and landowners.[63] After 1925, their daring increased; they dreamed of including in their fief not only the economic forces, employing and labor alike, but the state itself. They demanded the replacement of the *political state* by the *wholly corporative state,* and "self-government of the producers," in the style of Proudhon.

Mussolini had appointed at the end of 1925 a commission known as the "Eighteen" to prepare union and corporative legislation. The extremist majority of this commission proposed the following: "A national corporative organization shall be created which shall include all citizens divided *into different orders* according to their economic activity, and which shall absorb all existing institutions."[64]

But this idea alarmed the industrialists. Within this immense corporative machine, they feared they would be swamped by the plebeians, in their turn swamped by the masses. The industrialists would not agree to the suppression of their own organizations. "It is understandable," the Minister Rocco wrote, "how greatly the idea of a single organization for labor and production, with a single discipline, would *frighten* employers if the corporation were formed outside the state, under a regime of dangerous liberty."[65] The reactionary minority of the Commission of Eighteen replied to the majority: "The corporative reform reduces the state to a mere hierarchic federation of interests, in complete contrast to the modern conception of the state as the synthesis of all the moral and material interests of the nation."[66]

Mussolini was greatly embarrassed. On the one hand he did not want to cause the slightest distress to his financial backers and was, in his innermost convictions, won over to the reactionary concept of the all-powerful state. On the other hand, he had to lay a smokescreen and humor his plebeians. Therefore he made a rough compromise in the law of April 3, 1926 (supplemented by the regulation of July 1, 1926). *On paper,* he created corporations: "The employers' associations and the workers' associations *may* be united through central liaison bodies with a common superior hierarchy

(Art. 3). . . . The organizations thus joined constitute a corporation." In any case, these corporations would not exist at the base, on a *union* plane (mixed "unions"), but only at the top, on a *national* plane: "The liaison bodies . . . shall include the *national* associations, representing the different factors in production, employers and intellectual and manual workers, for a specific branch of industry."

The employers' independence was carefully preserved. Article 3 of the law of April 3, 1926, continues as follows: ". . . *but leaving intact the separate representation of employers and of workers.*"

Finally, the political state, far from dissolving into the corporation as the plebeians dreamed, granted the latter (in case it should be created at all) no life of its own: "The corporation is not a legal person but *an administrative organ of the state.*"

The following year, 1927, the "Charter of Labor" stated: "The worker is an active collaborator in the economic enterprise. . . ." But it added at once: "*of which the management as well as the responsibility devolves on the employer.*" This is far from collaboration between workers and employers "on an equal footing."

These "corporations," though almost emptied of all content, still displeased the industrialists. They demanded that their establishment be postponed, because the plebeians, masters of the federation of fascist "unions," were too strong and would indulge in an annoying amount of demagogy. Any formula for a corporative state, even an emasculated one, was capable of strengthening their influence and turning it against the employers. So the corporations were put off to a later date; the plebeians had to be liquidated first. It would be time to talk about a "corporative state" when the purge of the fascist "unions" had been completed, when every trace of the class struggle had been rooted out of them, and when they should be nothing more, from top to bottom, than a huge police apparatus. "We have time," Mussolini readily repeated.

To appease the ardor of the impatient, however, he pasted on everything the label: "*corporative.*" He set up a Ministry of *Corporations* in 1926, the function of which was to control more strictly the fascist "unions"; a National Council of *Corporations* in 1926 (reorganized in 1930), the members of which were appointed by the dictator, and which was merely a body for registering dictatorial decisions; and a *corporative* Chamber of Deputies, so called because the candidates were chosen by the dictatorship from a list presented by the occupational organizations, and the electors were required to be dues-paying members of these organizations. In 1931 he transformed the provincial Interunion Committees into provincial *corporative* Economic Councils. But the corporations themselves still did not exist.

A number of extremists continued to demand the *complete corporative state* and to babble on this theme. But they were no longer dangerous, for they had no social base. For the most part they were intellectuals and not men of action. So Mussolini let them talk freely, and he even gave them—in appearance—some satisfaction. In 1934, in fact, it was more necessary than ever to lay down a smokescreen, for the economic crisis had severely affected the working masses and unemployment was steadily increasing. The "mysticism" which had enabled the regime to keep up the enthusiasm of its partisans was beginning to grow stale. Mussolini therefore decided to strike an important blow. Through the law of February 4, 1934, he had a few high functionaries of the fascist "unions" enter the *employers'* economic organizations, which had a semi-governmental character and were christened "corporations"* for the needs of the cause, and he announced with a great fanfare that at last the corporative state had been born. He dug up all the old demagogic cliches: "The fascist era proclaims the equality of men in production."[67] "We must little by little teach the people to govern themselves. . . ."[68] "The workers must become more intimately acquainted with the productive process and its discipline. . . ."[69] "The worker will be liberated."[70] Corporatism tends towards a "higher social justice, towards a gradual lessening of the gap between great wealth and great poverty," etc.[71]

---

* For the real role of these organizations, see Chapter 9.

But the distance between words and reality is immense. "Collaboration" between employers and wage earners has not been instituted in the plant or in the "union," or on a local or regional scale, or even in the trade association. Neither in the factory nor in the "union" does the worker deal with his boss "on an equal footing"; nor does he participate at all in the management of the economy. To be sure, some fascist extremists insisted that the present system was only a beginning. Spirito and Bottai announced for "later" the "regional corporation," or even the corporation at the base—in the plant. But Mussolini destroyed these illusions, or unmasked this demagogy, by harshly declaring (to a journalist): "We do not aim to rebuild shop councils."[72] It is the "fixed determination [of the employers] . . . to refuse to agree to any revival of the old internal shop committees," writes Rosenstock-Franck.[73]

The "collaboration" exists only at the top, in the twenty-two "corporations." And what collaboration! A few docile functionaries of the dictatorship, substituted for the plebeians at the head of the fascist "unions" and supposed to represent the workers against the employers, are allowed to be present at the deliberations of those gentlemen. In the highly improbable case that the so-called "labor" representatives venture to assume a demagogic attitude at the council table, or dare not to cast their votes with those of the employers, three official representatives of the fascist state are there to add their votes to those of the bosses and automatically assure them a majority.

Such is the "Corporative State"!

In Germany

As soon as power was achieved, the Nazi plebeians impatiently clamored for a "corporative structure" (*Staendischer Aufbau*) to include employers' and workers' associations. Even before the independent unions were "coordinated," they tried to get their hands on the employers' organizations. On April 1, 1933, Dr. Wagener, head of the economic section of the National Socialist Party, staked out his claim in the German Federation of Industry. On April 6, the executive committee of the federation dissolved itself, and Wagener got it to assume the title of "Corporation of German Industry." He demanded that President Krupp retire, but the latter remained as president of the new "Corporation," flanked by two Nazi commissioners. For a time, Wagener had his own way in the employers' organization. He was appointed "Economic Commissioner of the Reich," and Krupp, after having been received by Hitler, announced that the employers' "Corporation" would be reorganized and the *Fuehrer-prinzip* (leader principle) would be applied. Its officers would be appointed from above and no longer freely elected.[74] "This reorganization," the *Temps* stated, "is to prepare the new corporative structure, patterned on that of fascist Italy, which will include the labor unions as well as the industrial associations."[75] It was asserted that the Fuehrer himself had been won over to corporatism. On May 31, he announced the promulgation of a law outlining the "corporative structure."[76] Alfred Rosenberg declared in June: "The corporative organization which is to be begun in Germany will represent real socialism, twentieth-century socialism."[77]

A committee was appointed to draw up the statutes of the new corporative state. Every plebeian had his plan, and each hoped that the new "structure" would have as its base his own fief and would increase his privileges. There was Dr. Wagener's plan, and the plan of Dr. Rinteln, leader of the "Combat League of the Middle Classes." But the plan that seemed to have the greatest chance of success was Dr. Ley's; he dreamed of nothing less than the absorption into his Labor Front of the entire economy, both workers' and employers' organizations: "The corporative structure of the German people," he exclaimed, "is completed in its main outlines! This very day I shall submit the finished plan to the Fuehrer. It will be one of the greatest works accomplished by the revolution! It is nothing less than the establishment of an organic tie between the workers and employees on the one hand, and the employers on the other, and their common integration into the economic organism."[78]

But the industrialists did not understand it this way. By July, 1933, big industry, supported by the Reichswehr, had pronounced its veto;

Hitler abruptly announced the end of the national revolution, and Dr. Wagener was removed. On July 13, the new Minister of Economy, Schmitt, assured the industrialists, not that the corporative structure was definitely abandoned, but that it was *postponed to better times.* The present organizations, he explained, were not yet sufficiently mature for such a splendid ideal, and there was danger that irresponsible elements might try to make adventurous experiments in this field.

The plebeians, however, would not admit their defeat. They had not lost all hope of achieving their goal. Dr. Ley continued to announce unperturbed the advent of corporations. In the middle of August, 1933, he declared: "The Labor Front and the corporative structure are two parts of a whole; one is inconceivable without the other. The Labor Front has no meaning if what it has achieved in the way of training and education is not translated into action by the corporative structure."[79]

Hitler, like Mussolini, was forced to make a rough compromise. He had to obey his financial backers, but he also had to lay down a smokescreen. He was still obliged to handle his plebeians carefully. By the law of January 20, 1934, he set up "confidential councils" in each business, which were represented as embryos of corporatism. The "confidential advisers" would "collaborate" with the employer and could require from the latter certain confidential information, particularly the inspection of his books. But these "confidential advisers"—whose names were originally submitted to the workers in a caricature of a plebiscite, but later were simply appointed by the boss—were the "confidential advisers" . . . of the boss. The same law also provided that experts in labor conflicts appointed by the Labor Front should be named "in agreement with the corporations . . . to the extent that a corporative organization of the economy has been achieved." But the corporations themselves remained in limbo, and the employers persisted in their opposition to any "corporative structure."

Therefore, when the *employers'* economic organizations, semi-official in character, were made into "occupational groups" by the

234 FASCISM AND BIG BUSINESS

law of February 27, 1934,* no "representative" of the wage earners
was even admitted; the plebeians still had too much influence for
their presence in these organizations to be without danger. The
author of the law, Minister Schmitt, stated specifically: "In the measures taken at present, there is no question yet of a corporative reform. You know that the Fuehrer has intentionally postponed the
solution of this problem, for he rightly believes that a corporative
structure should arise only slowly, with the development of events."[80]

But the plebeians were persistent; they fought every step. Driven
from one position, they retreated to a new line of defense. The law
of February 27, 1934, though a severe check for them, left a few
trump cards in their hands. They had at least been successful in
that the new employers' organizations had a pronouncedly governmental character, and the employers were in some degree regimented
in them; the "leader principle" was applied, and there were no more
deliberative assemblies. They hoped thus to be able somewhat to
control the activity of the industrialists from above. Another advantage was that they had succeeded in dismembering the Federation (now Corporation) of Industry into several different "occupational groups." Finally, they had obtained the appointment of a man
on whom they could count, Kessler, as "economic Fuehrer." He
seemed determined on dissolving the old private employers' associations, which had now become superfluous. Once this plan was
carried out, once the employers were staffed and controlled by the
plebeians of the party and the National Socialist state, perhaps it
would be at last possible to push them into the famous corporative
"structure."

But the old private employers' associations, particularly the Federation of Industry, stubbornly refused to let themselves be dissolved, and this was not one of the least causes for the crisis of June
30, 1934, following which Kessler was recalled (July 11). In his turn,
von der Goltz, associate and successor to Kessler, tried to dissolve
the recalcitrant associations. But he failed, and at the end of No-

---

* For the real role of these organizations, see Chapter 9.

vember, 1934, he was disgraced like his predecessor. And on December 2, the new Minister of Economy, Dr. Schacht, completed the destruction of the plebeians' work. He reconstituted the Federation of Industry by reuniting the seven "occupational groups" into one. Furthermore, he restored to the employers a large measure of autonomy. The "leader principle" was abolished in the "occupational groups," a general membership meeting was to be held at least once a year, and the administration of the head of the group had to be voted on by secret ballot. "It will always be necessary," Dr. Schacht declared, "for independent bodies to exist to advise employers, and *these bodies will always exist.*"[81] The plebeians of the National Socialist state and party had to give up the hope of "coordinating" the employers' organizations.

But no matter how bad the state of their cause, they still did not consider themselves beaten. Dr. Ley continued to demand his say in the economy. The employers became indignant. "Let nobody imagine," their organ, the *Deutsche Volkswirt,* stated on December 7, that "a second organization of German economy inside the Labor Front would be possible." It was time to settle things, and at the end of March, 1935, at the congress of the Labor Front in Leipzig, the "corporatist" plebeians finally had to capitulate.

Dr. Schacht himself came to announce that the era of competition between the Labor Front and the "occupational groups" was over. A "corporative" constitution was promulgated which satisfied all the employers' demands. For a smokescreen, collaboration between employers and "representatives" of the workers was provided, but only in the field of *social policy*—only regarding matters of wages and working conditions. The *economic* domain remained the private preserve of the employers, and the "representatives" of the workers were formally forbidden to enter. Dr. Schacht asked Dr. Ley to stop poking his nose into the economy.

At every step of the corporative state, the employers are represented twice. First, from an organizational point of view, they belong *both* to their own "occupational group" and to the "shop community" of the Labor Front. Then they are seated, on a district basis, *both* in the district economic commission and in the labor commission. On a national basis, they are represented *both* in the Economic Council of the Reich and in the Labor Council of the Reich. But to the *economic* organizations, commissions and councils, no "labor representation" is admitted. "Collaboration" exists only in the *labor* organizations, commissions and councils.

But even in this last, restricted domain, there is only a caricature of "collaboration." First, it should be noted that the Labor Front is eliminated not only from the *economic* but also from the *social* field. As a matter of fact, the "labor" delegates to the labor commissions are *exclusively* chosen from the members of the employers' "confidential councils" and are not necessarily responsible to the Labor Front. The secretaries of the Labor Front have no right to participate in the work of these commissions. Since the members of the "confidential councils" are appointed by the employers, the latter are sure to have before them in the labor commissions entirely docile creatures, *even more docile than the functionaries of the Labor Front would be.*[82] And if, in spite of everything, a disagreement should arise in these labor commissions between the employers and "labor" delegates, every precaution has been taken: the labor commissions have only a *consultative* vote, and the official representative of the state, the labor curator, flying to the aid of the employers, will decide.

9

Fascism in power:
Economic policy

The fascist state is not satisfied with reducing the workers to slavery and making a general massacre of wages possible. It restores capitalist profits in another way: through various *economic* expedients.

"Expedients" is the word. It is not a question of taking measures to set in motion once more, however feebly, the "normal" machinery of capitalism. It is not a question of reestablishing profits from the production and distribution of new wealth. It is, quite simply, a matter of restoring their revenues to capitalist enterprises by *artificial* means and at the expense of the masses.

These expedients, of course, are by no means specifically *fascist* or *National Socialist*. They are twin brothers to those used in other countries, differing only in *degree* and not in *kind*. What we are about to describe is not peculiar to fascism, and there is not, contrary to what the plebeian demagogues say, any kind of "fascist" or "National Socialist" economy. The fascist economy is only a sharpened form of the so-called "guided" capitalist economy, first tried in Germany during the First World War under the name *Kriegswirtschaft* (War Economy).

Nor are these expedients in any way "anti-capitalist." Only the

237

naive could ever have believed that fascism is an actual economic revolution, outmoding capitalism. But the massive scope of these measures drags the fascist state in deeper than foreseen at first. It must more and more reject solutions reputed to be "liberal" or "orthodox."

When fascism takes power, overflowing with gratitude for big business which financed it, its words and its deeds exhale the purest sort of laisser-faire economic doctrine. It announces its intention of favoring and protecting in every possible way private property and individual initiative. It rejects with horror the idea that the state might meddle in production. But the fascist state stands aside only so long as Messieurs Capitalists request it not to interfere in their private affairs. It imposes on them the lightest possible taxes, the most tenuous sort of control. But it is always ready to come running whenever these gentlemen cannot pull through by themselves. In any such crisis, it is immediately at their service, "socializing" their losses, refloating their enterprises, and keeping them alive with its orders.

In short the course of events soon forces fascism to give its program a serious wrench. Carried away by its eagerness to resurrect big business profits, it finds itself embarked, above all in Germany, on a huge armament program. Fascism speedily gets caught up in a system of wheels within wheels which insensibly conducts it from laisser-faire capitalism to autarky and a wartime economy.

Thus, starting from a desire to assure private enterprise maximum freedom, fascism is compelled to gradually bureaucratize the economy and is more and more trapped in the contradiction between what it would like to do and what it must do. Groping tortuously forward, it succeeds in maintaining the capitalist system, but only by restricting each individual capitalist's freedom of movement, and by sacrificing the other branches of the economy on the altar of heavy industry. Only the great capitalists continue to draw their profits, while the economy as a whole is paralysed and individuals of every class are ruined or put on short rations.

It is a well known fact among doctors that certain cures seem for a moment to overcome the disease; but the disease takes its revenge. Driven from one site in the body, it reappears elsewhere or in a different form. For a moment, fascism, by repairing the profit-making mechanism, seems to banish the illness that capitalism suffers from. But this only aggravates the disease. Charged with saving the system, it ends by plunging it into a worldwide holocaust.

Nor is this denouement peculiar to fascism. Every expedient that capitalism has resorted to in other countries has sooner or later led to the same result. Thus the authors of the "New Deal" in the United States temporarily succeeded in restarting the capitalist machine only by arms purchases even more gigantic than those in Germany. With the return of peace, American capitalism could survive only by remaining on a war footing—a nuclear war footing—that imperils the future of the whole planet.

1

No sooner is fascism installed in power than it hastens to give evidence of its good will. It restores to private capitalism a number of monopolies held or controlled by the state.

In Italy

Shortly after the March on Rome, Mussolini stated: "We must take from the state those functions for which it is incompetent and which it performs badly."[1] "I believe the state should renounce its economic functions, especially those carried out through monopolies, because the state is incompetent in such matters. . . ."[2] "We must put an end to state railways, state postal service, and state insurance."[3] Great monopolies were returned to private initiative, after having been made solvent. The match monopoly was turned over to a "Consortium of Match Manufacturers." The state also gave up running the telephone system (1925) and the execution of various public works. As for insurance, legislation in 1912 had created a state institution which was to become a monopoly at the end of ten years, but by a law of April 19, 1923, Mussolini turned life insurance over to private capitalism. Under socialist influence, municipal ownership had been considerably developed in Italy, but the Duce ordered that "the pace of municipalization be slowed down." A fascist admits that the powerful electric companies "do not even hide under polite formulas their desire to absorb—it would be better to say swallow up—the municipal power plants."[4] The *podesta* of Pola, Turin, etc., turned profitable sources of income over to the industrialists.

In Germany

As soon as the National Socialists came in, they announced that there "will be an end to all the attempts of recent years at nationalization. State enterprises will again be transformed into private enterprises."[5]

In 1932 the state had put the powerful *Gelsenkirchen* company on a sound footing by buying 125 million marks of stock, which assured it control of the "United Steel" trust. But Hitler was anxious to display his gratitude to the magnates of heavy industry, the Kirdorfs and Thyssens; so, through a series of complicated mergers, the state practically gave them back control of the business[6] and in March, 1936, returned its stock to the "United Steel" for 100 million marks.

After the bank crash of 1931, most of the big banks had come under state control. The Reich had acquired 90 percent of the capital of the *Dresdner-Bank* and *Danat* (merged); 70 percent of the capital of the *Commerz und Privatbank,* and 35 percent of the capital of the *Deutsche Bank und Diskonto Gesellschaft.* But the financiers demanded that their establishments be returned to private hands, and as early as December, 1933, the Minister of Economy, Schmitt, announced that "the Reich proposes to give up the important share it has had for two years in the capital of certain great credit establishments."[7]

At the end of 1933 an investigating committee composed of experts was appointed to study the question. Dr. Schacht at the same time stated in London that the "government of the Reich has no intention of making state influence over the banks eternal. . . ."[8] In

February, 1934, Dr. Reinhardt, state financial secretary and a big banker, declared in his turn that "the government is not thinking of nationalizing the banks. . . ."[9] Finally, on December 1, the report of the investigating committee appeared: all question of nationalizing the banks was definitely excluded. The *Deutsche Bank*, which as early as 1933 had got back nearly twenty million marks of its stock from the Reich (in return for giving the state a big building), could announce in March, 1937, that it had completed the repurchase of its stock from the Reich and had once more become a wholly private institution.[10] In August, 1937, announcement was made that the *Commerz und Privatbank* had bought the greater part of its stock back from the state,[11] and shortly afterwards a meeting of the directors of the *Dresdner Bank* let it be known that their bank too had finally become private again.[12]

In addition, the Reich had put a number of steamship companies and naval shipyards on a sound footing. In March, 1936, it returned the majority of the stock of the *Deutscher Schiff und Maschinenbau* to a group of Bremen merchants, and in September it ceded eight million marks of stock (out of a total capitalization of ten million) in the *Hamburg Sud-Amerika* to a Hamburg consortium,[13] etc., etc.

Likewise, National Socialism fought municipally owned enterprises. These were prosperous; even during the depression year 1932–1933 they had made profits amounting to 650 million marks. Therefore private industry coveted them. The very day that Dr. Schacht was appointed to the Ministry of Economy, July 30, 1934, he gave instructions to hasten the liquidation of municipal enterprises. As a first step, they were burdened after January 1, 1935, with a 20 percent tax on their profits.[14] Legislation on December 13, 1935, repealed the law of 1919 permitting "socialization" of power production. "Such an organization of the distribution of electric power is contrary to the basic idea of the National Socialist concept . . . " explained the preamble of the new statute, the avowed purpose of which was to put an end to the *disorder* brought into the development of electrical distribution by "municipal socialism." Henceforth *private* plants for the production and distribution of electric power were to be freed of all "unnecessary impediments," encouraged and favored in every way.[15]

2

The fascist state helps the industrialists to "make a profit" by granting them all sorts of tax exemptions.

In Italy

The Minister of Finance, de Stefani, stated: "We have broken with the practice of persecuting capital. A financial system based on the persecution of capital is a system tainted with insanity."[16] The new government on November 10, 1922, abolished the obligation to register securities—an obligation which to some extent prevented capitalists from evading the income tax—dissolved the committee to investigate "war profits" by a decree of November 19, and by legislation on August 20, 1923, abolished the inheritance tax on legacies remaining within a family.

The capital tax, instituted in 1920 and payable in annual installments, was called *stupidissimo* by Minister de Stefani. Through partial rebates and friendly arrangements with the Treasury, it was liquidated in a manner highly advantageous to those concerned.[17] In February, 1925, the supplementary tax on negotiable securities was abolished by law. A decree-law of June 23, 1927, established important tax exemptions with the purpose of facilitating the merger of corporations. Other instances of goodwill were the abolition of the 10 percent tax on capital invested in banking and industry, the cutting in half of the tax on managers and directors of corporations, the exemption of foreign capital from all taxation, and the abolition of the tax on luxury articles. As the Catholic don Sturzo wrote: "Fascist finance favors capitalist wealth."[18]

In Germany

Immediately on coming to power, the National Socialist Treasury Department directed its efforts toward a single goal: the assistance of capital. A law of June 1, 1933, supplemented by that of October 16, 1934, authorized industrialists to deduct from their taxable income all sums used to purchase new equipment. In addition, the state reimbursed owners for part of their expense in repairing houses, factories, or stores. Tax delinquents had the amount of their unpaid taxes reduced by half if they invested in the "fight against unemployment" loans. Families employing a maid could count her as a "minor child" and benefit by the corresponding tax reduction. Legislation on July 15, 1933, provided for tax exemptions on new business firms, on those using new processes or manufacturing new products, and on newly built dwelling houses.[19]

In April, 1934, the government granted huge tax reductions (about 500 million marks) "to facilitate the resumption of business."[20] The income tax for the fiscal year 1934–1935 was reduced to half of that for the fiscal year 1931–1932.[21] The fiscal legislation which came into effect on January 1, 1935, not only confirmed these reductions but also reduced inheritance taxes.

3

The fascist state helps the industrialists to raise their sales prices artificially by forbidding, through legislation, the establishment of new industries—that is to say, by relieving them of all new competition. The consumer pays.

In Italy

The decree of March 11, 1926, authorized the Minister of Finance to prevent the courts from registering charters of new companies with a capital exceeding five million lire, or permitting an increase in capital which would bring it to more than five million. By a decree-law of November 3, 1927, the opening of large industrial establishments in cities was made subject to previous authorization by the government, and a decree-law of November 18, 1929, extended this mandatory authorization to establishments working for national defense. A decree-law of July 18, 1930, provided that authorization must also be obtained for new shipyards, transportation companies, etc. The decree-law of June 12, 1932, on compulsory consortiums provided: "When the needs of certain branches of industry require it, the installation of new factories or the expansion of existing factories belonging to the consortium shall be subject to government authorization." Finally, the law of January 12, 1933, confirmed and generalized these various obligations.

In Germany

By the law of July 15, 1933, the Minister of Economy was given power to order, if necessary, within the framework of a given branch of economy, that "the creation of new enterprises, as well as any increased use of the productive capacity of existing enterprises, be suspended for a fixed period or subject to his authorization." But the law went still further than the Italian legislation: the Minister could even fix the degree to which the *present* productive capacity of existing enterprises might be employed.

The government has made great use of this law. In 1933 five decrees, and in 1934 seventeen, were promulgated extending to various industries the prohibition against founding new enterprises or increasing the productive capacity of old ones.

4

The fascist state also helps industrialists to raise their sales prices artificially—on the backs of the consumers—by legislation forcing "nonconforming" manufacturers to enter "compulsory agreements." It is well known that a trade agreement, no matter how many participate, almost never succeeds in including all the members of the industry. But, to have a decisive effect on sales prices, at least 90 percent of the total productive capacity of an industry must be included.[22] If the nonconformists cannot be conquered, state coercion is necessary.

In Italy

In the iron and steel industry a voluntary agreement had existed since 1928–1929. But the industrialists had not been able to establish an all-inclusive trade association through their own efforts and to get the better of the nonconformists. Therefore the state hastened to intervene. By a decree-law of December 31, 1931, it reserved the right to regulate the "means of forming compulsory associations for the various branches of the iron industry, in order to control the manufacture and sale of products."[23] The compulsory associations were formed at once.

Soon the measure was extended to all branches of industry. A decree-law of June 16, 1932, provided for "the formation of compulsory associations of industrialists exploiting the same field of economic activity, with a view to regulating production and competition." These compulsory consortiums were formed whenever requested "by a number representing 70 percent of the enterprises interested and 70 percent of the average production for the last three years."

In Germany

Through a law of July 15, 1933, power was conferred on the Reich Minister of Economy "to unite enterprises into associations, cartels, pacts, or similar agreements, or to join them to consortiums already existing, with a view to regulating the market, when this union or fusion seems necessary in the interest of the enterprises, of production as a whole, and of the community."

The German legislation immediately had its effect. In the highly centralized industries, thirty existing cartels were reorganized between July and November, 1933, the nonconformists were regimented, and production quotas imposed on each member. As for the less centralized industries (manufactured products), where cartellization was more difficult, twenty-eight new cartels were formed, including textiles, paper, food products, etc.

It would be a mistake to interpret this state intervention as "socialist" in character. It is brought about not in the interest of the community but *in the exclusive interest of the capitalists.* Furthermore the state is careful to apologize for meddling with things that are not its concern; it only *temporarily* departs from its traditional attitude of "nonintervention." The Italian Minister Bottai stated specifically in one of his speeches that the compulsory consortiums "must be considered as a *wholly exceptional* form of producers' associations."[24] The Reich Minister of Economy, Schmitt, also asserted: "In principle, I consider cartels and mandatory prices undesirable. If, in spite of everything, in difficult times, we have permitted and even forced the formation of a number of cartels—alas, a considerable number—it was in order to avoid serious economic disturbances."[25]

But how discreet this intervention! It is true that in both Italy and Germany the law provides for a certain amount of state "control." The Italian decree-law of June 16, 1932, gives the minister the right to require from the enterprises making up an association all records and documents he considers necessary for his information, and the administration can delegate a functionary to be present at the deliberations of the association. The German law of July 15, 1933, gives the minister vague "rights of supervision and intervention." But these attempts at control, timid as they are, have remained inoperative. "The Italian industrialists have always had a phobia of compulsory associations," writes Rosenstock-Franck. As a matter of fact, the law merely arms them with a means of pressure to force the nonconformists to yield peacefully to their demands without the state actually having to intervene. In Germany, also, the Minister of Economy has rarely had to use the power conferred on him by the law of July 15, 1933. Most of the new cartels were formed *voluntarily,* the law serving only as a means of pressure to force the consent of the nonconformists.[26]

5

The fascist state renders big business another service by generously refloating sinking enterprises. It takes over a block of the stock, but instead of using the opportunity to nationalize these enterprises, it preserves their character as private corporations and leaves the industrialists at their head. Its intervention is only *temporary,* and it hopes to be able—after it has made the companies solvent by standing all the expense and assuming all the risks—to restore to the private owners the stock it has taken over.

Similarly, when the state believes it necessary (for the needs of "national defense") to expand industries, or to open new ones which offer a commercial risk that private industry refuses to assume, it does not take advantage of the opportunity to create state enterprises. Instead, it creates *mixed* enterprises, in collaboration with private industry. The state furnishes its share of the capital, guarantees a return on the private investment, and alone stands all the risks in the hope that someday, when a profitable return from these enterprises is assured, it can hand them back to private initiative.

In Italy

Mussolini's first move when he took power was to put the powerful metal trust, *Ansaldo*, on a sound footing; he made it a gift of a 400 million lire subsidy. In 1924 a special body was appointed to liquidate, at state expense, banks and industries that had failed. One after the other, victims of the deflation crisis which began in 1926— the *Banco di Roma*, the *Banco di Napoli*, the *Banco di Sicilia*, and many other smaller establishments—were refloated and made solvent.

But it was chiefly after 1931, when the world depression spread to Italy, that the state was called on to contribute. The portfolios of the big commercial banks were full of depreciated industrial securities. One after another, the *Banco di Milano*, the *Credito Italiano*, and even the powerful *Banca Commerciale* went under, and the state flew to their assistance. One after another, three "autonomous" institutions were created but subsidized in reality by the Treasury. They were, to use Mussolini's expression, "convalescent homes" in which the state "pays the board bills."[27] The first of these, the *Society to Finance Italian Industry* (Sofindit), was founded in October, 1931, with a capital of 500 million lire, the greater part of which was supplied by the state. This institution, through the issue of public bonds guaranteed by the state, obtained 4 billion lire, which it used to purchase all the industrial securities held by the *Banco Commerciale* and other bankrupt establishments. A month later, in November, the *Italian Investment Institution* (Imi) was created, with a capital of 500 million lire also furnished by the state. The Imi issued bonds for 5.5 billion lire, guaranteed by the state, and maturing in ten years. This capital was loaned to private industry for long terms (a maximum of ten years), and each company put up a part of its stock as security. Finally, in January, 1933, the *Institute for Industrial Reconstruction* (Iri) was formed and issued bonds for a billion lire, maturing in from fifteen to twenty years and guaranteed by the state. Through its intervention, the state put back on their feet the biggest trusts in the country. For instance, at the end of 1933, the great *Piedmont Hydroelectric Company,* with liabilities of more than 600 million lire and stock depreciated from 250 to 20 lire, was saved after having been made solvent again.[28] In September, 1934, the metal trust *Ansaldo* was again reorganized with a capital of 175 million and authorized to issue bonds to the amount of 100 million guaranteed by the state.[29]

Fascism did not take advantage of the opportunity to nationalize these enterprises, the majority of whose stock it had acquired. "The state has three-quarters of the Italian economy on its hands," Mussolini exclaimed. "If I wished to inaugurate state socialism or state capitalism in Italy *(which is not the case),* I would have today the necessary and sufficient objective conditions for doing so . . ."[30] Bottai agreed that in Italy they did not want—*quite the contrary*— "to speed up the movement of expropriation begun by the depression."[31]

However, when the masses are discontented, it is necessary to throw a little dust in their eyes. In March, 1936, fascism announced the "nationalization" of Italian banks. Mere bluff! Although it held, as we have seen, an important percentage of the stock of the big credit establishments, such as the *Banca Commerciale,* the Bank of Rome, and *Credito Italiano,* the fascist state was careful not to nationalize the big banks. It was satisfied to call them "public banks," by virtue of which their stock had to be registered and owned exclusively by Italian citizens. Nor was the Bank of Italy nationalized; it was merely proclaimed a "public institution," which meant that its stock had to be registered and owned solely by semi-state institutions or *"public" banks*. But these latter, as we have just seen, remained *private* institutions. Twelve out of fifteen directors of the Bank of Italy had to be elected at a general stockholders' meeting, and this permitted the capitalists who directed the "public banks" to remain masters of the bank of issue.[32]

Fascism also made a great stir about "nationalizing big industry." What was involved? Mussolini announced in a speech in March, 1936, that "big industry working directly or indirectly for national defense, and also that which has developed to the point of becoming capitalist or supercapitalist, will be organized into large units . . . assuming a special character within the orbit of the state." He had in view, particularly, a formula for "a mixed enterprise, for which the state and private individuals will together furnish the capital and organize the management in common."[33]

Strange "nationalization"! The capitalists go out the door and come back in through the window. Even if the state holds 51 percent of the stock, and the capitalists hold or control only 49 percent, the latter remain masters of the enterprise for all practical purposes. What, in fact, is this state whose delegates now sit on the boards of directors beside the capitalists? It is the fascist state, the accomplice of big business. There is no indiscreet meddling to be feared from it. The state is present merely to furnish capital and orders, guarantee profits, and assume all the risks.

Here are a few examples. In 1936 the state and the big *Montecatini* trust underwrote jointly the capital for the *Azienda Nazionale Idrogenazione Combustibili,* a company to produce synthetic gasoline. In April, 1937, the *Institute for Industrial Recovery*—that is to say, the state—acquired stock amounting to more than 50 percent of the capital in the *Ansaldo, Odero-Terni-Orlando, United Shipyards of the Adriatic.*[34] In June there was formed, under the auspices of the *Institute for Industrial Recovery,* a *Finance Company for the*

Iron Industry, with a capital of 900 million lire, in which the trusts, *Ilva, Terni, Dalmine,* etc., participated with the state.[35]

In Germany

The Nazi state did not need to refloat sinking industrial enterprises and banks; the preceding governments had looked after that. But it took no advantage of the opportunity to nationalize those companies of which it held the majority of the stock. Quite the contrary; as we have seen, it returned this stock to private capitalism as soon as it could. The Reich substituted itself for private initiative only when it could not do otherwise—for instance, when it was a question of creating unprofitable enterprises, in which private capital would not invest. These enterprises were given, as in Italy, a *mixed* character: the state guaranteed a certain return on the capital invested—that is, it alone assumed all the risks. It was in this way that they set up the *Hermann Goering Reichswerke fuer Erzbergbau und Eisenhuetten* (Reich Mining and Iron Works), a stock company with the purpose of exploiting low grade iron ore: the stock was underwritten by both the Reich and big industry. The *Temps* correspondent pointed out that "the legal form of the stock company *safeguards the rights of private property.*"[36] The *Bergwerkszeitung,* the organ of heavy industry, *was surprised that the creation of the company was considered abroad a measure for nationalization.* "The state," it said, "spares private industry the risk of investing new capital and leaves it the responsibility of sharing voluntarily in the execution of great new projects."[37] Furthermore, General Hanneken, a department head in the Ministry of Economy, told the "occupational group" for the iron industry that "as soon as possible the *Goering-Werke* will be returned to private ownership."[38]

While awaiting the happy day of "reprivatization," the National Socialist state and the great capitalists conspire like pickpockets in managing the joint state-private enterprises. An idea of the close interpenetration of the state and private industry achieved in the "mixed" enterprises can be obtained from the supervisory board of the big *Rheinmetall-Boersig* (a subsidiary of the *Goering-Werke*), composed of the following: four representatives of big capital (Boersig, Karl Bosch of the *I.G. Farben,* a representative of the *Deutsche Bank,* and one from the *Dresdener Bank*); a representative of the old aristocracy converted to National Socialism (the Duke of Saxony-Coburg-Gotha); two state representatives (the State Secretary Trendelenberg and a representative of the Ministry of Finance); a representative of the Army (General Thomas, of the Department of War Economy in the Ministry of War); and finally, two representatives of the *Goering-Werke* and one from the *Reichskreditgesellschaft,* a semi-state credit establishment.[39]

6

Of all the expedients employed by the fascist state to restore capitalist profits, those we are now going to examine are by far the most important—not only because they have a decisive effect on increasing capitalist profits, but also, and primarily, *because they involve fascism in a fatal course which leads it gradually to autarky and "war economy."*

In Italy as in Germany, the industrialists are faced with a two-fold want as a result of the depression. On the one hand, private customers are lacking because of the reduced purchasing power of the masses; on the other hand investors, having had their fingers cruelly burnt, withhold their savings from industrial investments. So the fascist state hastens to intervene, replacing both the missing customers and the missing investments. In Italy, in 1932, 90 percent of the new stock and bond issues came from semi-state financial institutions, and only 10 percent from private companies.[40] In Germany in 1934, 70 percent of the new securities issues came from the state, and only 30 percent from the private sector. In 1935, "capital formation for the needs of the private sector falls far short of these needs."[41] In certain cases, National Socialism encourages companies particularly favored by state orders to practice self-financing. Thus the profits of the Krupp works, for example, which rose in 1935 to ten million marks, were entirely reinvested in the economy.[42]

There is nothing specifically *fascist* about this expedient. In all

252 FASCISM AND BIG BUSINESS

industrial countries today heavy industry, having become parasitic, survives only thanks to state orders. If there is a difference, it is to be found in the disproportion, much more striking in Italy and Germany than elsewhere, between the national income and the huge expenditures undertaken.

State orders are of two sorts: *great public works for the sake of prestige,* generally yielding no return, and *orders and works for "national defense."* It is rather difficult to draw a strict line of demarcation between the two sorts of outlay; but as the second is intensified, the first tends to go into the background. Part of the outlay for public works, it is also true, arises out of "national defense," particularly highway and railroad projects.

GREAT PUBLIC WORKS

Between October, 1922, and June, 1934, Italian fascism expended 43 billion on public works, not including works connected with the railways, of which more than 28 billion were actually paid out.[43] Most of this expenditure was unproductive, and the state was sinking its billions without a return. The railway deficit was chronic (900 million lire in April, 1935), but new lines were constantly built. Foreign trade was falling off, but enormous sums were spent for improving such ports as Genoa, Trieste and Venice and for building big luxury liners. Motor traffic was very light (one-fifth that of France), but millions were swallowed up in building magnificent motor highways. By June, 1934, there were 544 kilometers of these new highways, though the high tolls on them kept away many who might use them. Mussolini himself confessed that the motor highways were only a "glorious anticipation."[44] Finally, the fascist state sank millions in city improvements, such as the "embellishments of the Eternal City" (costing a half-billion lire), the Ministry of Air building, etc. A fascist has admitted in a propaganda pamphlet that the economic return from the great sums expended "will be appreciable only in the distant future."[45] But *in the meantime,* these great works have permitted a few industrialists, a few cement and iron merchants, to build fortunes.

In the end, expenditures for armaments took precedence over outlays for public works. In February, 1936, the head of the fascist federation of industrial workers, Tullio Cianetti, told the *Matin:* "For reasons of economy, the government has stopped most of the big works."[46]

In Germany

Immediately after taking power the Nazis launched a vast program of public works which, according to their own paper, the *Voelkischer Beobachter,* were "non-profit making." On May 1, 1933, Hitler inaugurated the first "work battle." On June 1 the legislation for "making work" was promulgated. The Reich granted the "states," municipalities, and other public institutions credits without interest charges—in many cases granted outright—for great "auxiliary" public works. A billion marks were appropriated for this purpose, spread over five budgetary years.

On March 21, 1934, Hitler, inaugurating the second "work battle," announced that another billion marks were to be swallowed up in the bottomless pit of public works. In the same period, the Reich undertook to build a 7,000 kilometer network of motor highways at the astronomic cost of a half-million marks a kilometer. By December, 1937, 2,000 kilometers had been completed, and Hitler announced, "Every year we will complete another thousand kilometers."[47] In spite of the deficit of the German railways (a half-billion marks in 1935), new lines were undertaken at the cost of a billion marks.[48] The depression paralyzed river shipping, but twenty-eight million marks were devoted to building locks in the canal connecting the Elbe and the Oder.[49] Finally, the National Socialist state sank millions in city improvements such as the new party buildings in Munich, the railway station for "party congresses" in Nuremberg, the gigantic Air Ministry in Berlin with 2,500 rooms, etc. The state has gone in debt, but a few cement and iron merchants have amassed enormous sums.

Gradually the speeding-up of rearmament has reduced the importance of public works. As early as June 13, 1934, the Minister of

Finance told the Leipzig *Herrenklub:* "In the future, we shall not undertake any more . . . 'auxiliary' works to combat unemployment." Dr. Schacht, when he became economic dictator, strenuously opposed continuing these subsidies that offered no return. In spite of the strong resistance of the Nazi plebeians, particularly Dr. Ley, he prevented a third "work battle" being opened in the spring of 1935.[50]

ORDERS AND WORKS FOR "NATIONAL DEFENSE"

In Italy

Ever since it came into power, Italian fascism has supported heavy industry with its "national defense" orders. For seven or eight years it spent the "trifle of five or six billion lire a year to give the country an army, navy and air force that had no relation to the needs of national defense."[51] But it was chiefly after 1934 that the armament program was speeded up. The index of industrial production, which was 75 for the year 1934 (as against 100 in 1928), suddenly rose to 105 in April, 1935—an increase manifested almost exclusively in heavy industry. "The industries in a position to work for the army are the ones that show the greatest development."[52] The cost of the Ethiopian war, according to the most conservative figures—for instance, those of the fascist Professor Arias[53]—has been estimated at thirty billion lire for the fiscal years 1934–1935, 1935–1936, 1936–1937. The Minister of Finance, Thaon di Revel, admitted in a speech to the Chamber[54] that between July 1, 1934, and March 31, 1938, the government had laid out thirty-six billion lire for "extraordinary expenses," and he anticipated that another twelve billion would be needed for the fiscal year 1938–1939. The greater part of these sums obviously went for war orders, and into the strong boxes of heavy industry.

In Germany

National Socialism, as soon as it got into power, threw billions into rearmament. While the slump in industries producing consumers' goods continued, heavy industry worked at full capacity. For example, on May 1, 1935, Herr Krupp von Bohlen told his employees that his blast furnaces, steel mills, rolling mills and machine shops were working *to the limit of their capacity*.[55] An English publication, *The Banker*,[56] estimated the expenditure for armaments from the fiscal year 1933–1934 to that of 1936–1937 to be more than thirty billion marks. The State Secretary of Finance, Reinhardt, stated publicly that the "economic recovery of Germany" had put her *more than forty billion marks in debt*.[57]

The barons of heavy industry took in fabulous profits. "New fortunes are being built . . . the mark is circulating; luxury is again appearing. . . ."[58] "Rearmament has placed a *gigantic proportion* of the economy in the service of state needs," declared the *Voelkischer Beobachter*. "Supplying the army *is a blessing for the economy*. . . ."[59]

7

Very naturally the question arises: Where does the fascist state find the resources that permit it to become the principal customer of heavy industry, to finance big public works for prestige, and especially to pay for munitions orders? Where does it get the money to put into the pockets of the big capitalists?

Fascism uses old "tricks." Its procedure is no different than that of the governments of the belligerent countries between 1914 and 1918: it issues paper and ruins the national currency at the expense of all the people who live on fixed incomes from investments, savings, pensions, government salaries, etc.,—and also the working class, whose wages remain stable or lag far behind the rise in the cost of living.

But this inflation is camouflaged. After the First World War financial techniques were polished; fascism did not forget the grave social consequences of the open inflation which, in Germany in 1923, nearly propelled the desperate middle classes towards the proletariat. It would be too dangerous to just run the printing presses openly, for all to see. Mussolini proclaimed himself "deflationist" as the state's indebtedness mounted. The leaders of the Third Reich rejected inflation with horror. Thus Dr. Dreyse, Vice President of the *Reichsbank*, explained: "National Socialism cannot repeat the deception of scarcely a decade ago—inflation—a deception whose victim was precisely the mass of government officials, workers, employees, small rentiers, etc. It would run the risk of thereby preparing the way for communism."[60] In April, 1933, Dr. Schacht declared: "The policies of the *Reichsbank* have but one aim: maintaining the stability of the mark."

The enormous expenses of the fascist state do not appear in the official budget. The Italian budget may seem to be balanced or even to show a surplus; but the real deficit, according to the calculations of the fascist Professor Arias,[61] reached more than twelve billion for 1935–1936, and more than sixteen billion for 1936–1937. In Germany, the billions for rearmament cannot appear in the budget for the very good reason that no budget has been published since that for the fiscal year 1934–1935.

Nor do fascism's expenditures appear in the circulation of paper money. This has indeed increased, but in infinitely smaller proportions than the expenditures. In Italy it rose from thirteen billion lire on December 31, 1934, to fifteen-and-a-half billion on April 30, 1937. In Germany it rose from five-and-a-half billion marks in June, 1933, to eight billion at the end of September, 1938.

An abundance of paper is issued. But it is not banknotes, but rather commercial paper and short-term bonds.

In Italy

The fascist state issues Treasury bonds generally maturing in a year. These amounted to 10.5 billion lire in 1934. In addition it pays for its orders with "promissory notes," due at a more or less near date, which its creditors discount at the banks. The report of the budget commission for the year 1933 admitted that "balancing the budget is delayed by the undertaking of heavy expenditures for which payment is deferred. The state is buying on the instalment plan, using one of the worst inventions of the American inflationary spirit."

In Germany

German rearmament is financed chiefly by so-called "make work" drafts, issued for a period of six months, but renewable at maturity.

The state gives these drafts to the industrialists, who get them discounted at the banks. Their total sum is difficult to estimate, but it must amount to around *twenty or thirty billion marks.* The system is convenient because it is accompanied by a minimum of publicity, but it offers grave dangers. When the time comes that the banks, overloaded with this paper, can no longer meet their obligations to their depositors, they will be obliged to have the paper rediscounted at the *Reichsbank,* and the paper in circulation will be suddenly doubled or trebled. This hypothesis is by no means groundless. Indeed, we find it in a memorandum transmitted to Hitler by the Ruhr industrialists in June, 1937.[62]

The danger in fact is so real that the Reich government, after April 1, 1938, gave up the system of "make work" drafts, issuing in their stead the Treasury's new "delivery bills." The bills would only be issued for a period of six months and would not be eligible for rediscount with the *Reichsbank*; their issue would be strictly limited to an amount which can be repaid at maturity from "normal" budgetary sources; and the amount of bills issued would be made public. In August, 1938, these bills reached a total of 3 billion marks.[63]

But every time this short-term paper matures, the fascist state is forced to honor its signature. The more drafts and Treasury bonds it puts into circulation, the more perilous become the dates of maturity, the greater grows the risk that it will be driven simply to print paper money, and the greater the danger of the credit inflation—the camouflaged inflation—becoming just plain inflation. Therefore the fascist state tries to "fund" its floating debt—that is to say, convert it into a long-term debt and place the burden on the future. And it succeeds in this only through coercion, by a forced loan.

To force private individuals to buy its long-term paper, it is compelled to exercise especially severe control over all financial establishments that handle savings—savings banks, and various semi-state institutions and banks. In both Italy and Germany this control has the alleged object of "protecting savings"; the state pretends to see to it that the financial institutions maintain sufficient liquid assets to meet their obligations. But its real concern is quite different. Its right to supervise their management makes it possible to discover whether all the available funds of the depositors have been placed at the disposition of the state; in short, the fascist state forces those with small or moderate savings to convert their savings—their available funds—into state paper, the income of which is every day losing more of its purchasing power, and the principal may vanish into thin air in case of government bankruptcy or a monetary crisis.

This obligation is all the more painful and unjust because big capital alone, as if by accident, escapes it. As a matter of fact, the magnates of heavy industry conceal in their balance sheets the enormous profits they make from the state's war orders; they hasten to convert them into "real values" by reinvesting them in their own businesses and using them to set up new productive machinery. Thus they evade the strong arm of the state.

In Italy

By legislation of February 10, 1927, the savings banks, which handle considerable money (about thirty-four billion lire in 1934), were reorganized, unified, grouped into provincial and regional federations, and placed under the tutelage of the state. In similar fashion, the state intervened as the final authority in the management of so-called independent institutions such as the National Insurance Institute, the Institute for Workmen's Accident Compensation, etc. Decree-laws of September 7 and November 6, 1926, forced banks not merely to submit monthly and annual balance sheets to the Bank of Italy but subjected them to inspections by the latter. The Minister of Finance could take away the licenses of establishments evading this control.

At the end of 1935, withdrawals of funds from savings and commercial banks were severely restricted. In March, 1936, the need of procuring "new capital" at any cost for the Ethiopian war led to a reinforcement of the control over credit establishments, and an "inspection service to protect savings and credit extensions" was created. All establishments handling savings and credit were put under the control of this inspection service and had to show their balance sheets and undergo periodic inspections.[64]

This system made it possible to absorb all savings accounts in the forced loan. The forced loans badly hurt the possessors of small and moderate savings and real estate owners, but heavy industry escaped them. To be sure, a decree of August, 1935, ordered companies to invest all profits in excess of 6 percent of their capitalization in state securities (a latter decree, on October 20, 1937, raised the limit from 6 to 8 percent). But the big companies take care not to distribute their enormous armament profits; they conceal them in the books and thus evade the obligation of converting a part of them into state paper.

In Germany

"All the savings of the German people should be put in the service of rearmament," the Minister of Finance, Schwerin von Krosigk, declared.[65] The savings banks, which administered enormous sums (about thirteen billion marks), were placed under strict state control by a law of December 5, 1934. They were subject to the supervision of a "control office for credit institutions," with its headquarters in the *Reichsbank*, which could demand all sorts of information. The "control office" gave instructions for investing the funds under its administration.[66] Measures were also taken to prevent savings depositors from drawing out too large sums.

The state likewise intervened in the management of allegedly independent establishments such as national institutions for health insurance, unemployment insurance, workmen's compensation, etc.

As for the banks, whose deposits amounted to about two billion marks, they were also subjected, by the law of December 5, 1934, to strict control by the state. They had not only to transmit their balance sheets regularly to the "control office" but to undergo all sorts of inspections and check-ups. The state closely supervised all individual bank accounts, prevented withdrawals by force if need be, and made certain that all available funds in the banks were converted into state paper.[67] The Reich banking commissioner could forbid any financial institution failing to observe the fixed regulations to continue its activity.

It should be noted in passing that these measures profoundly altered the character of the German banks: "Instead of playing, as formerly, a prominent role in the distribution of credit to private economy, they have become veritable holding companies for state securities and bodies destined chiefly to facilitate the work of the public Treasury."[68]

The system made it possible to levy tribute on German savings. Whenever the Reich needed to borrow in order to amortize its short-term debt, it dug into the resources of the savings banks, semi-governmental institutions, and great commercial banks. Thus the Reich heavily mortgaged the future. It has been estimated that the annual servicing of these loans (interest and amortization), which in 1936 represented 158 million marks, will amount to 1,220 million in 1944, and even more in the years to come.[69]

Thus small and moderate sized savings accounts were mobilized into the service of the Third Reich and forced to swallow up state paper with a nominal value, while big industry transformed its enormous profits into "real values." To be sure, the law of December 4, 1934—extended for three years in December, 1937—forced companies to place their profits in excess of 6 or 8 percent of the paid-in capital in a special account in the *Golddiskontbank,* to be invested in state securities. But the magnates of heavy industry had no trouble concealing their profits in their accounts and evading the law. As a matter of fact they carried on tremendous "amortization" operations. Equipment which normally should be amortized in ten or fifteen years was written off in two or three. In four years the Rhenish-Westphalian mining industry thus succeeded in "amortizing" more than half the value of its declared capital. In the single year of 1937, the amortization of machinery of the *I.G. Farben* amounted to 28 percent of the total value of the machinery, and that of the *Rheinmetall-Boersig* trust to 27 percent of the total value of its declared assets, etc. Heavy industry is not naive enough to invest its profits in state paper that overnight might lose all value; it prefers to devote its profits to acquiring new manufacturing equipment. This, too, no doubt, might some day depreciate, but iron is always iron and worth more than paper.[70] Hence it is not surprising that the law of December 4, 1934, brought into the special account in the *Golddiskontbank* in 1935 and 1936 only thirty million marks, twelve million of which was paid in by the *Reichsbank*.[71]

But the floating of long-term loans has definite limits; the savings available annually are not inexhaustible. To pay off its short-term debt when due, the fascist state, in addition to forcing loans, is compelled to give the tax payer another turn of the screw. The mass of the people, in both Italy and Germany, are already crushed by taxes, and as far as they are concerned the fiscal sponge cannot be given another squeeze without danger. Therefore the fascist state, whose sole concern up to the present has been to grant tax exemptions to the possessing classes, is forced, despite itself, to send the tax collector after them. Yet the least discriminated against are still the magnates of heavy industry, whose profits and surpluses are cleverly hidden. So the fascist state finds itself tangled in a dilemma: on the one hand, the needs of rearmament and autarky require extensive amortizations by the big manufacturers and reinvestment of their profits in their own plants in order to expand production; on the other hand, the state's need of procuring fiscal revenue immediately and at any cost in order to fill up the worst holes in the Treasury requires that the companies should not evade the tax. Caught between these conflicting requirements, the fascist state refrains from exercising the draconian control over big industry which alone could provide a full yield from the tax on the companies.[72]

In Italy

A decree-law of October 19, 1937, levied on the declared capital and surpluses of commercial companies an exceptional tax of 10 percent. (This rate was reduced by three-quarters for companies shown to have a deficit for the last three fiscal years, and by half for those whose last balance sheet showed a deficit.) The tax is payable in fifteen instalments between March 10, 1938, and June 10, 1940, but all sorts of exemptions and compensations were provided. A half of the tax could be paid by turning over to the state a sufficient amount of the company's stock, and the companies were authorized to revise their balance sheets (taking into account the devaluation of the lire) and under certain conditions to distribute their surpluses. This tax might have brought in three to six billion lire.

In Germany

In September, 1936, the income tax on companies with an income of more than 100,000 marks, which formerly paid 20 percent on their income, was raised to 30 percent. On July 30, 1938, it was increased to 35 percent for 1938, and to 40 percent for 1939 and 1940. This tax yielded 1,553 million marks in 1937.

In August, 1938, there was talk of instituting a new tax called the "*Wehr Steuer*" (National Defense Tax), which would raise the rate on private incomes to 30 percent.[73]

Almost all the annual reports of the big companies at the beginning of 1938 complained of the increased taxes.[74] As a matter of fact, the tax burden, which in 1928–29 was 18.5 percent of the German national income, in 1937 reached 28.6 percent. With fourteen billion marks, the tax revenue for 1937–38 was already more than double the respective figure for 1933–34. But big capital has up to the present borne only a small share, in proportion to its enormous profits, of this greatly increased tax burden.

8

All these expedients, no matter how varied, ingenious, or even daring they may be, do not prevent the old laws of political economy from taking their revenge. Gradually the hidden inflation produces the same effects as open inflation: *the purchasing power of money is lessened.* But fascism wants to conceal this depreciation—or at least put off as long as possible the moment of its open appearance—and it wants to preserve as long as possible the artificial value of the currency. It succeeds to a large extent by police terror and by secrecy. But these extraordinary measures are effective only within the national boundaries; they have no effect abroad. Fascism is thus driven to a new expedient: that of placing a wall around the national currency.

In Italy

After 1934, the real depreciation of the currency was manifested in the flight of capital abroad and a consequent withdrawal of gold that was constantly reducing the metal reserves of the Bank of Italy. The reserve of 7,105 million lire at the end of February, 1934 (compared with 12,106 million lire on January 1, 1928), fell to 3,394 million on December 31, 1935.

In order to preserve the fictitious value of the currency, fascism was forced to build a wall around it. By radical measures, it prohibited the flight of capital. Two decree-laws of May 27, 1934, set up a rigorous control over foreign securities held by Italians, prohibited all transactions in foreign stocks and exchange except those necessary for commercial requirements, and forbade the exportation of Italian bank notes and checks. These measures were reinforced by the decree of December 8, which made the export of merchandise dependent on delivery to the state of all foreign exchange received in payment; all banks, companies, businesses, and private individuals had to declare and put at the disposal of a "National Exchange Institute"—that is to say, the Treasury—all their foreign credits. Every Italian subject had to declare before December 31, his holdings in banks or companies having their home offices outside Italy. In May, 1935, every Italian owner of foreign securities or Italian securities issued abroad had to deposit them in the Bank of Italy. On August 28, it was decided that all foreign securities possessed by Italians were to be acquired by the National Exchange Institute in return for 5 percent Treasury bonds maturing in nine years. A decree of October 8 forbade anybody on leaving Italy to take out more than 2,000 lire.

These severe measures, however, did not prevent the decrease in buying power of the currency inside the country. On October 5, 1936, Mussolini, who at the time of the 1927 stabilization had sworn to defend the lira "with the last drop of his blood," decided to devalue it at 41 percent of its 1927 rate. But this surgical operation likewise failed to save Italian currency. Its real depreciation continued.

In Germany

After 1934, the real depreciation of the German currency was likewise apparent in the flight of capital abroad and the resulting gold withdrawals, which had reduced the ratio of gold to banknotes from 20 percent at the end of 1932 to 1.5 percent on December 31, 1934.

To halt the outflow of gold, the National Socialist government had to prevent the exodus of capital by radical measures. It began by suspending partially, then totally, interest payments on the foreign commercial debt. After July 1, 1934, a total moratorium was declared on all transfers relating to the commercial debts, including those reverting to the Dawes and Young loans,* and on July 1, 1935, this moratorium was extended. A decree of October 2, 1934, prohibited any German traveler on going abroad from taking more than ten marks. And finally, came the famous decree of December 1, 1936: *"Anyone under German jurisdiction who knowingly and out of vile interest or any other base motive sends his fortune abroad, or leaves it there contrary to the legal provisions, thus causing grave injury to German economy, is subject to the death penalty. His fortune is to be confiscated."* This decree was followed by another on December 15 giving the guilty a period of grace expiring January 31, 1937, for the repatriation of their exported capital.

---

* By these loans, Germany's conquerors converted the "reparations" into commercial debt, thus charging Germany for payment of interest to bond-holders and for amortization of the principal.

But these extraordinary measures obviously could not prevent the buying power of the mark from shrinking inside the wall. In June, 1937, in their memorandum addressed to Hitler,[75] the Ruhr industrialists estimated that depreciation at 40 percent. It must be at least 50 percent. However, in Germany, the national leaders did not dare to resort, as they had in Italy, to a devaluation. They feared the psychological effects—because of the terrible memories of the past. In 1937 Dr. Schacht proudly presented the mark as "the only currency of a great country which has not been devalued."[76] Furthermore, a devaluation of the mark under present conditions not only would do serious psychological harm but would be incapable of checking the continuous drop in the buying power of German money. As long as the Reich devotes colossal sums to rearmament, it would be vain to hope to maintain a stable real value for the mark even after devaluation. In its hermetically sealed glass cage, the mark continues to lead a purely artificial existence.

9

One expedient leads to another. Fascism is now forced to place a wall around not only the currency but the whole national economy. To forbid the flight of capital is not enough. It is necessary to prohibit all withdrawals of gold not justified by an urgent need for importations. Only the import of materials needed in the manufacture of armaments and not produced domestically can be authorized; other imports are tolerated only if the former have not already exhausted the available foreign exchange.

Such a system leads to rigorous state control of foreign trade. And since imported goods must be replaced by domestic products, the state is forced to create *ersatz* industries, artificially and at great expense.

Fascism thus embarks, without having wanted to, on autarky, not the utopian autarky promised before the conquest of power, which was to "assure the satisfaction of the needs of every member of the community" and the "precedence of Labor over Money" (Chapter 4), but a veritable *blockade* resulting in poverty for the masses and a tendency towards rising prices, contained nonetheless by draconian price controls.

In Italy

In 1934, the unfavorable balance of foreign trade came to 2.5 billion lire. Gold withdrawals were alarming. Furthermore, by the beginning of 1935, all foreign trade was subordinated to military requirements: it was necessary that "in case of war the nation should have at its command the indispensable means of winning a victory."[77] A decree of February 18, 1935, made licenses issued by the state necessary for the importation of any foreign products. Importers of war materials were granted these licenses without difficulty, but others had to obtain from some exporter an import license issued to him in payment for what he had exported.

The fascist government denounced the trade agreements made with foreign countries on the basis of the "most favored nation clause" and substituted a barter system. It endeavored to limit purchases from any country to the amount of Italian products that country would buy.

After August 1, the state took over the monopoly of foreign purchases of certain raw materials: coal, copper, tin, nickel, cotton, wool, fuel oil, etc. At the beginning of 1936 a state department was created for foreign exchange with the special responsibility of regulating imports and exports.

On March 2, 1937, the fascist Grand Council decided on "the maximum achievement of autarky as far as military requirements are concerned and *the total sacrifice, if necessary, of civilian requirements.*" In June, 1937, the board of directors of the "Finance Company for the Iron Industry," which had just been formed, received this telegram from Mussolini: "If any sector attains the maximum of autarky, it should be the iron sector!"[78] On October 11, the central corporative committee, meeting in Rome, constituted itself the "supreme commission for autarky," for the avowed purpose of "coordinating, controlling and stimulating all activities . . . with a view to achieving autarky."[79]

The cost of this "autarky" is high. An industry for manufacturing substitutes was created by dint of state participation, subsidies, guaranteeing of profits, etc. In this way a company formed to manufacture synthetic gasoline, the *Azienda Nazionale Idrogenazione Combustibili,* was guaranteed a return of from 6 to 8 percent. Three factories were built at great expense to make synthetic gasoline from Alban bitumens, Tuscan lignites, Sicilian schists, etc.

But autarky, despite every effort, could not make it possible for Italy, poor in raw materials, to get along without the rest of the world. In 1938, she produced only 10 percent of the coal she consumed, and she would scarcely be able to produce more than a third of her requirements under any circumstances. The Italian iron industry is dependent on foreign countries for 50 percent of its raw materials. Mussolini admitted this himself.[80] During the first four months of 1937 alone, Italy had to import 1,300,000 metric tons of petroleum products. In 1938, the wheat shortage was estimated at between ten and twenty million quintals. The foreign trade balance for 1937 showed a deficit of six billion lire, far above that of the previous years.

The very fact that, in spite of autarky, imports were still large made it necessary to use every means of stimulating exports. Commenting in the Chamber on the unfavorable trade balance, Minister Guarneri stated that imports had been reduced to the *absolute minimum.* Very little could be done as far as they were concerned to establish a favorable balance of trade. Exports alone remained, and the Minister insisted on the strict necessity of fighting to win more markets: *"Either export or disappear!"*[81] But the facilities granted exporters work a hardship on domestic consumption. Imports of raw materials for manufacturing export commodities come *after* imports of raw materials for armaments, but they come *before* imports of necessities for domestic consumption. The exporter, after being forced to turn over to the state 75 percent of the foreign exchange he received for his shipments, is free to use the remaining 25 percent for importing raw materials to be reexported after they had been fabricated into manufactured products. The domestic consumer is the last served—if any foreign exchange is left.

Such were the limits and shortcomings of autarky. Moreover, for the fascist leaders, autarky was not a panacea but a *makeshift*. "The head of the Italian government," the Rome correspondent of the *Temps* wrote, "*does not look at the problem from a dogmatic viewpoint.*"[82] He would be satisfied with the "indispensable minimum of autarky. . . ." But fascism was caught in a fatal chain and had no choice.

In the meantime the popular masses are paying for the experiment. The cost of living is going up, despite dictatorial price controls, and there is a scarcity of necessities—of consumer goods. The consumer can only tighten his belt.

In Germany

In 1934, Germany's unfavorable trade balance reached 285 million marks. Foreign trade was moreover subordinated to the requirements of rearmament. "The Minister of Economy does not hesitate to import metals and raw materials intended solely for war industries, but he restricts imports required to feed the nation."[83] After 1934, the Reich government began to reduce the amount of foreign exchange at the disposal of importers. The law of March 23, 1934, provided a control office with powers to grant or refuse import licenses, as the case might be, for each classification of imported products. Control offices were set up successively for cotton, wool and hemp, nonferrous metals, rubber, and copper. On September 11, Dr. Schacht decided to increase the number of control offices to twenty-five, so that all imports without exception should be subject to government control. Nothing could be imported without the office concerned first authorizing the necessary foreign exchange. The imports authorized (except in the case of raw materials needed for "national defense") were proportional to the foreign exchange procured by exports.

On August 26, 1934, Dr. Schacht announced that all commercial agreements made by Germany would be denounced—or modified through negotiations—in order to conform to the new organization of foreign trade. Germany henceforth would buy from a country only to the extent that the latter absorbed German goods.

On April 27, 1936, Goering, the strong-arm man, was given supreme authority in all questions relating to raw materials and foreign exchange. At the Nuremberg Congress in September, 1936, Hitler announced a "four-year plan" to make Germany independent of the rest of the world, and in October Goering was appointed dictator of the "four-year plan." He was in command "of all the authorities, including the highest authorities of the Reich, and all party bodies."[84] At the end of November, 1937, following the departure of Dr. Schacht from the Ministry of National Economy, the administration of the "four-year plan" was merged with this Ministry and absorbed it.

Carrying out the four-year plan required the investment of between six and eight billion marks.[85] Whether it was profitable was not taken into account. As the Ruhr industrialists said, perhaps somewhat ironically, in their memorandum to Hitler:[86] "The state does not look at the plan for raw materials from the point of view of production costs. What is decisive for it, in the face of the dangerous scarcity of raw materials, is the purely quantitative question." In fact, the Reich did not shrink from any sacrifice. Using every method—financial investments, subsidies, tax exemptions, guarantees of prices, orders and profits, etc.—it encouraged the manufacture of substitutes. For instance, it guaranteed the *Braunkolen Benzin A.G.*, making synthetic gasoline from lignites, the amortization of its equipment in ten years and a 5 percent return on the capital invested.[87] Eleven factories were set up to make synthetic gasoline from lignites, coal, etc. The Reich also furnished the greater part of the capital for the *Herman Goering Reichswerke fuer Erzbergbau und Eisenhuetten* set up in July, 1937, to process low-grade iron ore.

But this enormous effort met with serious limitations when it came to prices. The excessive cost of many synthetic products made it difficult to substitute them for natural products in peacetime. For instance, the minimum price of Leuna synthetic gasoline at the beginning of 1936 was 140 francs a hectolitre, according to General Serrigny, while natural gasoline cost 22 francs a hectolitre at the port of Hamburg.[88] Even granting that the price of synthetic gasoline may have gone down since, the difference is still great. "If the difference in prices remains what it is today—and it is considerable—" wrote the German correspondent of the *Temps*, "they will limit themselves to manufacturing small quantities of the new products, but the factories will be equipped for rapidly increasing production in time of war. . . ."[89]

These feverish efforts, these huge expenditures, however, have not succeeded in lifting the "foreign yoke" from Germany, where industry is primarily manufacturing and essential raw materials are lacking. Colonel Thomas, head of the war economy department of the Ministry of War, admitted in a lecture: "Neither thorough exploitation of natural resources, including the *ersatz* or synthetic materials, nor restricting to the minimum the requirements of a country, *can make it independent to the point of ceasing entirely to import.*"[90] In 1937, national production supplied only between 20 and 25 percent of the needs for raw materials. Thanks to the "four-year plan" it will be able to supply 30 or even 40 percent, but not more. Under the most favorable conditions, the production of metal ores could at most supply 50 percent of the requirements. In 1937, iron production was only seven million metric tons, while consumption was twenty-eight million metric tons. The production of liquid fuels (natural and synthetic) would not supply more than 50 percent of the requirements. In wartime, because of these serious deficits, the Third Reich, despite its victories and its potential, proved to be extremely vulnerable.

Despite these measures, the trade balance for the first half of 1938, although it had been more favorable during the three preceding years, showed a deficit of 114 million marks.

If imports continued to be as heavy, the trade balance could be made more favorable only by increasing exports. At all costs, it was necessary to find foreign markets, but this could be done only by cutting the prices of German goods abroad artificially and selling them *at a loss*—in other words, by impoverishing the country. A law of July 1, 1935, authorized the Minister of Economy to levy an annual tax of 720 million marks on German industry as a whole for a "dumping" fund, and the state added 300 million marks to this sum. From this fund a bonus proportionate to their losses was paid exporters, enabling them to cut their sales prices from 25 to 50 percent below the domestic prices. But the tax on industry as a whole was in reality passed on to *all the consumers.* "In industrial circles, it is not believed possible to make this heavy sacrifice *without an appreciable increase in domestic cost prices. These will necessarily be reflected in a rise in living costs.*"[91]

When the trade balance became unfavorable again in 1938, the Minister of Economy, Funk, decided to increase the amount of foreign exchange allotted to exporters for the importation of raw materials needed for their manufactures.[92] As in Italy, the domestic consumer came last of all in the distribution of foreign exchange.

Such were the results of German autarky. To tell the truth, in resorting to it Dr. Schacht never considered it anything but an unpleasant expedient. He never ceased to repeat that he did not like autarky in itself, and that he preferred regular and active international relations.[93] He considered it an "expedient one is forced to resort to under certain circumstances" and not as a "true economic system."[94]

As in Italy, the popular masses pay for the closed economy. The necessities of life are scarce or expensive, most often both. To this is added an invisible rise in prices, taking the form of a lowering in the quality of goods—a rise that may be estimated as actually increasing prices by from 10 to 15 percent.[95] The scarcity is particularly marked in those food products (butter, fats, pork) for which Germany depends on foreign countries, and the importation of which was severely limited. "Rearmament," Goering exclaimed, "has cost us gigantic effort. We needed raw materials which had to be obtained from abroad. We had to decide whether to use our foreign exchange to buy minerals or other things. Either we would buy butter and give up our freedom, or we would choose freedom and give up

butter. . . ."[96] "Let us tighten our belts! It will do us good!" Goebbels
advised the unfortunate consumer.[97]

10

Thus from expedient to expedient—following no preconceived
theory but in a purely empirical fashion, perhaps without having
foreseen exactly where the road was leading which excessive armaments was forcing it to take—fascism arrives at a "war economy"
similar to that of the belligerent countries between 1914 and 1918.
The only difference between yesterday and today is that the economy
of 1914–1918 was a *wartime* economy in the proper meaning of the
word, while the present fascist economy is war economy *in peace
time*.[98]

After 1919, when peace was restored, the capitalists, impatient to
recover their full freedom of action, demanded the liquidation of
"war economy." In Italy, Mussolini was even subsidized by them to
carry on a campaign in his paper, the *Popolo d'Italia*, against the
"statism" inherited from the war.[99] Today, thanks to the financial
assistance of big business, fascism is in power. And what does it
do?—or rather, what is it forced to do? Revive "war economy."

The distinguishing characteristic of this economy is the continuous extension of the functions of the state. The state is the supreme
director of the whole economy; the state becomes the sole customer
of industry; the state drains off all private savings; the state monopolizes foreign trade; the state controls prices; the state freely disposes
of labor; the state allots raw materials; the state determines in what
sectors of economy new investments are necessary and decides on
new manufactures, etc., etc. "We have reached a point," Mussolini
exclaims, "when if . . . the state went to sleep for twenty-four hours,
it would be enough to cause a catastrophe."[100] And in Germany, according to Dr. Schacht: "More than ever before, individuals are nothing without the state. . . ."[101] "Only the state can be at the helm."[102]

The state directs the economy. But what is there behind that abstraction, the state? Who directs the state?

The bureaucracy of the fascist state is obviously incapable of solving such new and complex economic problems as have arisen. "It is clear," as the *Temps* says, "that if the state undertakes to direct national economy, it has to have an infinitely more complicated administrative apparatus than it has today."[103] Therefore, the bureaucracy, while putting on a show of proud independence, lets itself be "advised" by those who are "competent"—*namely, the capitalist magnates*. They become the economic high command—no longer concealed, as previously, but *official*—of the state. *Permanent* contact is established between them and the bureaucratic apparatus. They dictate, and the bureaucracy executes. Such is the real role of the "corporations" set up in Italy by the law of February 4, 1934, and of the "occupational groups" set up in Germany by the law of February 27, 1934, prototypes of the "organizing committees" of Petain.

What is the avowed purpose of the Italian "corporation"? "To give its advice on all questions in any way relating to the economic field for which it is constituted whenever it is requested by the public authorities concerned."[104] And the avowed purpose of the German "occupational groups"? "To organize systematic contact between the industrialists and the services of the Ministry of Economy."[105]

Inside the "corporations" and "occupational groups" problems concerning the "war economy" are determined jointly by the industrialists and the state bureaucracy: the division of import quotas of raw materials for armaments, the storing of raw materials and commodities for time of war, the creation of industries to make substitutes, the increasing of exports, etc. And, quite fittingly, whenever there is anything to be divided, the magnates reserve the lion's share for themselves.

In Italy

The Italian "corporations" in 1934 were given the task of forming consortiums for the purchase in the world market of raw materials to be divided among the different manufacturers.[106] After February, 1935, when the import restrictions began, "committees with a corporative base" were entrusted with distributing the import quotas and licences.[107] In the beginning of 1936, it was announced that "the corporative technical committees are preparing and carrying out the maximum exploitation of all national reserves and resources. . . . The work of the corporations is firmly directed toward these objectives."[108] For instance, the corporation for the metallurgic and machine industry was particularly concerned with the problem of special metals for airplane construction.[109] On October 11, 1937, as we have seen, the central corporative committee, made up of representatives of the twenty-two corporations, became the "supreme commission for autarky" with broad powers. At the same time, the "corporations" sought to reduce the cost of production in order to increase exports. "The new corporations," wrote *Giornale d'Italia*, "are preparing a favorable basis for overall study and coordinated action which the problem [of exports] requires, in every phase of production."[110]

The "occupational groups," whose leaders "were frequently identical in practice with the heads of the cartels,"[111] collaborated closely after September, 1934, with the various import control offices set up at that time. Working hand in hand with them, the state perfected its huge program for manufacturing substitutes. When the dumping fund was established in 1935 to stimulate exports, the "occupational groups" collaborated both in collecting this fund and in parcelling it out among the exporters. One of their principal aims was to "rapidly and rationally develop export trade," (Kessler) to "develop export trade by any means" (von der Goltz and Schacht).

11

However, a few innocent people are still convinced that under a fascist regime the big capitalists have no power over the state, but that, on the contrary, the state rules the capitalists with a rod of iron. Whence comes this persistent illusion? The fascist plebeians have a large share of responsibility for its spread. In fact, they take their wishes for reality, and would have others do so also. Indeed they would like to reverse the roles and use the "war economy" and the "corporations" to subject capitalism to the authoritarian rule of the state—that is to say, *to themselves.* As masters of the economy, they would possess wealth and power. Also a little verbal demagogy seems useful to allay the discontent of their rank-and-file. But they no more manage in this field than any other to go from words to deeds. The capitalists vigorously defend themselves against these pretensions. Faithful to economic liberalism, they accept the war economy only under the force of circumstances and insist on being in charge of it. They will not stand for the plebeians taking advantage of it to imprison them in an ever more stringent "statism." They fear that the "corporations" or "professional groups" may be diverted from their original aim, strictly limited in space and time, so that they are caught in their own trap. *The rulers of the fascist state formally condemn and repudiate all "socializing" tendencies.* They draw the line between temporary measures capitalism may resort to and the idle dreams of some who, following a preconceived scheme, would transform this "statism" into a permanent system.

In Italy

The *Lavoro Fascista* claimed to see in the "corporative" system an "anti-bourgeois" and a "truly revolutionary transformation of the national Economy."[112] "Some fascists," the *Temps* correspondent in Rome noted, "found even in the sanctions an *excellent opportunity* for speeding up the application of the corporative system and accustoming the whole population, without distinction between rich and poor, to defer to the national interest. . . ."[113]

Against such tendencies, big capital reacted vigorously. The Federation of Industry, the employers' private organization, continued to exist independently outside the "corporations," even though it had no legal status in the "corporate state." It held annual congresses, and the one in 1934 was even graced by the presence of *Il Duce* himself. The president, Pirelli, took advantage of the occasion to remind the representative of the state that it must not interfere in the management of production. Doubtless state intervention is sometimes necessary—for instance, to rescue a bankrupt firm—but it "need not be so general. . . . Economic laws must not be violated." As for the employers, they will never deviate "in any case whatsoever" from "the principle of private property and individual initiative."[114]

The Duce multiplied his assurances. The corporations in Italy would continue to be merely bodies for contact between the state and the industrialists—*and nothing more*. They would not be used to dominate private industry; they would not themselves manage production. Mussolini gave his formal promise: "Does it have to be repeated again that the corporations are not an end in themselves?"[115] "The corporations are state bodies, but not merely bureaucratic bodies of the state."[116] "There is no question of state socialism, because the fascist state has no intention of monopolizing production; nor does it seek to restrain individual initiative and still less to injure private property rights. . . ."[117] He refused to consent to a development that would lead "*de plano* to state capitalism . . . the bureaucratization of the national economy."[118] "I believe that none of you wants to bureaucratize the economy—that is, congeal the reality of economic life, a complex and changing reality. . . ."[119] "We have no intention of multiplying by ten the already imposing figure of state employees."[120]

In Germany

The plebeians of the *Voelkischer Beobachter* wanted to see in the formation of the "occupational groups" "economic construction directed by German socialism."[121] "The National Socialist state has the economy in its hands. . . . The nebulous 'economic laws' of liberalism . . . are no longer valid; they are replaced by the will and purposes of the state. . . . After twenty-one months in power, National Socialism has become master of the economy."[122]

At the end of 1937, the plebeians believed conditions were favorable for a new wave of "leftism." The *Voelkischer Beobachter* and other Nazi papers let loose a campaign against the enormous armament profits.[123] Dr. Ley's Labor Front, and Walter Darre's Food

Corporation went so far as to demand the *nationalization of war industries.*[124]

The anger of the big capitalists had been periodically aroused by such ideas. They would not consent to the "occupational groups" leading to anything but the specific aim assigned to them. "These organizations must not be allowed," wrote the *Frankfurter Zeitung,* "to become an end in themselves. The bureaucracy of these groups needs to be seriously limited. *Their privileges must not be enlarged beyond what they have been up to the present.* . . ."[125] The specter of a "socializing" statism continued to annoy the industrialists: "Industrial circles dread seeing the National Socialist state try to put an end to the great difficulties confronting it by intervening in the internal management of business. . . ."[126] And the employers' organ, *Der Ring,* uttered a cry of alarm: "A sort of forced economy is being born, similar to that during the war. The effects are even more extensive and deeper and *can only too easily lead to a situation in which the independence of private industry would disappear and be replaced by the direction of the state authorities.* It is all the more necessary to look this danger in the face because such a development would not correspond to the principles that presided over the creation of the new Reich."[127]

In January, 1938, industrial circles especially feared nationalization of the armament industry of the Reich, "which certain information presents as imminent."[128] Their spokesman went to see Hitler in Berchtesgaden and protested vehemently against any plan for nationalizing war industries.[129]

The rulers of the Third Reich categorically dispelled this anxiety. Dr. Schacht rejected any attempt to use the "occupational groups" to increase bureaucracy or statism. In no case should these groups strip the head of a business of his personal responsibility. The individual enterprise should work independently as far as possible and not be led on a leash by dozens of groups. Any excessive organization would lead fatally to the disappearance of the spirit of initiative.[130] No nationalization of Economy. "Private Economy must continue its efforts and activity. . . ."[131] "The state alone cannot take over a mechanism as vast and ramified into so many branches as that of the economy. Stimulation of individual interest is and will remain the foundation of all economic activity. National Socialism has established the principle that the state should guide the economy, but not become an entrepreneur itself. . . ."[132]

In November, 1937, Dr. Schacht left the Ministry of Economy, but his successors, Goering and Funk, spoke the same language. In a speech delivered at the Koenigsberg fair, Funk declared: "Nothing could be more false than to claim, as some do abroad, that Germany plans to introduce a system of economic controls and state capitalism excluding private initiative. . . . We cannot dispense with the creative power of the individual. . . . We are not fashioning a dogmatic economic policy but a policy of success."[133] On January 31, 1938, a Berlin dispatch announced: "Those close to General Goering *deny that nationalization of heavy industry is contemplated. . . . Nationalization would only be a hindrance by bureaucratizing industry and killing the initiative of the industrialists.*" On February 7, Funk, on formally taking over his functions as Minister of Economy, stated: "The four-year plan must not impede individual initiative. . . . Private and public economy are not competitors; they should supplement one another."[134] It is significant that the military men who shared in the direction of the "war economy" and the "four-year plan," although favoring a strict control of industry *in the interest of "national defense,"* disapproved of the "anti-capitalist" campaigns of the plebeians and declared themselves unmistakably against all nationalization. For instance, Colonel Thomas, head of the "war economy" department of the Ministry of War, declared peremptorily: "The execution is left as far as possible to private initiative. German war economy will not socialize war industry. . . . The entrepreneur and the merchant should make money. That is what they are for."[135]

12

As the four-year plan and autarky are put into effect, the circles of big German industrialists show signs of uneasiness and anxiety, and display a lack of enthusiasm. This is not because the "socializing" tendencies of the plebeians have a chance of winning out; they still have none. Nor is it because capitalist profits are in any immediate danger; those accumulated in the preceding years have given the industrialists enormous reserves, and the profits they are still making are more than respectable. At the bottom of their uneasiness is a very clear impression that the regime they wanted and put in power, from which they alone have benefited, and which they have sucked to the marrow, has passed its prime. Gradually, imperceptibly, margins of profit are growing narrower. In the early years, the government showered tax exemptions upon them; now the war economy is costing them heavy taxes (see above). In the early years, the government allowed them, through compulsory cartellization, to fix monopoly prices; now the needs of war economy are forcing the state to a stricter control of cartels and prices. They wonder what the effect on prices and the situation of the cartels will be when the *Goering-Werke* starts throwing large quantities of iron and steel on the market.[*] In the early years, the regime assured them rates of profits surpassing anything they had known for a long time; now their forced participation in the *ersatz* industries (with profits guaranteed) assures them a return no higher than the market rates. Truly they have reason to look sour! And, as if to give tangible evidence of their anxiety and of the narrower margins of profit, the big industrial stocks at the end of July, 1938, start to tumble on the Berlin Stock Exchange.

At the same time, bureaucratic restrictions are daily becoming more unendurable. One of the mouthpieces of big capital, the *Deutsche Volkswirt*, exclaims: *"Woe to the industrialist who accidentally fails to fulfil his obligations! The furies are unleashed, in spite of the fact that it is scarcely possible any more for him to perform all the duties continually imposed on him. . . ."*[137]

---

[*] It is asserted that the *Goering-Werke* should some day produce six million tons of unfinished steel--almost as much as the biggest trust, the United Steel, which produced 6,280,000 tons in 1936–1937.[136]

So the industrialists start grumbling not only about the plebeian demagogues but about the man who has done the most for them, who is entirely devoted to them, who would doubtless readily dispense with subjecting them to restrictions were he not himself forced to insure the success of the "four-year plan" at all costs. Between them and Hermann Goering the clashes are growing frequent. On December 17, 1936, Goering, having assembled the "three hundred leaders of the economy," assured them of "the need for an immediate industrial mobilization of Germany." His statements, according to the Berlin correspondent of the *Temps, occasioned great surprise among the listeners, and Goering harshly took the industrialists present to task. He reproached them for their laxity in putting into effect the great idea of the four-year plan.*[138] In December, 1937, in the periodical, *The Four-Year Plan,* Goering wrote: "Business must realize that it lives, in the last analysis, only by accomplishing the great tasks entrusted to it and *not by balancing accounts of profits and losses.*"[139]

Another conflict in interests causes a section of big industry to look with disfavor on the "four-year plan." Export industry complains that it has been sacrificed. In spite of subsidies from the dumping fund, German exports are declining in all the foreign markets, and this is aggravated by the circumstance that world economy is itself in decline. In a memorandum addressed to Chancellor Hitler in June, 1937, the spokesmen of the export industry, particularly of the Rhenish-Westphalian coal barons, state their grievances.[140] Exports are strangled by all sorts of formalities that "transform the exchange of goods into a purely bureaucratic activity." Export industry lacks raw materials: these are reserved almost exclusively for the armament industry. It lacks labor: "They insist on borrowing the best workers from certain branches of industry" in order to assign them to war or synthetic products industries. It lacks capital: it is unable to grant foreign customers the big credits made necessary by increasing competition. It lacks markets: the result of autarky is to isolate German economy from the world market. "It has been shown," the memorandum sadly notes, "that the foreign trade of the principal countries in the world does not necessarily depend on the German market. . . ." So the export industry demands that engines be reversed and contact resumed with world economy. But—and they do not mince words—*it is impossible "to bring back into the orbit of world economy an economy functioning to the detriment of the domestic value of its currency and carrying on solely such activities as rearmament and autarky."*

Dr. Schacht became the spokesman of the export industry. On April 13, 1937, he went to Brussels and there stated to the press "that he would like to stabilize the currency at a new rate, and that he believed he could give assurance of Germany's readiness to collaborate in such an undertaking. It would make for freedom of trade. . . ."

But the partisans of the "four-year plan" and extreme autarky, supported by those sections of heavy industry living on autarky and "war economy," won out, at least for the time being, and on November 26, 1937, Dr. Schacht had to leave the Ministry of Economy, where he was replaced by Funk, Goering's puppet.

The uneasiness, both of big industry in general and of the export industry in particular, is not unrelated to the political crisis of February 4, 1938 (See Chapter 7) that led to the retirement of Marshal von Blomberg and General von Fritsch. But that crisis, as we have seen, ended in a compromise. And apparently on the economic plane also it led to a compromise between the outright partisans and the half-hearted supporters of the "four-year plan." Dr. Schacht, at the end of November, 1937, had been named minister without portfolio, which permitted him to continue to participate in government deliberations. In March, 1938, he was reappointed president of the *Reichsbank* for a four-year term. On several occasions, Goering and Funk publicly paid him homage. In the words of the *Frankfurter Zeitung,* "Schacht goes out and stays in."[141]

Although the Reich government continues to carry out the "four-year plan," it is obviously striving to appease the industrialists in general and satisfy in particular a few of the demands of the export industry by increasing the latter's quotas of raw materials and foreign exchange. In July, 1938, Goering appointed a "media-tion commissioner," one Neumann, and charged him with finding a "compromise between war economy and the export interests."[142]

The commotion of the general call-to-arms, which permitted Hitler to discard the Munich pact, seemed to have granted Hitler a respite from the contradictions of the German economy. The Danubian and Balkan countries, whose economies complemented Germany's, were to become satellites of "greater Germany." If Germany had succeeded in embracing these countries in one huge customs union, she would have immediately obtained the markets which her export industry desperately needed and the raw materials essential to her war economy.

But German imperialism's imperialist adversaries fully grasped the danger presented by such a strengthening of the economic potential of the Reich. And they forestalled it, at first by purchasing—with gold—the "friendship" of the Danubian countries, and then by deliberately proceeding to the point of armed conflict.

Hitler, for his part, knew that the markets of Central Europe would not suffice for long to lift German capitalism out of its difficulties. He did not hesitate to pick up the gauntlet flung by his opponents, and he hurled himself into the conquest of the world market. The juggernaut began to roll—and it would not stop for years.

13

It should be noted that if big industry has only a moderate enthusiasm for autarky, the hermetically-sealed economy, the sections of light industry working for domestic consumption have still more cause for complaint. They pay dearly for the enhanced domination of heavy industry, through higher prices for machinery, fuels, etc. They see their markets constantly growing smaller because of the lessened buying power of the masses. On account of the preference given the importation of products to be used in armaments, they suffer a serious scarcity of raw materials and undergo a severe crisis. In Italy this is the case of the woolen industry, real silk, and the like; and in Germany, of textiles, clothing, hides and leather, radio, etc.

In 1937, the hide and leather industry was working only thirty hours a week, and textiles, twenty-four. For the latter, the index of hours worked (taking 1929 as 100) was only 82.9, and in the garment industry it was 84.9.

14

As for the middle classes—the very ones whose discontent put fascism in power—they are simply bled white.

Just as during the last war it was *those with fixed incomes* (from savings, investments, pensions and salaries) who paid for the armaments, so now they are paying for rearmament, and their existence becomes ever more difficult as the national currency loses its purchasing power in the country.

The *small manufacturers and independent craftsmen* suffer both from a scarcity of raw materials and a lack of markets. The National Socialist party in Germany promised "to favor them by orders of the Reich, the states, and the municipalities." But there is no longer any question of keeping this promise, for the very good reason that armament orders go exclusively to heavy industry.[143] Fascism in both countries promised to "reverse engines," to go back to an economy of small producers, and throttle the great capitalist monopolies (Chapter 4). But as we have seen, when it gets in power it only strengthens in every possible way the monopolies it promised to render harmless (see above); it merely intensifies the tendencies of capitalism toward concentration and mechanization. In Italy, after asking, "Are we going . . . to destroy the machines . . . or limit their use?" Mussolini answers: "That solution is childish. . . . Going backward has never been profitable."[144] In Germany, Dr. Schacht makes fun of a certain "artisan romanticism for the past," and reminds the reactionary petty-bourgeois that "the spinning-wheel has been replaced by the spinning-machine, the water-wheel by the electric motor. . . . An industry which does not use these modern machine methods of production cannot meet the competition of other countries on an international plane."[145]

In both countries, the condition of small and medium-sized industry is deplorable. In Italy, in 1934–35, when the twenty big companies with a capital over 250 million lire reported a net profit of 675 million lire, 9,144 companies with capital of less than one million reported a net loss of 95 million. At the same time, 649 companies with capital less than 10,000 lire lost 60.94 percent on their capital investment, and 290 companies with capital between 10,000 and 25,000 lire lost 92.29 percent.[146]

In Germany, the number of companies having a capital between 5,000 and 1,000,000 marks dropped from 7,512 in 1931 to 3,850 in 1937.[147]

Small merchants are particularly brutally disappointed by fascist economic policy. On the one hand they are not protected, as they had hoped, from the murderous competition of department stores. On the other hand, they are caught in a pincers between rising wholesale prices, brought about by shrewd mergers, and the freeze on retail prices.

In Italy

In Italy, the big stores, far from declining since the advent of fascism, have constantly grown, to the detriment of small trade. The magnate Volpi rejoices on the floor of the Senate at certain measures "aiming at the gradual abolition of small trade and the creation of big, centralized, commercial enterprises which the authorities can more easily supervise."[148]

The little merchants are overwhelmed with taxes, which go up every year. For instance, a decree of November, 1937, raised the sales tax from 2.5 to 3 percent and provided that any sale amounting to more than one lira was taxable, whereas previously sales of less than 10 lire were exempt.[149]

The small tradesmen pay, too, for the discrepancy between rising wholesale prices and retail prices which are artificially kept down by the government. A decree-law of December 16, 1926, set up municipal supervisory commissions to license merchants and regulate retail prices. In December, 1930, a general 10 percent cut in prices was decreed, and the Black Shirts brutally forced the small tradesmen to change their price tags. In April, 1934, the fascist state repeated the performance. It got the Federation of Commerce to decide that all merchants who did not consent to another 10 percent cut would be expelled from the association to which they belonged. This was ruthlessly enforced by closing shops and retail stores. Between January, 1934, and January, 1938, the index of wholesale prices for the twenty principal food products went up from 100 to 141, while the index of retail prices for the same products rose only from 100 to 129.[150]

In Germany

In Germany, the big stores are neither "communalized" nor limited in their activity, as National Socialism promised. The Third Reich has been content to forbid . . . restaurants in department stores—and only if abolishing them does not endanger "the soundness of the business" (law of July 15, 1933). Later, a decree of February 1, 1935, again authorized department stores "of first rank" in big cities to "serve food."

Rudolf Hess announced, in Hitler's name, that "in view of the economic situation, the party leadership considers undesirable any action that would ruin the big stores. . . . It therefore prohibits members of the NSDAP from undertaking any action whatever against them. . . ."[151] In the spring of 1934, the National Socialist Federation of Commerce and Industry again asserted there was no question of closing the big stores.[152] Not only is the activity of the big stores not restricted, but the National Socialist state has come to their rescue (Karstadt, Tietz) with millions. The figures for the business done by the department and "one-price" stores have constantly grown, while 16,000 small tradesmen (7,000 in Berlin alone) have been forced to close up shop.[153]

Small tradesmen are squeezed even harder than in Italy between rising wholesale prices and officially controlled retail prices. A "commissioner to regulate prices" was appointed November 5, 1934. He exercised strict supervision over retail prices, and the little merchants who sold for more than the fixed prices were heavily fined (as much as 1,000 marks) and had their shops closed. At the same time, a big campaign for lowering prices was entrusted to the Brown Shirts, who repeated against the "Aryan" small tradesmen their 1933 exploits against Jewish merchants. In his proclamation to the Nuremberg Congress in 1935, Hitler stated: "We will act brutally against those who . . . try to raise prices, and we will not hesitate, if need be, to send them to concentration camps."[154]

Through the "corporations" as well, the small manufacturers and merchants, to whom fascism had demagogically promised *independent* corporations (Chapter 4), are turned over, bound hand and foot, to the great monopolists, their direct enemies.

In Italy

Until 1934, the small manufacturers had no independent organization, but rather a federation attached to the General Federation of Industry, the powerful organization of the big industrialists. As for the small merchants, they were organized not separately but in the fascist Federation of Commercial Associations—that is, placed directly under the tutelage of the owners of big stores. After 1934, small tradesmen and manufacturers, instead of obtaining independent representation, were regimented into the twenty-two new "corporations," according to their branch of economy. Because, in any one of these, they formed only a small uninfluential minority, their representatives in fact were strictly dependent on the big capitalists.[155]

For example, the small manufacturers and craftsmen have two (out of thirty) representatives in the Wood Products Corporation, one (out of fifty) in the Textile Corporation, two (out of fifty) in the Metallurgy and Machines Corporation, three (out of forty-three) in the Garment Corporation, one (out of twenty-three) in the Book-Paper Corporation, one (out of twenty) in the Extraction Industries Corporation, and two (out of twenty-five) in the Glass and Ceramics Corporation. Trade has only three employers' delegates and three "employees' representatives" in the corporations for Wood, Textiles, Chemical Products, and Garments; four of each in the Corporation of Metallurgy; two of each in Book-Paper and Glass-Ceramics; and one each in the Extraction Industries. And these trade delegates represent, *without distinction,* both small tradesmen and the department stores or chain stores.

In Germany

Two independent corporations were formed at the beginning of May, 1933—a Corporation of Retail Trade (exclusive of big stores) and a Corporation of Artisans. At the head of both was placed the leader of the middle classes, Dr. Rintelen. But these corporations did not preserve their independence long. Dr. Rintelen was soon ousted from their leadership, and when, in 1934, the whole of the German economy was divided into "occupational groups," the Corporation of Retail Trade became the "occupational group of commerce," and the Artisans' Corporation became the "occupational group of artisans." Both groups were placed under the strict control of the Minister of Economy—in other words, the high command of big industry. Furthermore, the Group of Commerce henceforth included not only the small merchants *but also the department stores and chain stores.* The board of directors had three members, one of whom owned a big chain store company and another a big department store.[156]

10

Fascism in power:
Agricultural policy

Fascism, as we have seen (Chapter 1), is subsidized before the conquest of power not only by the industrialists but also by the big landowners. Once victorious, it tries to check the drop in the profits of the latter as well as the former. By doing so, it both pays a debt of gratitude to the landowners and furthers another aim: the achievement of autarky and the nation's independence in foodstuffs. For the big estates lend themselves much better to intensive, scientific, mechanized farming than do small tracts of land.

Fascism, moreover, for political reasons wants to create beside the big landowners a restricted layer of medium-sized farmers, recruited from the reliable supporters of the regime, so as to be sure of a dependable social base on the land.

Finally, fascism's agricultural policy tends to reconcile what it calls the "interests of agriculture" and the "interests of industry"—in reality those of the big industrialists and big landowners—on the backs of the poor peasants and urban proletariat. It does not protect the small peasantry against capitalism; on the contrary it completes capitalism's invasion of the land.

1

To win the support of the small peasants, fascism does not hesitate to make demagogic demands for the division of the big estates. But once it has conquered, it takes care not to touch them. If it turns over a few thousand hectares for "colonization," it is only as a smoke-screen. These measures leave the big estates almost intact; fascism in reality opposes dividing up the land and tries to reassemble large and medium-sized farms at the expense of the small peasantry.

In Italy
Italian fascism trampled its promises under foot. Even in June, 1922, at the first congress of the fascist "unions," Mussolini soft-pedalled the agrarian revolution.[1] During the summer of 1922, the draft of a law for colonizing the *latifundia* was introduced into the Chamber by the Catholics and passed. It provided for expropriating, with compensation and through a National Institute for Colonization, certain big estates that were not cultivated or were badly cultivated by their owners. But this plan, timorous as it was, the fascist parliamentary group fought bitterly, and after the March on Rome Mussolini's first care was to withdraw it before it was considered by the Senate. On January 11, 1923, the government annulled the "Visochi decree" of September 2, 1919, which had temporarily legalized a number of cases of occupation of fallow land by the peasants. The unfortunate squatters, after having first cultivated the land at a loss and then improved it with the sweat of their brows, were forced to give it back to the former owners without compensation.[2]

After 1923, fascism never touched the big estates. To be sure, it tried to pass off the "general land improvement" project as opening the way for a redistribution of Italian soil. But there was a vast difference between words and reality. A fascist, G.C. Baravelli, wrote in a pamphlet on the subject: "The fascist regime believes in the fundamental importance of private ownership of the land. It leaves the landowners where it finds them. . . . It respects the principle of property . . . *with the utmost scrupulousness.*"[3] When the Chamber on December 12, 1934, voted on the second land improvement law, the Minister of Agriculture, Acerbo, gave assurance that the law was enthusiastically received by the landed proprietors, and that it did no injury to sacred property rights—"those rights that, after the war, fascism defended and saved from attacks on all sides."[4] Owners who could not assume their share of the expense of land improvements (the other and larger share was borne by the state) *could*, according to the law of December 24, 1928, have all or part of their property expropriated, with compensation of course, by the "land improvement consortium" to which they belonged. But in Rosenstock-Franck's opinion,[5] expropriations before 1934 were not numerous. The few estates expropriated were turned over by the landowners' consortium, not directly to small settlers, but to speculative land companies which, after the improvements had been made, sold them for as much as possible. "Expropriation is carried out not for the benefit of all but for the profit of companies with strictly limited interests. A system farther from any kind of socialism could not be imagined."[6]

The law of December, 1934, doubtless corrected some of these abuses by the provision that expropriated land was thereafter to be improved and allotted by the state itself, through the agency of the fascist Institute for Land Improvement. In addition, it made expropriation compulsory in case the owners could not pay their share of the improvement costs. But the farm crisis hit the small farmers much harder than the big agrarians (see below), and it was chiefly the small farmers who were expropriated. Moreover, the compensation was based on the capitalization as estimated from the net income on the property, and, since the income of the ruined small owners was little or nothing, their land was purchased at paltry prices.

Finally, the improvements were very expensive—between 10,000 and 20,000 lire a hectare. The state was therefore faced with a dilemma: either dispose of the expropriated land at prohibitive prices after it was improved, making the sale impossible, or practically give it away to privileged settlers. Since the condition of the public finances did not permit such generosity on a large scale, "colonization" continued to be very restricted. In 1935, G.C. Baravelli wrote that "the full and complete repurchase of a very large part of the national soil is now only *a question of time.*"[7] This was really a confession which at that time *it had not even begun.*[8]

In January, 1936, an English journalist asked Rossoni, the minister of agriculture, why fascism had not undertaken an agrarian reform. The latter answered: "We cannot confiscate the property of the landowners. *We are fascists, not socialists.*"[9] Mussolini, in March, 1936, stated that "agriculture—in its structure—does not permit extensive transformations. No substantial innovation in the traditional form of Italian agricultural economy. . . ."[10]

Not only did the fascist state fail to "divide the land," but its policy clearly tended to reconstitute large and medium-sized holdings at the expense of the small peasants. Ever since the end of the feudal regime, the peasants had enjoyed the right of collective use of certain lands coming from the old feudal fiefs and still nominally owned by the heirs of the old lords. The law of June 8, 1924, restored these lands to their nominal owners. Similarly, the peasants had enjoyed other rights (especially that of pasturing their stock) in the "communal lands," such as the *tratturi* of central and southern Italy. The big agrarians in the course of time had ended these privileges. Immediately after the war, the peasant municipalities took their stolen lands back from the usurpers. Once fascism was in power, the big agrarians appropriated them again on an even larger scale.[11]

The few estates that were devoted to colonization, after they had been improved, were not distributed to small settlers but were divided into medium-sized farms. For instance, on the drained Pontine marshes the fascist state installed a few thousand families of so-called "war veterans"—in reality carefully selected fascists—who were granted 50,000 hectares divided into only 2,773 farms.[12]

In Germany
The Nazis too went back on their promises. The first Minister of Agriculture of the Hitler government was none other than

Hugenberg, the big landowners' man. It is well to point out that among the Junkers were a number of prominent Nazis: for instance, the Duke of Saxony-Coburg-Gotha, of the NSKK (Nazi motor corps) with 10,182 hectares; the Prince of Hesse, intimate friend of Goering, with 7,013 hectares; Marshall von Blomberg, with 2,345 hectares; Count Schwerin von Krosigk, Minister of Finance, with 3,846 hectares; etc., etc.[13] Not surprisingly, division of the big estates was postponed *sine die*. Hitler stated that "large rural property could have the right to exist legally on condition that it is worked for the common good of all citizens."[14] He appointed as commissioner for domestic colonization another representative of the Junker landowners, Baron von Gayl, a former minister of the Papen government. Instead of expropriating and dividing the big estates that had long ceased to be profitable, Hugenberg put them on a sound footing at the expense of the state (law of June 1, 1933, see below). His rival and successor in the Ministry of Agriculture, Walter Darre, followed exactly the same policy: "In agreement with the Chancellor," he declared, "I shall not touch any property, whatever its size, if it is economically sound and can support itself."[15]

By proclaiming *inalienable* the "hereditary farms" (law of September 29, 1933)—and the big estates in certain cases could benefit by the "hereditary farm" legislation—the Nazi state completely closed the door on any prospect for real "colonization."[16] For example, the Leinfeld estate in Wurttemberg, belonging to Baron von Neurath, was declared "inalienable and not subject to seizure" on February 2, 1935.

But although "colonization" was dead and buried, the word was still served up in various sauces. The Nazi press from time to time put forth glittering and grandiose projects for "colonization," such as that announced by the *Gruene Woche* in January, 1934, for the creation of 190,000 new farms; and Darre set up a "special committee for domestic colonization" in October, 1934. But in reality "colonization," far from progressing, was receding. Whereas in 1932, there were 9,046 new farms with a total area of 102,000 hectares alloted to small settlers, in 1933, the figure fell to 4,914 totalling 60,297 hectares. In 1936, it was 3,308 (60,358 hectares) and in 1937, only 1,785 (35,942 hectares).

A very small part of these lands, it should be added, came from the big estates. In 1933, the Nazis, as a matter of form, asked the Junkers to allot a certain part of their property for colonization, but this "charitable" step had practically no success. The few little plots of ground turned over were generally situated on the edge of these estates and unsuited both in location and quality for colonization. The debt relief law of June 1, 1933, provided that the restoration of solvency to the properties should be accompanied by the donation of a certain percentage of the land; but in practice the Junkers got rid of a few tracts, chosen from among the least valuable, at exorbitant prices. As a matter of fact, nearly all the lands alloted to colonization came not from the big estates but from the public domain, or from waste or swampy tracts reclaimed at little expense by the "labor service."

Instead of dividing the big estates, the Nazis followed a policy which definitely tended to increase large and medium-sized estates at the expense of the small holding.

The lands devoted to "colonization" were not distributed to small settlers but were divided into a limited number of medium-sized farms. Of the new farms, there were 60 percent with more than ten hectares in 1933, and 70 percent in 1934. The beneficiaries of this "colonization" were chosen from among the most reliable partisans of the Nazi regime. The primary purpose of the "hereditary farm" law of September 29, 1933, was to form a limited stratum of big and medium-sized farmers—a "new nobility of blood and soil," in the words of Walter Darré[17]—that would assure the regime a social base on the land. On January 1, 1935, about 700,000 farms (out of about 5.5 million in Germany) were declared to be "hereditary farms." They were proclaimed inalienable and could be inherited only by a single heir (the oldest or the youngest son, according to the region)—a device that prevented division of the property and reduced the disinherited children to the status of proletarians.

In order to create sufficiently large hereditary holdings, the Nazis in many districts confiscated small farms or took the use of certain lands from the poor peasants. For instance, by a decree of February, 1934, the government of Baden withdrew from the peasants their age-old right—for which they paid a small tax—to use the communal lands known as *Allmend* for pasturage. These communal lands, representing 17 percent of the area of Baden, were used to create "hereditary farms" for a few favored Nazis. In Hesse, a government decree of December 27, 1934, expropriated in the same way and for the same purpose 192,000 hectares of peasant lands (13.8 percent of the area of the state). In the swampy region of the Roehn a drainage plan was adopted, the sole purpose of which was to expropriate tens of thousands of wretched peasants with tiny holdings in order to put a few hundred "hereditary farmers" on the improved land.

2

The fascist state helps the landowners exploit their workers. The agricultural laborers are deprived of their independent unions, fixed hours of labor are no longer guaranteed, medieval forms of exploitation are imposed on them, they are excluded from unemployment insurance, and their wages are cut below the subsistence level. The result is that many of them try to escape their wretched condition by pouring into the cities, and the rural districts are depopulated. But access to the centers is severely forbidden them, and they are pitilessly herded back onto the land. Various archaic systems are revived, such as the payment of wages in kind, in order to bind them more securely to the soil.

In Italy

After the war farm laborers (*braccianti*) were organized into powerful unions and bargained with the landowners on an equal footing (Chapter 1). Fascism began by destroying these unions and forcing the laborers to join fascist "company unions" (Chapter 8). The unions of farm workers had been supported by the socialist municipal governments, but by the law of February 4, 1926, the fascist state abolished the elected municipal councils and replaced them by mayors (*podesta*) appointed directly by the government. In every commune, the *podesta* was naturally a big landowner or rich peasant. The law of December 30, 1923, excluded the *braccianti* from unemployment insurance. The old union contracts were cancelled and replaced by so-called contracts which cancelled all the gains formerly won by the rural proletariat In many contracts the feudal custom of a workday "from sunrise to sunset" was revived.[18] The contract for the province of Mantua, for instance, stated as a principle that the average workday should be eight hours but provided numerous exceptions for extra hours with no compensation.[19]

The new contracts also effected enormous wage cuts. In the province of Milan, for instance, wages were 50 percent lower than those of the pre-fascist period.[20] In 1930 the average wage in agriculture was 30 percent below that before the war and 40 percent below that of 1919. Between 1930 and 1938 it went down about 20 percent more. Although Mussolini had declared that in no case should the daily wage go below 8 lire,[21] it went lower in many regions. In the Ferrara district it fell to 6 lire 60 in 1934, as compared with 19 lire 71 in 1925. The *Corriere Padovano* admitted: "The condition of agricultural workers in our province could without any exaggeration be described as tragic."[22] Furthermore, wages were cut another 20 to 25 percent during the winter months on the pretext of "encouraging the agriculturalists to employ more labor in order to combat winter unemployment."[23] Similar cuts were provided for "agricultural and land improvement enterprises" with the "exceptional purpose of being directed to the reduction of unemployment."[24] Lastly, the *braccianti* worked only 80 to 150 days a year—a fact which made their average daily income almost nothing. In the province of Forli, the actual earnings of a farm laborer were 1,297 lire a year, or 3 lire 55 a day.[25]

These wretched living conditions drove the rural proletariat to emigrate to the cities. But the fascist state was on the watch. Rural workers were forbidden to leave their villages and look for work elsewhere. "Domestic emigration" (this influx into the cities) was made impossible. Silone tells of the *carabinieri* forbidding "any workman to get aboard a train so as to go and work anywhere else."[26] The provincial governors, through legislation in 1928, were authorized to prevent the emigration of the rural population if they believed it advantageous to do so.[27] The laborers were herded back into the country without mercy.

To bind the rural proletariat more closely to the soil, fascism revived a particularly odious archaic custom, payment in kind— something that had always been the dearest desire of the landed proprietors.[28] The *bracciante*, according to the *Temps*, "with less cash at his disposal" would be "less eager to move about constantly."[29] He would be more firmly chained to his exploiter, for whom the system would be pure profit since he could dispose of his own products in the form of wages.

"Collective sharecropping," about which fascism has made a great noise, and which allegedly would "deproletarianize" (*sbracciantare*) the *braccianti*, was nothing but a revival of wages in kind. Instead of receiving daily wages, a certain number of farm laborers or families of workers "shared collectively" in the produce of the land. The "sharecroppers" therefore ceased to be wage-earners, though they did not become tenant farmers. The share-tenant had a right to half the crops, but the "collective sharecroppers" were entitled to only a third of them. And even this third was not guaranteed; it was set only as a "basis," and could vary according to the productivity and organization of the farms. The "sharecropper" could also be dismissed at any time by his landlord, like any wage-earner—in which case he would lose "all right to share in the proceeds no matter what the period of his previous employment in the enterprise."[30] In short, he was closely bound to his master, but the obligation was all on his side; he had all the duties and no rights.

In addition, the landowners set aside their worst land for "sharecropping," the hardest to cultivate, particularly that which had just been cleared.

In the spring of 1938, the fascist government devised a new form of slavery for the farm laborers: it sent them to till the soil of the big German landowners. Thirty thousand of them were thus conscripted, given a uniform and a police cap, and supplied with a "little guidebook for the agricultural worker abroad," in which they could read: *"Thanks to the regime, you are leaving in organized service, as an Italian, as a soldier in the great fascist army of labor. . . ."* In Germany, their wages were 7 lire 60 a day![31]

In Germany

After World War I, the farm laborers, particularly numerous in the Eastern provinces, began to achieve their emancipation. They flocked into the independent unions and won better working conditions and union contracts from the Junkers. But the victory of National Socialism reduced them again to the condition of serfs. Their unions, "coordinated" on May 2, 1933, along with all the other labor unions, were really dissolved in March, 1934, and they were forcibly regimented in the "Reich Food Supply Corporation," whose local section leaders were the Junkers themselves. In September, 1933, farm laborers were excluded from unemployment insurance. Feudal methods of exploitation reappeared: the Junkers once more subjected their serfs to severe disciplinary penalties, fines, and even corporal punishment. Although in theory the length of the workday—of the work year—was regulated, there were many deviations in practice, and overtime work was miserably paid.[32]

After May 1, 1934, when the law "for the regulation of national labor" went into effect, many union contracts were annulled or amended by the labor curators. Almost everywhere the latter sanctioned wage cuts as great as 25 percent.[33] Moreover they authorized the employers to deviate from the established rates,[34] and with their complicity many contracts, though still in effect on paper, were openly violated or evaded by the Junkers. The result was that the laborers' wages, already very low, went below the subsistence level. A Nazi functionary, Gutsmiedel, had to concede that "the wages and living conditions of the laborers are catastrophic," with wages often only equalling 50 to 70 percent of unemployment compensation for industrial workers.[35] "It is a secret to nobody," wrote the *Temps*, "that on the still numerous big estates in Germany, farm laborers are wretchedly paid."[36]

The Reich government did all it could to drive down agricultural wages. It handed over to the Junkers nearly half a million urban unemployed who were forced to work for almost nothing. We have seen that, by the decree of August 28, 1934, unmarried men under twenty-five lost their jobs in the cities. These were sent to the country as *agricultural helpers* and forced to toil like beasts of burden for the Junkers. The cash wages to which they were entitled, but the actual payment of which depended solely on the employer's pleasure, were much less than the unemployment allowances. The state also placed at the disposal of the Junkers members of the "labor service," as well as adolescents who, by the law of April 1, 1934, had to spend a "year on the land" after leaving school. The arrival of the Italian *braccianti* further depressed farm wages.

The conditions of the rural proletarians grew so bad that *even when they had work,* they left their villages and poured into the cities, hoping to find a less wretched existence. The authorities fought against this exodus, herding the farm workers back to the big estates, where they were again "more than ever at the mercy of the Junkers who exploit them."[37] The law of May 15, 1934, for instance, strictly prohibited urban businesses from hiring employees who had worked in agriculture during the preceding three years, and a decree of February 28, 1935, provided that farm workers to whom the previous law applied should be expelled from the cities immediately and sent back to the country on pain of criminal prosecution.

Likewise, to bind the rural proletariat more closely to the soil, the Nazis considered replacing cash wages with payments in kind. A Nazi functionary, Kraeutle, said that "labor must again be closely bound to the farm," and that "everywhere payments in kind must again be introduced."[38]

In the same way they tried to revive the archaic caste of the

Heuerlinge, which had survived in only a few regions. The *Heuerlinge* was an agricultural worker to whom the big landowner alloted a bit of land in return for a specified number of days of work on the master's land. For the leader of the peasantry of Oldenburg, extension of the *Heuerlinge* system was "the most efficacious way to stop the exodus from the land and attach the farm worker to the soil."[39]

3

The fascist state also helps the big landlords to make further extortions from their small tenant farmers and share-croppers.

In Italy

After 1922, farm rents increased by from 600 to 700 percent, an exorbitant rise which made it impossible for small tenants to continue as independent farmers and drove them back into the proletariat.[40]

The share-croppers, who had succeeded after the war in improving their contracts, now lost all they had gained. In the contract made in 1920 for the province of Bologna, for example, the tenant kept for himself from 60 to 70 percent of the crops. In the 1929 contract he received only half. In certain regions medieval clauses, presumably gone forever, reappeared. Such was the following section from the contract for the province of Taranto, made in 1935: "The share-cropper and members of his family will be respectful and obedient to the landlord. They promise to make bread, do the laundry, etc., as well as deliver wood, straw and other products to the landlord's house, either in the country or in the city. Furthermore, the share-cropper is absolutely forbidden to be on bad terms with his neighbors." A law of February 11, 1923, exempted landowners from levies for insurance and made the tenant farmers responsible. A decree of September 10, 1923, annulled the provision that kept landlords from putting share-croppers off their land without the sanction of a committee representing both parties. The landlords reassumed the right to impose fines on their tenants for trivial offenses.[41]

The share-croppers were regimented into the fascist Federation of Agriculture, which drew up the contracts imposed on them. The leaders of the Federation were either big landowners or their creatures. For instance, Prince Torlonia, a big landowner, was also a provincial president of the Federation, in which capacity he imposed a contract on the tenants that the *Lavoro Fascista* itself conceded "the most unscientific, uneconomic and unfair that could be imagined."[42]

It is significant that on one occasion, when Razza, president of the fascist Federation of Agricultural Workers, tried to bring the share-croppers into his organization, the big landowners vetoed the plan in the Senate. Not that Razza was moved by any philanthropic motives—the plebeian was only seeking to enlarge his own "social base"—but the share-croppers would have benefited by being grouped with the farm laborers—at least they might have gained a few rights. Instead, the fascists gave in to the landowners, and the text of the legislation finally adopted on share-cropper contracts provided no wage scale and none of the other safeguards customary in contracts for labor paid in cash wages.[43]

The fascist press does not conceal the harsh living conditions of the share-croppers, who make *even less than day laborers.* "Unfortunately," writes the economist Perdisa, "it is true that where the land is cultivated on shares, the income has fallen so low that the peasants are forced, in spite of their great attachment to the land, *to hire out as farm hands.*"[44]

In Germany

It is true that the Nazis have given the little tenant farmer a semblance of protection in the law of April 22, 1933. But in reality it is reduced to this: in case the landlord terminates the lease, the farmer can be evicted only at the end of the year. And even this provision does not apply if the farmer is behind in his rent payments. Moreover, the law of September 29, 1933, creating the "hereditary farms" dealt a harsh blow to the small tenants, for it specifically provided that rented farms cannot be declared "hereditary farms." Many Junkers and rich peasants hastened to terminate the leases on their farms in order to take advantage of this law.[45]

4

The fascist state gives the big landowners and well-to-do peasants all sorts of favors—tax exemptions, subsidies, debt relief, etc.—which scarcely benefit the little dirt farmer.

In Italy

Tax exemptions. The decree of January 4, 1923, based the agricultural income tax on the *net* income for the owner who does not farm his own land—that is, on his income after deducting wages paid—but based it on the *gross* income for the dirt farmer who is his own hired hand. As a result, the tax rate paid by the working-farmer is often higher than that paid by the big landlord (about 10 percent, as against 5 percent).

The law of January 7, 1923, provided for a general revision of land assessments. As this was carried out under the control of the big landowners, almost everywhere the dimensions recorded and values assessed for the enormous estates were ridiculously small. Thus the taxes of the big owners were greatly reduced in comparison with those of the little dirt farmers.[46] On top of that, through a decree of August 1, 1927, and a law of June 28, 1928, the fascist state granted the big owners all sorts of tax exemptions. According to statistics published in a fascist paper, the working-peasant in the plains regions paid an income tax of 240 lire a hectare, while the non-working landlord paid only 131.[47]

Subsidies for general land improvement. Under the law of December 24, 1928, providing for land improvement, the fascist state handed out enormous subsidies to the big landowners. The general land reclamation program properly speaking (reforestation, prevention of erosion, drainage, distribution of electrical power, communications, etc.) was almost entirely paid for by the state (its share was from 75 to 92 percent). Property improvements were subsidized by the state only to the extent of 33 percent of the cost, on the average, although the state might pay as much as 45 percent for the installation of electric power or even 75 percent for the construction of rural aqueducts. The fascist state on July 1, 1934, had already spent more than 4 billion lire towards a 7 billion work program.[48] The property owners contributed much less than this. Rosenstock-Franck points out that "a minority of big latifundists" dominated the land improvement consortiums.[49] The "general land improvement" has meant largely the improvement, at government expense, of big estates which formerly were cultivated only in part.

Subsidies for "The Battle of Wheat." The fascist state also favored the big landowners and rich peasants after 1925 by instituting a yearly "national contest" of wheat growers. The prize winners received big cash prizes. For instance, in 1932 the winner in the medium-sized farm classification received 38,000 lire.[50] In the 1937 contest the prizes amounted altogether to nearly 650,000 lire, and among the prize winners were 60 archbishops and bishops and more than 2,000 priests.[51] But only the great landowners and rich peasants in Italy grow wheat for the market; the working-peasants either produce only the wheat needed for their own consumption and are not in a position to obtain high yields, or else they devote themselves to other activities (stockraising, vine-growing, olive or mulberry growing, etc.). Hence the rewards in the "national contest" are not for them.

In Germany

Tax exemptions. The "hereditary farms" created by the law of September 29, 1933, were wholly exempt from the inheritance tax and the real estate tax. The law of September 21, 1933, granted large-scale farms a reduction in the tax on the total revenue from produce marketed. Another law, on October 16, 1934, altogether exempted from this tax the wholesale trade in agricultural products, a measure chiefly benefiting the big farms. The Junkers also profited from tax exemptions for the acquisition of new machinery, automobiles, construction of new buildings, etc. (Chapter 9). The working-peasants on the other hand, were burdened with new taxes. In 11,000 communes where it was not yet in effect, the poll tax—particularly unpopular in rural districts—was introduced. In addition the peasants had to pay all sorts of levies and taxes to the "Reich Food Supply Corporation," a costly bureaucratic body with a monopoly on marketing agricultural products.[52]

Moratorium. Through the law of February, 1933, the state applied to the entire Reich the moratorium on farm indebtedness instituted by Bruening for the Eastern provinces, and extended it until October 31, 1933, when it was again extended until December 31. On that date it was finally lifted. But in the meanwhile, the fortunate beneficiaries of the "hereditary farms" law had won permanent protection against forced sales, since their properties were declared exempt from seizure and inalienable. But soon the big banks protested against this all-too-convenient way of escaping the obligation of paying one's debts. By a law of December 1936 they won the concession that no "hereditary farm" could henceforth be established when the owner's debts exceeded 70 percent of the value of the farm. "In many cases," wrote the correspondent for the *Temps,* "peasants had their property declared 'hereditary farms' for the sole purpose of evading their creditors. The new regulations are primarily aimed at putting a stop to these abuses."[53] The most heavily indebted farmers were thus no longer protected.

Moreover, the law on hereditary farms did not apply to the great mass of working peasants. These were no longer covered by any moratorium. However, the government was obliged to grant them a few exemptions. For instance, they were temporarily allowed the benefit of another moratorium—that applying to non-agricultural real estate. But under the terms of this latter moratorium, forced sales were suspended only for a period of six months. Once this term expired, there was no further legal obstacle to the forced sale of debt-ridden farms. Certainly the Nazis tried to smooth the change-over, but gradually forced sales resumed. In the last four months of 1934 they increased 91.6 percent over the same period in 1933. In 1935 they were even greater, and they affected very small farms above all.

Debt reduction. The government of the Reich, by the law of June 1, 1933, reduced farm debts to two-thirds the "value" of the farm and lowered the interest rate to 4.5 percent. But this law applied chiefly to big and middle landowners because as a matter of fact the little peasant farmers were indebted not to the banks, but to artisans, tradesmen, relatives, village usurers, etc. Moreover the law based the "value" on the unit price of January, 1931, augmented, *in the case of small farms only,* by a high percentage. Since the indebtedness of small peasants to the banks rarely exceeded two-thirds of the value of their farms when thus calculated, the debt reduction law was of no use to them. In fact on June 1, 1934, a year after the law was promulgated, it had been applied to only 60,000 farms out of 5.5 million.

Subsidies in the Eastern provinces. To the Junkers and rich peasants the Nazi government continued to distribute *Osthilfe* credits (emergency subsidies to the Eastern provinces).[54] In December, 1932, before Hitler took power, out of 132 millions in credit distributed, 60 millions had been granted to farms of more than 100 hectares. Although the Nazis had demagogically denounced this scandal, once in power they made it even worse: by November 1, 1934, 213 million marks had been paid to farms of more than 125 hectares, 194 million to farms between 7.5 and 12.5 hectares and only 33.5 million marks to farms of less than 7.5 hectares.[55]

Subsidies for the "Production Campaign." In an attempt to make Germany self-sufficient in its food supply, the Nazis waged a noisy "production campaign" from the end of 1934 on, giving big subsidies for increased production. The law of April 1, 1935, appropriated 100 million marks in the 1935 budget to "encourage agriculture." Total credits of a billion marks were provided for the duration of the four-year plan, to be used for the improvement of the soil and farming methods. A subsidy of 100 marks per hectare was granted for transforming meadows into cultivated fields. All sorts of bonuses were instituted for increased production,[56] to encourage the growing of turnips, flax, hemp, etc. But these numerous subsidies went chiefly into the pockets of the big and medium-sized landowners, who alone were in a position to expand or undertake intensive production of the desired crops.[57]

5

The agricultural policy of fascism with regard to tariffs and prices favors the big landowners and rich farmers almost exclusively at the expense of the small peasants. In both Italy and Germany, in fact "the technical division of products corresponds to an economic and political division of property and classes."[58] The big landowners and rich farmers, because their holdings are larger and they can use scientific methods, have a monopoly in the production of grain. The small peasants, on the other hand, produce almost no grain for the market but devote themselves to other activities, such as stock raising, truck farming, etc. But fascism assures profitable prices almost solely to the grain growers. As a matter of fact, the industrialists are opposed to any increase in prices of agricultural products which could have an adverse effect on their own costs. Fascism avoids sacrificing agriculture to industry when the products of large scale farming are involved, but it is less ardent in the defense of other commodities, produced chiefly by small peasants. In short, it manages a compromise that safeguards the interests of both the big landowners and the industrialists, but that is paid for by the small peasants.

In Italy

The government's whole concern was for the grain growers. Tariffs on wheat were raised successively from 27.50 lire in July, 1925, to 40.40 in September, 1928, to 51.40 in May, 1929, to 60.60 in June, 1930, and to 75 in August, 1931.[*] This tariff protection insured the wheat growers artificially raised market prices, at the expense of the consumer. Professor Mortara has calculated that as of 1931 the tariff had cost the consumer one and a half billion lire. In addition, they were indirectly protected by a legal requirement that 95 per-

---

[*] For the purposes of comparison, the lira has been calculated here at the stabilization rate of 1927.

cent domestic wheat should be used in flour. Finally, to maintain the price, the state subjected the market to a number of regulations covering collective sales, storing of surpluses, and advances on harvests; for example, farm loan banks gave growers an advance of eighty lire for every quintal of wheat stored.

While this policy of protection and keeping up prices was very favorable to the big farmers, it was less advantageous for the middle peasantry. (As the little peasant does not produce grain for the market, he is not taken into account.) In the first place, some farm loan banks gave advances on stored wheat only for comparatively large quantities. Since the middle peasant had not such quantity to market, he could not benefit from these advances and was compelled to sell his wheat as soon as it was harvested, at a less favorable price. Secondly, after February, 1936, the peasant was no longer free to dispose of his own crop because he was compelled to deliver it to a state body and could keep only three quintals for his personal use. (Attempts are being made to reduce this to two quintals.)[59] Since the quantity allowed the peasant was insufficient for his needs, he was forced either to buy his bread for more than it would cost if he made it himself, or to increase his crop through great sacrifices. It was naturally much more difficult for him than for the large scale grower to do this.

Gaddi writes, "to increase wheat production in a country where the amount of uncultivated land is not great, it is necessary to basically transform agricultural economy . . . and reduce other more profitable crops. . . . The yield must be increased by greater use of machinery and chemical fertilizers and by investing more capital in the land . . . The average yield per hectare which formerly was ten or eleven quintals, has today reached thirteen quintals. This average, however, includes the average yield of eight quintals for the small farmers of Sardinia and an average yield from twenty-five to thirty quintals for the big capitalist landowners of Lombardy."[60]

The small producers of commodities other than grains were treated as poor relations. Industry had long shown itself hostile to general tariff protection for all farm products. When the world depression began, the prices of farm products without sufficient protection (particularly the products of stock and poultry raisers: meat, milk, butter, eggs, and cheese) collapsed, leaving no margin of profit. In 1933 milk brought no more than thirty or forty Italian centimes a litre.[61] Markets for agricultural products that were exported (wines, olives, raw silk) simply vanished. The devaluation of the lira in 1927 had already dealt them a harsh blow; the world crisis and Japanese competition (in the case of silk) deprived them of their remaining markets. "Italian agricultural exports are falling vertically."[62] A silk cocoon, for example, which in prosperous times sold for as much as 35 lire, was worth only 3.50 in 1933.[63]

Today the state fixes all prices, but the margin of profit for secondary farm products (particularly from cattle) is still insufficient. In addition, the government has placed enormous taxes on cattle and farm animals. The annual tax on a goat has been raised to twenty lire, with the result that goats declined from 3,100,000 head in 1926 to 1,795,000 in 1936.[64] In short, autarky is causing agricultural exports to lose their last markets.

The little peasants are literally ruined, "up to their ears" in debt.[65] At the end of 1934 the newspaper *Terra* estimated farm indebtedness at ten billion lire.

In Germany

Up to 1932 the governments of the Weimar republic protected almost exclusively the Junkers, the growers of wheat, and sacrificed the small peasants who went in chiefly for stock raising. The Nazis easily won over the small peasantry by promising them the same protection as the big grain growers. On first coming to power, they had to pretend to keep their promises. In his speech of March 23, 1933, to the Reichstag, Hitler proclaimed: "We must proceed to rescue the German peasant. . . . Without the counterbalance of the German peasant class, Bolshevist lunacy would have already submerged Germany. . . ." And he raised by from 300 to 500 percent the tariffs on the principal secondary products (eggs, cheese, meat, etc.).

But after this fine start, the agricultural policy of the Third Reich proved disastrous for the small and middle peasantry. By the laws of September 13 and 26, 1933, a state bureau was created, the Reich Food Supply Corporation, with a view to "fixing prices" of the principal farm products. Regulation was first applied to the production of wheat. "Our aim," said Walter Darre, "is to arrive at a fair price for every farm product and first of all for grains." A ton of rye, worth RM 152 in Berlin in January, 1932, rose to 172 in May, 1935; a ton of wheat rose from 185 to 212. This policy of price fixing almost exclusively favored the Junkers and rich farmers. It favored much less the middle peasants. The small peasant, not producing wheat for the market, is not concerned here at all.

Firstly, the "fixed prices" for grains were determined for each month of the year, on a sliding scale: the longer after harvest, the higher the price. But, as the middle peasant was not in a position to store his produce, he had to sell his crop as soon as harvested, and at the lowest price. Moreover, the "fixed prices" were good only for a certain minimum quantity (for example, a full carload, fifteen metric tons), and the middle peasant, being unable to supply that much at one time, had to accept less favorable prices.

Secondly, the peasant after June, 1934, was *forced to deliver* his crop to the "Reich Food Supply Corporation." Out of the 1934, 1935, and 1936 harvests he was allowed a fixed (and insufficient) quantity for his own consumption. An ordinance of July 22, 1937, however, compelled him to turn over *all* grain suitable for bread-making that he harvested, and extremely severe penalties (fines up to 100,000 marks and prison sentences) awaited him if he tried to evade the law. Hence, for him, the advantages of the "fixed prices" were more than offset by his inability to use his own produce for his family and for feeding his stock (see below).

In May, 1934, the "fixed price" system was also applied to the products of stock raising. However, the situation of the little cattle raiser—that is, of the great majority of small German peasants—was not bettered—quite the contrary.

Firstly, the cattle and milk bureaus, etc., were much less anxious to raise the market value of the products for which they had a monopoly than to check their rise. Because these products figure so largely in the budget of industrial workers, capitalist circles were exercising a strong pressure to keep them from rising so high as to force wage increases. As a result, the price index of dairy products is 10 percent below the prewar level, while that of grains is 15 percent over.[66]

Secondly, the dairy farmer could no longer freely dispose of his products and take them directly to the market. Before the advent of National Socialism he generally made his own butter and cheese and sold them directly to the consumer. Now he no longer had the right to turn his own milk into butter and cheese but was compelled to deliver fixed quantities of milk to the monopoly organization, and the prices he received were very low. For instance, a Silesian peasant who used to sell his milk directly to his customers for twenty-two pfennigs a liter, now gets no more than fourteen pfennigs, out of which he must turn over two pfennigs as a commission towards the administrative expense of the bureau. The same milk is sold in the city through the bureau for twenty-four pfennigs.[67]

The result was that the peasants refused to turn over their milk. So stubborn was their resistance that in December, 1935, Goering ordered the *Gestapo* to proceed vigorously against the recalcitrants. "Sabotage of milk deliveries by farmers," stated an official communique, "is an act of treason against the people of the nation. Anybody displaying passive or open resistance is committing a crime against the national community."[68]

Thirdly, small cattle raisers suffered from the dizzy rise in the price of feed for their livestock, which they seldom grew themselves. In Germany, in fact, the big landowners are almost the only ones producing feed grains: small cattle raisers, not producing them themselves, have to purchase them on the market. Because German production of feed crops was short about 1.5 million metric tons a year—that is, between 25 and 30 percent of the requirements[69]—the government in 1933 raised the tariffs on imported feeds to prohibitive rates both to encourage their cultivation and to economize on the foreign exchange at its disposal. Feed soon became very expensive, and prices went even higher when the 1934 harvest turned out to be unusually poor. This was fine business for the Junkers, who raised feed, but disastrous for the little cattle and poultry raisers whose stock consumed it. Unable to procure the necessary feed at prohibitive prices, the latter had to slaughter their stock and give up poultry raising. The result was a noticeable falling off in their production of milk, butter, eggs, and later, meat (particularly pork)—in a word, in their income.

Those farmers who also produced wheat or rye could resort at least to feeding these grains to their stock. But the ordinance of July 22, 1937, strictly forbade the feeding of any grains that could be made into bread, under the same severe penalties noted above. Almost simultaneously it was announced that because of a lack of foreign exchange, it would no longer be possible to import sufficient foreign feeds such as barley and maize to replace the rye forbidden to animals![70]

To these various causes of discontent, was added the severe strain which the execution of the "four-year plan" put on the German peasantry. The farmers were incessantly appealed to and harassed. They were ordered to put more land into cultivation, increase their yield, or raise some new crop or other. They were constantly under suspicion. For example, the decree of March 23, 1937, provided that in case a farm was not cultivated in such a way as to contribute what it should to feeding the German people, the authorities concerned could intervene, either by warning the farmer or ordering him to carry on cultivation in line with the needs of the national food supply. Furthermore, the management of the farm could be placed under the control of a commissioner, or the farmer be forced to rent his land or entrust its cultivation to an experienced person.[71]

German soil, however, is not very fertile; to increase its yield or put the poor land into cultivation is very costly. In spite of the subsidies distributed by the Reich, in spite of the 30 percent cut in the price of nitrate fertilizers and the 25 percent cut in potash ordered in the decree of March 23, 1937, the effort demanded of German agriculture was increasingly burdensome, especially for the small and middle peasantry. A secretary in the Ministry of Agriculture, Backe, had to admit in an article that the value of agricultural production in 1937 had increased only 163 million marks, while farming expenses had increased 335 millions. Costs were devouring profits.[72]

"Among the farmers," the German correspondent of the *Petit Parisien* wrote, "there is a growing lack of interest in their daily work since Nazism completely rewrote agricultural legislation. It is very doubtful that the German peasants feel much enthusiasm for the new order. All official publications and speeches end with pathetic appeals to farming circles, to their spirit of sacrifice, even of abnegation. These appeals . . . are not unnecessary."[73]

6

Fascism not merely increases the profits of the big landowners and rich peasants; it often opens new rural outlets for industrial and finance capitalism—already bound to landed property by a close community of interests. To win over the small peasants, the fascist demagogues promised to free them from exploitation by the banks, the big agricultural machinery trusts, the fertilizer trusts and the power trusts; they promised to emancipate them from the big speculators and middlemen with a monopoly on farm products, who buy cheap from the producers and sell dear to the city consumers. But once in power, the fascists do exactly the opposite and aid in every way capitalism's penetration into agriculture.

In Italy

Fascism's agricultural policy ("land improvement," "the Battle of Wheat," and tariff protection for wheat) resulted both in raising the profits of the big landowners and rich peasants and in giving industrial and finance capital new rural outlets. Rural electrification enriched the big power trusts; intensified cultivation brought the big machinery consortiums large orders for farm machinery; and the manufacturers of fertilizers also profited greatly from "the Battle of Wheat." "Italians go around whispering," said Rosenstock-Franck, *"that the Montecatini Co. was the victor in the wheat battle."*[74] At the beginning of 1938 a financial journal reported that the position of *Montecatini* was still splendid (there was talk of a dividend of eleven or twelve lire instead of ten), "if only because of the increased sales of fertilizers, especially nitrates, of which five million quintals were produced for the 1937–38 campaign instead of the three millions produced formerly."[75]

In Germany

The agricultural policy of the Nazis enriched the big landowners and also the big capitalist dealers in agricultural products—the food wholesalers, the farm machinery and fertilizer trusts. "The Hitler government," according to Steinberger, "surrounded agriculture with a practically closed circle of cartellized industries, which made the peasants' markets and production strictly dependent on both trade monopolies and industrial cartels."[76] One of the primary functions of the "Food Supply Corporation" was to assure capitalist middlemen more extensive production and markets, *by forcing the small producer out of the market.* We have seen how this occurred in the case of milk. But it should be pointed out that the profit resulting from the spread between the price the peasant received and what the consumer paid was not pocketed by the Food Supply Corporation, which acted only as agent, but by the big capitalist or cooperative dairies. (The latter were generally managed and financed by the Junkers.) Another example was in the sugar refining industry, where a decree of November, 1934, assigned each peasant grower of beet sugar to a specific refinery, to which he was bound for life. These refineries bought beets from the peasants at ridiculously low prices and sold sugar to the consumers at an enormous profit.

The agricultural policy of Nazism opened new markets in the countryside for the big industrial cartels which produced fertilizer and farm machinery. Gone are the days when the Nazis promised the peasant liberation from the capitalist yoke. In one of his speeches, Dr. Schacht glorified the mechanization of agriculture, so profitable to big industry: "We must not forget that products of capitalist industry, such as harvesting machines and tractor plows, are indispensable for an agriculture proposing to feed sixty-five million people. An agricultural policy that would prevent progress in this field could not win the 'battle of production' or serve the interests of the people."[77]

Conclusion:
Some illusions that must be dispelled

We hope that this study has thrown a little light on the real nature of fascism. In the preceding chapters, we have tried to correct many erroneous opinions regarding the subject. In conclusion, a few particularly dangerous illusions remain to be dispelled.

1

One of these illusions consists in regarding fascism, despite the horror it inspires, as a *progressive* political phenomenon, as a *passing* and even *necessary,* though painful, stage. Rash prophets have announced ten times, a hundred times, the imminent and inevitable crumbling of the fascist dictatorship in Italy or Germany under the blows of the victorious revolution. They have asserted that fascism, by driving class antagonisms to their highest degree of tension, is hastening the hour of the proletarian revolution, or even, as one Stalinist with a dry sense of humor would suggest, that the "proletariat could conquer power only by passing through the hell of the fascist dictatorship."[1]

However, events have demonstrated with tragic clearness that the moment the working class allows the fascist wave to sweep over it, a long period of slavery and impotence begins—a long period during which socialist, and even democratic ideas are not merely erased from the base of public monuments and libraries, but, what is more serious, are *rooted out of human brains*. Events have proven that fascism physically destroys everything opposing its dictatorship, no matter how mildly, and that it creates a vacuum around itself and leaves a vacuum behind it.

This extraordinary *power to survive* by annihilating everything except itself, to hold out against everything and everybody, to hold out for years in spite of internal contradictions and in spite of the misery and discontent of the masses—what is behind it?

The strength of the dictatorship rests first of all in its extreme centralization. Such a regime, observes a French newspaper, cannot "by its very nature endure the slightest trace of federalism or autonomy. Like the Convention, like Napoleon, it must seek complete centralism, the logical consequence of its system and the necessary means to insure its permanence."[2] Mussolini and Hitler strengthen, to the utmost, the authority of the central government and suppress even the faintest trace of individualism. In Italy the powers of the provincial governors have been considerably increased. "It must be clear," a communication from the Duce informs them, "that authority cannot be divided. . . . Authority is single and unified. If it were not, we should fall back to a disorganized state."[3]

In Germany the seventeen "states," whose rights to their own governments and parliaments were preserved by the Weimar Constitution, have been gradually suppressed and transformed into mere provinces of the Reich, directly administered by representatives of the central government, the *Statthalter*. Extolling his centralizing work, Hitler boasts of having "given the people the constitution that will make them strong."[4]

Marx in his time was able to rejoice because the executive power, while becoming ever more concentrated, simultaneously concentrated against itself all the forces of destruction.[5] And certain of our contemporaries, such as Edouard Berth, with a somewhat too simple conception of the dialectic, imagine that by centralizing to the utmost, fascism is working automatically for the revolution.[6] But fascism, at the same time that it centralizes, *destroys in the most radical fashion the "forces of destruction" themselves.*

Fascism, in fact, has brought the methods of police repression used in modern states to the highest degree of perfection. It has made the political police a truly scientific organization. The Italian *Ovra*, the German *Gestapo*—real "states within the state," with tentacles extending into all classes of society and even into every dwelling house, with enormous financial and material resources, and with limitless powers—are in a position literally to annihilate at birth every attempt at opposition wherever it appears. They can arrest anyone they wish at any time, "put him away" on a remote island or in a concentration camp, even execute him without a semblance of a trial.

One could call such a regime a "smooth block of granite where no hand may find a hold."* The *Temps* correspondent was at least partly right when he wrote of Italy: "Opposition has completely disappeared. . . . With the system of the totalitarian state, no hostile propaganda is possible."[7] And Goebbels, too, when he asserts: "The enemies of the regime are completely put down; there is no longer any opposition worthy of the name in the whole country."[8]

Added to these methods of police repression is the state of "forced disunity, dispersion, and helplessness" in which fascism keeps the working class.[9] Certainly, it has not succeeded in suppressing the class struggle, a sociological phenomenon which it is granted to no regime, however perfected, to stamp out. The class struggle continues underground. If it is not recognizable at first glance, this is because it takes forms somewhat different from those we are used to. It is manifested, for instance, through the demagogy of the plebeians in the "fascisized" or *"gleichgeschaltet"* unions, etc., etc. Cer-

---

* The metaphor was brought up by Elie Halevy in a newspaper article. It was related to me, but I have not been able to locate the exact reference.

tainly, neither in Italy nor Germany can the regime boast of having all the proletariat with it; quite the contrary. Mussolini himself is forced to confess: "I cannot say that I have all the workers [with me]. . . . They are perpetual malcontents."[10] In Germany the elections to the factory "confidential councils" have twice (April 1934 and April 1935) constituted a stinging defeat for the regime.

According to the later admission of Dr. Ley himself, scarcely 40 percent of the electors voted in 1934.[11] In 1935 at least 30 percent of the electors abstained or voted against.[12] In 1936, 1937, and 1938, the elections were "postponed" as a precautionary measure, and in June, 1938, it was decided that the "confidential men" would no longer be "elected" but appointed by the head of the company.

This latent discontent, however, finds it almost impossible to express itself or to organize. The working class is atomized and disintegrated. It is true that protest movements have appeared here and there, but they are stifled immediately. They are restricted to isolated plants and known to few workers outside the plants where they occur; in each factory, the workers believe they are alone in their resistance. Not only are the ties broken between the workers in different factories, but even inside large enterprises contacts no longer exist between employees of the various departments, and it is very difficult to reestablish them.[13] Even when the embryos of illegal unions are formed with heroic effort, they are almost always nipped in the bud.[14]

No doubt there are militant Socialists and Communists who distribute illegal leaflets at the peril of their lives, but they are only a heroic and constantly decimated phalanx. The workers lose their passivity only when an event *abroad* reveals to them that they are not alone, that beyond the frontiers other workers are struggling. . . . Thus the great strikes of June 1936 in France, in spite of the care of the fascist press to minimize their importance, had a profound echo among the workers of Italy and Germany. On April 18, 1937, Rudolf Hess made a violent anticommunist speech at Karlsruhe, which the Berlin correspondent of *Information* commented on as follows: "Inside Germany this speech tends to put a stop to the discussions

which have arisen among the popular masses of the Reich, despite
the censorship, as a result of the promulgation of the forty-hour
week law and new social laws by the Blum cabinet."[15]

And while fascism puts its adult opponents in a position where they
can do no harm, it imposes its imprint on the young and shapes
them in its own mold. "The generation of the irreconcilables will
be eliminated by natural laws," Mussolini exults. "Soon the younger
generation will come!"[16] Volpe speaks lustingly of the "virgin material which has not yet been touched by the old ideologies."[17] "Our
future is represented by the German youth," Hitler declares. "We
will raise it in our own spirit. If the older generation cannot become accustomed to it, we will take their children from them. . . ."[18]
"We want to inculcate our principles in the children from their most
tender years."[19]

And Goebbels asserts that as long as the youth are behind Hitler,
the regime will be *indestructible*.[20] At the age of four in Germany,
and at six in Italy, the child is taken from his family, enrolled in the
militarized formations of fascism, and subjected to an intensive
stuffing with propaganda. The dictatorial state puts in his hands a
single newspaper, a single textbook, and educates him in an incredible atmosphere of exaltation and fanaticism.

This training accomplishes its aim. In Italy the results were tangible: "The youth can no longer even conceive of socialist or communist ideas," Gentizon writes.[21] A militant worker, Feroci, con-
firms this: "A youth that has never read a labor paper, never attended
a labor meeting, and knows nothing of socialism and communism
. . . that is . . . what makes for the real strength of Mussolini's regime."[22] In Germany the results were even worse.*

Doubtless there is something fascist education cannot stifle, and
which does not need to be taught—the class instinct. No amount
of propaganda will ever prevent the young worker from feeling he

---

* Cf. the admirable novel by Stuard Engstrand, *Printemps Norvegien 1940 (Nor-
wegian Spring 1940)*, which appeared in London in 1944 in French.

is exploited. Pietro Nenni, while far from claiming that the Black Shirt youth has already succeeded in freeing itself from the fascist grip, states that in Italy "many young people are socialists without knowing it and without wanting to be."[23] *Il Maglio,* the weekly paper of the fascist unionists of Turin, complains that among the youth there is a certain lack of understanding of fascist "unionism." "It is natural that there should be a few young people who, while recognizing that the abolition of all forms of class struggle is an absolute necessity . . . still believe that labor's material interests can better be assured by strikes and the methods of struggle used up until yesterday in labor conflicts. . . ."[24]

In Germany as well, countless young people who believed literally that the Third Reich would be *their state* and who saw instead the consolidation of all the old capitalist exploitation, were bitterly disappointed. But it is extremely difficult for the youth in either country, in view of the mental training they are given, to get rid of the false ideas with which they are indoctrinated, to clarify their revolt, and without guidance, to do for themselves the work of a century of socialist action and thought. The confused awakening of their class consciousness leads some of them to the "left wing" of fascism or National Socialism; it does not make them into militant revolutionists.

Of course their families can, to a certain extent, combat in the home the influence of the fascist educators. But the state is on the watch; during all his leisure hours, the child is taken out of his home and systematically incited against "adults" in general and his parents in particular. Very often a tragic conflict divides the two generations—the old which has remained faithful at heart to socialist ideas, and the new which rebels against the old and treats it as an enemy.

(Addition to the 1964 Edition)
[Moreover, with consummate skill fascism in power follows a policy which, for lack of a better term, I will call "dust in the eyes." This consists of disguising or blurring its real countenance, to some

degree, in the eyes of a quite large section of the popular masses.

In the first editions of this book, preoccupied above all with exposing the vile acts of fascism, I neglected to mention these various types of window-dressing. In the light of hindsight, I feel that this underestimation must be rectified, for these devices played a substantial role in the surprising staying power of that monstrous regime.

Among the expedients which assured fascism a certain amount of popularity, some have already been analysed in the chapter devoted to the "Fascist Mystique," and it would be useless to review them here.

But there are others, not "idealist," but rather *material*, which permitted Hitler's and Mussolini's regimes to lure the masses, who were otherwise aloof, if not outright hostile. These were:

1. The massive reabsorption of the unemployed by big and indisputably useful public works, particularly the motor highways, and, above all, armaments manufacture.

2. The dictatorial control of capital export and price levels—techniques all the more remarkable considering that the "left" governments, of the Popular Front type, have shown themselves incapable of putting them into practice.

3. Above all, the gigantic "social welfare projects," often quite well equipped and organized, providing collective recreation for the workers. (*Dopalavoro, Kraft durch Freude*).

The fearsome police methods forged by fascism certainly worked strongly for its survival. But it would be an error to consider it a completely unpopular regime, maintaining itself in power only by terror. Certainly it bends the masses under its yoke, but it likewise wrings from them a measure of support.]
(End of the Addition to the 1964 Edition.)

2

Another illusion about the duration of fascism must be dispelled. Certain people try to deduce from the economic and political contradictions which have developed in the fascist regime that the days of the dictatorship are numbered. One fact is undeniable: the men of wealth who financed fascism and brought it to power were not satisfied with their creation.

In the first place the regime is terribly expensive. The maintenance of the excessive state bureaucracy, the party, and the numerous semigovernmental bodies often with overlapping functions costs unheard-of sums and adds to the financial difficulties of the government. "All the chief administrative bodies of the state," the Berlin correspondent of *Temps* has observed, "are duplicated, so to speak, by the organs of the National Socialist Party. . . . The party penetrates into the Ministries, but it also preserves, on the fringes of the traditional administrative bodies, its own organs. . . ."[25]

In their memorandum of June 1937 to Hitler, the industrialists wrote: "It used to be estimated that there was one functionary for every twelve persons in productive occupations. Today if the official party organizations and the semi-official and corporative services, with their functionaries and employees, are included, *it is estimated that there is one person on the state payroll for every eight persons in productive occupations.*" Abandoning any attempt to "estimate the amount of personal and material expenses required by the administrative machine," the authors of the memorandum complained of the "incalculable losses arising from a lack of contact between the old and the new authorities, and the overlapping of functions between the old and new state services and the party."[26]

For their part, the big industrialists also have to directly meet a certain number of incidental expenses: "voluntary contributions" extorted by the party and its "welfare" undertakings, various subscriptions, "graft," and seats on the board of directors of the big companies for the "upper crust" of the fascist leaders, etc. But this burdensome parasitism, the importance of which must not be exaggerated, is less annoying to big business than the demogogic agitation indulged in by the fascist plebeians which, despite purges and repressions, never entirely ceases.

Moreover, while big business approves of an aggressive foreign policy that brings it new armaments orders, it is afraid lest the fascist leaders, in seeking a diversion from the wretchedness of the people, provoke a premature war which will result in the isolation of the country and its defeat. It is especially significant that in the autumn of 1935 it was the fascist leaders Farinacci, Rossoni, and others, who urged Mussolini into conflict with England, while the big bourgeoisie, the General Staff, and the Crown, on the other hand, advised moderation and caution. Likewise in Germany, when Hitler decided in March 1937 to remilitarize the Rhineland, it was the Nazi top bureaucracy—Goering, Goebbels, and others—who urged him on to the adventure while the big capitalists and their representative, Dr. Schacht, as well as the Reichswehr generals, were wary, not of the act itself, but of the rash form it took.[27]

At the end of December of the same year, General von Fritsch pointed out that neither the Reich nor the German army could undertake any action that might lead to war in a short time, and he went so far as to threaten to resign his command if his expert advice was disregarded.[28] We have since learned that on the eve of the Second World War the majority of generals desperately, but in vain, warned Hitler against the risks of that military adventure.

Neither does big business look without a certain amount of anxiety on the symptoms of "delusions of grandeur" displayed ever more obviously by the dictator. This development is really inevitable, for in proportion to the elimination of the plebeians and the relegation of the party to a secondary position, it is necessary to inflate the "Man of Destiny" all the more to conceal behind his person the real nature of the fascist state: a military and police dictatorship in the service of big business. It was necessary to follow Spengler's advice: "Nothing has meaning anymore but the purely personal power exercised by the Caesar [in whom] the omnipotence of money disappears."[29] Thus in Italy, the dictatorship of the fascist party gradually gave place to the personal dictatorship of the Duce. In Germany, during the last election campaigns, "there [was] very little question of National Socialism and much—to the exclusion of almost everything else—of Herr Hitler."[30] But the dictator himself is taken in by this booby-trap. The same mishap befalls him as befell Louis Bonaparte: "Only . . . when he himself now takes his imperial role seriously . . . does he become the victim of his own conception of the world, the serious buffoon, who no longer takes world history for a comedy, but his comedy for world history."[31] Mussolini and Hitler end by literally becoming egomaniacs. And the big capitalists must increasingly reckon with the boundless pride, the changing humor and whims of the Duce or the Fuehrer.

And finally, the economic policy of fascism, however favorable it may be, is not entirely satisfactory to its former underwriters. Although they eagerly pocket the fabulous profits from armaments orders, they are terrified at the possible consequences of this policy. They are haunted by the thought of a financial catastrophe that would spark a middle-class uprising against them. They also reproach the fascist government for increasing its expenses at an "imprudent" pace. They also fearfully note that the "war economy" regime is constantly imposing more burdensome state regulations on them, that it is forever eating away at sacrosanct "private initiative."

Therefore the industrialists are not wholly content, and in the minds of some of them the idea begins to germinate of throwing overboard once and for all the fascist plebeians and *their leader himself,* and of completing the already far-advanced transformation of the fascist totalitarian regime into a purely military dictatorship.

But they have second thoughts. They dare not deprive themselves entirely of the incomparable and irreplaceable means of penetrating into all the cells of society which they have in the fascist mass organizations. Above all, they hesitate to deprive themselves of the services of the "Man of Destiny," for the mystic faith in the Duce or the Fuehrer, though declining, is not yet extinct. "The present order in Germany," the *Temps* states, "exists and continues only thanks to the popularity of the Chancellor and the faith of the German masses in Herr Hitler's actions. . . ."[32] "The Fuehrer is unquestionably more popular than the regime."[33] The "Man of Destiny," however much of a nuisance he may be, is still necessary. Even his madness is useful; he alone can still perform the psychological miracle of turning the discontent and wretchedness of large strata of the people into enthusiasm and faith.

But most of all, the industrialists are apprehensive lest a radical change in the regime, such as they desire, should cost much bloodshed. They dread a civil war, even a short one, in which "national" forces would oppose one another: they fear nothing so much as what in Germany was called in anticipation, a "new June 30." Therefore the bourgeoisie hesitates. But one cannot entirely discard the hypothesis that one day the advantages of a "strong state" without a Mussolini or a Hitler, would seem to them to outweigh the disadvantages.*

3

If fascism is not progressive *politically*, it is no more so *economically*—notwithstanding what certain people think. Stripped of all appearances, all the contradictions which dim its real face, all the secondary aspects which hide its essential character from so many, and all the circumstances peculiar to any one country, fascism is reduced to this: a strong state intended to artificially prolong an economic system based on profit and the private ownership of the means of production. To use Radek's picturesque figure of speech, fascist dictatorship is *the iron hoop with which the bourgeoisie tries to patch up the broken barrel of capitalism.*[34] Here some clarification, however, is necessary: the "barrel," contrary to what many believe, was not broken by the revolutionary action of the working class; fascism is not the bourgeoisie's answer to an attack by the proletariat but rather "an expression of the decay of capitalist economy."[35] The barrel fell apart of its own accord.

Fascism is, to be sure, a defensive reaction of the bourgeoisie, but a defense against the disintegration of its own system far more than against any nearly nonexistent proletarian offensive. The working class, in fact, paralyzed by its organizations and its leaders in the hour of the decay of capitalist economy, did not know how to take

---

* See the preface to the edition of March, 1945.

power and install socialism in place of an economic system whose very defenders admit is gravely wounded and failing fast.

As to the nature of the crisis, fascism itself has no illusions. "The crisis," Mussolini admits, "has penetrated the system so deeply that it has become a systemic crisis. It is no longer a wound, but a chronic disease. . . ."[36] In spite of the fact that fascism demagogically promises the reabsorption of unemployment and the resumption of business, it is in fact less ambitious. It merely tries to check, through artificial means, the fall in the profits of a private capitalism which has become parasitic. In spite of its verbose demagogy, it has no great designs; it lives from week to week; it aspires to nothing more than to keep a handful of monopolists and big landowners alive through wage cuts, state orders and subsidies, seizure of small savings, and autarky. And in order to prolong the reign of this oligarchy, at the price of a restriction of free enterprise, it hastens the ruin of all other layers of the population—wage earners, consumers, savers, working farmers, artisans, and even industrialists manufacturing consumer goods.

Those naive people who, outside Italy and Germany, fall into the trap of fascist demagogic lies, and go around saying that fascism is a "revolution," that fascism has "gone beyond" capitalism, are advised to study the following letter from a worker published by the Nazi daily, the *Voelkischer Beobachter:*

> Nobody concerned with economic questions will believe the capitalist system has disappeared. Although it is true that methods of public financing have assumed a different character—a character of coercion—capital, or at least what is generally understood by this word, has never been so powerful and privileged as at the present time. . . . The economy accumulates enormous profits and reserves; the workers are invited to wait, and to console themselves while waiting by undergoing a whole series of preliminary conditions. The big ones make profits, and the little ones receive drafts on the future. If that isn't capitalism in the specific sense of the word, I would like to know what capitalism

means. . . . One group is making immense profits at the expense of the rest of the population. That is what used to be called capitalist exploitation. . . .[37]

"This isn't National Socialism: this is simply capitalism," another correspondent wrote to the *Voelkischer Beobachter* on June 13. And the official organ of the Nazi party cynically replied that if the government had wanted to divide among the workers the two billion or so of big business's increased profit, it would have placed itself *"in flagrant opposition to the economy."*[38]

Economically, then, fascism is in no way "progressive." It does not "go beyond" capitalism, but, on the contrary, is a form of what Lenin called *capitalism in decay.*[39] Fascism uses every possible means of "dragging out" the process of decomposition.[40] It nurses the abscess instead of opening it with the surgeon's knife. Far from leading to socialism—namely the collective ownership of the means of production—it devotes all its energy and resources to blocking the spontaneous movement which tends, as the crisis is prolonged, to bring private economy into the hands of the state. It intensifies to the utmost the conflict between the social character of production and the private ownership of the means of production. While it could socialize, without striking a blow, whole sectors of the economy, it respects and shores up private capitalism as far as it can. It does not lead to socialism even by a roundabout road; it is the supreme obstacle to socialism.

4

Moreover, on the international plane, fascism merely aggravates the tendency of the whole capitalist system to national isolation and autarky. By detaching the economy from the international division of labor, by adapting the "productive forces to the Procrustean bed of the national state," fascism brings, "chaos into world relations." For the future work of socialist planning, it creates "colossal additional difficulties."[41]

At the same time fascism aggravates and brings to their highest degree of tension the contradictions resulting from the uneven development of the capitalist system, and thus hastens the hour of a new division of the world by force of arms—the hour of that "relapse into barbarism" which Rosa Luxemburg foresaw in case the proletariat should be slow to fulfill its class duty and achieve socialism.[42]

Nevertheless, it is not correct to say that *fascism means war.* Bela Kun not long ago attacked this self-interested lie: "The slogan that fascism, which is *one* of the political forms of bourgeois rule . . . means war, is designed . . . only to free again and always from all responsibility one of the groups of imperialist powers that mask their war preparations under democratic forms and pacifist phrases. . . . The old slogan of Marxist anti-militarism—that of the revolutionary struggle against imperialist war—was differently expressed: *capitalism means war.*"[43] War is the product of the capitalist system as a whole. Tomorrow's war will not find the *democracies* opposing the *dictatorships.* Behind ideological pretexts, imperialist realities are concealed. Tomorrow's war will find the *satisfied* nations, who long ago got their "places in the sun" and divided the planet among themselves through blood and iron, opposing the *hungry* nations—the late-comers who also demand their share in the feast, if need be through blood and iron. One group is ready to make war to force a new division of the world; the other is ready to make war to prevent this division. This is an elementary truth that can never be repeated too often in these troubled times when, for many people, anti-fascism has become synonymous with *chauvinism.* Fascism must be fought not from the outside by imperialist war but from within by proletarian class struggle. There is only one way to hasten the fall of Mussolini and Hitler: that is to encourage the Italian and German workers to fight at home. And how can they be encouraged? By example! By fighting in our own countries!

5

There would be a final illusion to be dispelled if the triumph of National Socialism in Germany had not dealt it the death blow: the illusion that fascism is a *local* phenomenon, a "specifically Italian" phenomenon, or one "peculiar to backward and predominantly agricultural countries," to which the great industrial nations, the "great Western democracies," are immune.

The time is gone when the Italian don Sturzo could write that "in England, France, *and Germany,* there is a strong 'political class' equal to its task. . . . " and that we shall undoubtedly never see "a March on London, Paris, *or Berlin*";[44] or when Nitti could seriously assert: "Any fascist enterprise in the countries which have reached a high degree of economic civilization would only be a vain experiment. . . . *In Germany the democratic parties and the republic are solidly established.*"[45]

The time is gone, too, when the German Social Democrats could write: "Fascism, in its Italian form, corresponds to Italian conditions. The organized strength and highly developed political education of the German working class, as well as the relative weakness of the non-proletarian masses in Germany in comparison with Italy, make such a brutal crushing of democracy impossible in our country . . .";[46] or when the Bolshevik Martinov could say: "Fascism of the pure type will be our chief enemy only in backward and semi-agricultural countries."[47]

In Italy as in Germany, fascism was rather the specific product of the most advanced form of capitalism—monopolistic heavy industry. However, in these two countries certain special causes accelerated its development; in particular, the fact that after the First World War, these two countries found themselves in the position of "proletarian" nations, vis-a-vis the wealthy countries. This had the following results: on the one hand they had to struggle with acute economic difficulties much sooner than the more favored industrial powers; on the other hand it was much easier to graft nationalism onto the concept of social reform and thus stir the fanaticism of the popular masses.

It is not at all an excluded possibility that the same profound causes that drove the Italian and German industrialists to finance fascist gangs, and then to bring fascism to power, may produce the same effects elsewhere. Here and there in the world, the trusts entrust to the "strengthened state," if not the "strong state," the task of restoring their profits. We observe the progressive erosion of the "democratic" institutions and the spread of a masked fascism.

As for an open fascist dictatorship, however, the bourgeoisie, wiser by the precedents of Italy and Germany, is hesitant to take such a step. But can we say for sure that they have renounced it? It would, without a doubt, be both more prudent and more precise to assume that the bourgeoisie is holding this ultimate trump card in reserve.

<h1 style="text-align:center">6</h1>

In every way, the lesson of the Italian and German tragedies is that fascism is in no way foredoomed. The socialist movement could have, and should have, exorcized it if it could have torn itself out of its paralysis and impotence; if it had outstripped its adversary; if it had beaten fascism out in winning, or at least neutralizing, the impoverished middle classes; and if it had seized power before fascism—not in order to prolong the capitalist system for better or worse (as too many governments brought to power by the working class have done), but to put the financial backers of fascism (the heavy industrialists and the big landowners) out of action: in a word, if they proceeded to the socialization of the key industries and the confiscation of big land-holdings. In conclusion, any antifascism is a frail illusion if it confines itself to defensive measures and does not aim at smashing capitalism itself.

But such is not the perspective of "popular fronts." Their hucksters cling to the rotten plank of bourgeois "democracy" and turn their infantile smiles towards the "less reactionary" capitalist groups, to save themselves from the "more reactionary." They await salvation from a Giolitti or a Bruening, who will deliver them in the end, bound hand and foot, to a Hitler or a Mussolini. If they have a weakness for suicide, it's their business. But others, who wish to live, have already chosen between fascism and socialism.

REFERENCES

Preface to 1965 edition
1. Trotsky, *Against National Communism! (Lessons of the "Red Referendum")*, *Workers' Control of Production*, *The Turn in the Communist International and the Situation in Germany*, *The Only Road*, *What Next?*, *Bonapartism and Fascism* (all reprinted in *The Struggle Against Fascism in Germany*), *Whither France*, *The Soviet Union and the Fourth International*.

Foreword
1. The quotation from Clara Zetkin is taken from a report she made to the plenary session of the Executive Committee of the Communist International in Moscow, June, 1923.

Chapter 1
1. Marx, *Capital* (Molitor French translation), Vol. X.
2. The part played by "fixed costs" was made particularly clear by the German Professor Schmalenbach in a lecture in Vienna, June, 1930.
3. Professor Bonn, *Das Schicksal des deutschen Kapitalismus,* (French translation), 1930.
4. Rossi, *La Naissance du Fascisme* (L'Italie de 1918 a 1922), Paris, 1938.
5. *Ibid.*
6. *Ibid.*
7. Perroux, "Economie corporative et systeme capitaliste," *Revue d'Economie politique,* September–October 1933.
8. Rossi, *op. cit.*
9. Volpe, *Historei du mouvement fasciste,* (in French), Rome, 1935.
10. Cf. Steinberger, *Die Agrarpolitik des Nationalsozialismus,* 1935.
11. Bonn, *op. cit.*
12. Cited by G. Raphael, *Krupp et Thyssen,* 1925.
13. Stinnes, interview in the *Deutsche Tageszeitung,* February 25, 1919.
14. Thyssen, statement to the *Journal des Debats,* February 7, 1924.

331

15. *Landarbeiter oder Kleinbauer?* National Socialist propaganda pamphlet, 1932.

16. Erwin Topf, *Die Gruene Front,* 1933.

17. Gumbel, *Les Crimes politiques en Allemagne* (1919–1929).

18. Konrad Heiden, *Historei du National-Socialisme* (French translation), Paris, 1934.

19. July, 1920. Cited by Beaumont and Berthelot, *L'Allemagne, lendemains de guerre et de revolution,* 1922.

20. Rathenau, *Le Triple Revolution* (essays), (French trans.), 1921.

21. Gumbel, *op. cit.*

22. Knickerbocker, *Allemagne: fascisme ou communisme?* 1932.

23. Statement published in *Der Ruhrarbeiter,* Labor Front paper, May 1, 1936.

24. Hitler, speech at Coburg, October 19, 1935.

25. Heiden, *op. cit.*

26. Benoist-Mechin, *Histoire de l'armee allemande,* V.II, 1938.

Chapter 2

1. Ignazio Silone, *Der Fascismus,* 1934.

2. Trotsky, *The Only Road,* 1932.

3. Bernstein, *Socialisme theorique et social-democratic pratique,* (French translation), 1899.

4. H. de Man, *Pour un plan d'action,* 1933.

5. Kautsky, *Le Marxisme et son critique Bernstein,* (French translation), 1899.

6. Laurat, "*Le Plan et les Classes Moyennes,*" lecture published in *Crise et Plan,* Paris, 1935.

7. Russo, *Mussolini et le Fascisme,* 1923.

8. Herisson, "Le National-socialisme et la protection des classes moyennes," *Revue Economique Internationale,* March, 1934.

9. Rivaud, *Les Crises allemandes,* 1932.

10. Moeller van den Bruck, *Le Troisieme Reich* (French trans.), 1923.

11. Herisson, *op. cit.*

12. Feder, *Kampf gegen Hochfinanz,* collected articles and speeches.

13. Cited by Mussat, *De Marx a Hitler,* 1933.

14. Cf. Sternberg, *Der Niedergang des deutschen Kapitalismus,* 1932.

15. Trotsky, *Whither France?* 1936.

16. *Communist Manifesto,* 1848.

17. Herisson, *op. cit.*

18. *Ibid.*

19. De Man, *op. cit.*
20. Deat, *Perspectives socialistes,* 1930.
21. *Ibid.*
22. Mussolini, speech in July, 1923.
23. Cf. Nicoletti, *Le Fascisme contre le paysan,* 1929.
24. Cited by Carlo Rossi, *L'Eglise et le fascisme,* 1933.
25. A. Rossi, *La Naissance du Fascisme,* Paris, 1938.
26. *Ibid.*
27. Cf. *Masses,* number devoted to "Spartakus," August 16, 1934.
28. Rivaud, *op. cit.*
29. *Ibid.*
30. Sternberg, *op. cit.*
31. Volpe, *Histoire du mouvement fasciste,* (in French), Rome, 1935.
32. Article of Pietro Nenni, *Peuple,* December 24, 1934.
33. Cf. *Le capitaine Conan,* 1934, by the French novelist Vercel.
34. Marinetti, *Le Futurisme,* 1911.
35. Cited by R. Patry, "Les Origines du mouvement de jeunesse," *Revue d'Allemagne,* November, 1927.
36. Wilhelm Reich, *The Mass Psychology of Fascism,* 1933.
37. *Revolution proletarienne,* November, 1932.
38. Silone, *op. cit.*
39. Salvemini, *La Terreur fasciste,* 1929.
40. Silone, *op. cit.*
41. Aniante, *Mussolini,* 1933.
42. *Masses,* No. 15, 1934.
43. Harold D. Lasswell and Renzo Sereno, article in *American Political Science Review,* October 1935, cited by Robert Marjolin, "Le recrutement des chefs fascistes," *Europe Nouvelle,* August 1938.
44. Mussolini, speech of December 5, 1922.
45. *Arbeitertum,* organ of the National Socialist shop cells, May, 1933.
46. Daniel Halevy, *Courier d'Europe,* 1933.
47. Suarez, article in the *Temps,* November 14, 1933.

Chapter 3
1. Ernst Krieck, *Education nationale-socialiste,* cited in *Cerveaux en uniforme,* Paris, 1934.
2. Mussolini, speech to the Senate (discussion of union legislation) April 3, 1926.
3. Hitler, *Mein Kampf,* 1925.
4. Mussolini, *Le Fascisme, doctrine et institutions,* 1933.

334 FASCISM AND BIG BUSINESS

5. Mussolini, Popolo d'Italia, January 19, 1922.

6. Mussolini, speech of October 5, 1922.

7. *Roma Fascista*, June 21, 1931.

8. Hitler speech to the Nuremberg Congress, September 13, 1935.

9. Leo XIII, Encyclical *Rerum Novarum*, 1891.

10. Mussolini, *Le Fascisme, doctrine et institutions*, 1933.

11. Hitler, speech to the Nuremberg Congress, 1933.

12. F. Engels, *Ludwig Feuerbach*.

13. Marcel Martinet, "Le Chef contre l'Homme," *Esprit*, January 1, 1934.

14. Mussolini, article in *Popolo d'Italia*, cited by Cambo, *Autour du fascisme italien*, 1925.

15. Cited by Gaston Raphael, *Krupp et Thyssen*, 1925.

16. Moeller van den Bruck, *Le Troisieme Reich*, (French trans.), 1923.

17. Hitler, *Reden* 1920–1923.

18. Count Sforza, *Les Batisseurs de l'Europe moderne*, 1931.

19. *Official Correspondence of the N.S.D.A.P.*, reprinted by the *Temps*, September 15, 1934.

20. *Morning Post*, January 31, 1934.

21. Rudolf Hess, speech in June, 1934.

22. *Temps*, December 19, 1933.

23. *Temps*, February 13, 1935.

24. Goebbels, *Kampf um Berlin*.

25. Goebbels, letter to Hitler, cited by Pernot: *L'Allemagne de Hitler*, 1933.

26. Goebbels, *Revolution der Deutschen*.

27. Prince zu Hohenlohe, "Son Redempteur," *Pariser Tageblatt*, July 16, 1934.

28. Rudolf Hess, speech of February 26, 1934, in Munich.

29. Boettcher, *Rasse und Recht*.

30. Martinet, *op. cit.*

31. Gorgolini, *Le Fascisme*, 1921.

32. Mussolini, speech of October 24, 1922.

33. *Temps*, July 26, 1933.

34. *Temps*, February 12, 1933.

35. *Temps*, April 28, 1935.

36. *Temps*, June 25, 1935.

37. Oath taken in chorus by crowds at National Socialist public meetings, *Temps*, May 2, 1935.

38. Volpe, *Histoire du mouvement fasciste*, (in French), Rome, 1935.

39. *Temps,* July 26, 1933.
40. Article from *Dagens Nyheder,* Copenhagen, reprinted in *Lu,* February 10, 1933.
41. Rosenberg, *Das Wesensgefuge des Nationalsozialismus.*
42. *Temps,* November 10, 1935.
43. Volpe, *op. cit.*
44. P. Gentizon, *Temps,* July 26, 1933.
45. Hitler, *Mein Kampf.*
46. *Temps,* August 25, 1935.
47. *Temps,* September 21, 1935.
48. *Temps,* February 26, 1934.
49. *Temps,* September 13, 1935.
50. Hitler, speech to Nuremberg Congress, *Temps,* September 8, 1934.
51. Hitler, *Mein Kampf.*
52. Goebbels, *Kampf um Berlin.*
53. Hitler, speech at Coburg, October 19, 1935.
54. Hitler, *Mein Kampf.*
55. Konrad Heiden, *Histoire du national-socialisme,* (French translation), 1934.
56. Hitler, *Mein Kampf.*
57. Gustave Le Bon, *Psychologie des Foules,* 1896.
58. Hitler, *Mein Kampf.*
59. Volpe, *op. cit.*
60. Pierre Frederic, *Revue des Deux Mondes,* March 1, 1934.
61. *Temps,* September 16, 1935.
62. *Temps,* March 15, 1936.
63. Martinet, *op. cit.*
64. Gorgolini, *op. cit.*
65. Gregor Strasser, *Kampf um Deutschland,* collected articles and speeches.
66. Rosenberg, *Der Mythus des XX Jahrhunderts.*
67. Marx, *Critique of Political Economy,* preface, 1859.
68. Jaures, *Idealisme et materialisme dans la conception de l'histoire,* 1896.
69. Antonio Labriola, *Essai sur la conception materialisme de l'histoire,* 1902.

Chapter 4

1. Cited by Rosenstock-Franck, *L'Economie corporative fasciste,* 1934.
2. The term is from the Nationalist Corradini.

3. Volpe, *Histoire du Mouvement fasciste,* (in French), Rome, 1935.
4. Cited by Henri Massoul, *La Lecon de Mussolini,* 1934.
5. Cited in *La Reforme syndicale en Italie* (in French), Rome, 1926.
6. Cited by Konrad Heiden, *Histoire du national-socialisme* (French translation), 1934.
7. Moeller van den Bruck, *Le Troisieme Reich* (French trans.), 1923.
8. Gregor Strasser, *Kampf um Deutschland.*
9. Goebbels, *Revolution der Deutschen.*
10. Cited by Rosenberg, *Der Weltkampf des Faschimus,* 1927.
11. Cited by Valois, *Finances italiennes,* 1930.
12. Cf. Herisson, "Le national-socialisme et la protection des classes moyennes," *Revue Economique Internationale,* March, 1934.
13. Goebbels, *Der Nazi-Sozi,* 1931.
14. Gorgolini, *Le Fascisme,* 1921.
15. Lanzillo, article of September 7, 1920.
16. Malaparte, *L'Italie contre l'Europe* (French translation), 1927.
17. Hitler, *Mein Kampf.*
18. Winnig, *Vom Proletariat zum Arbeitertum,* 1930.
19. Feder, Otto Strasser, *Aufbau des deutschen Sozialismus.*
20. Cf. W. Prion, "Les Problemes de la Reforme bancaire en Allemagne," *Revue Economique Internationale,* June, 1934.
21. *Das Programm der NSDAP,* edition of 1932.
22. Gorgolini, *op. cit.*
23. Bottai, *L'Organisation corporative de l'Etat,* 1929.
24. Goebbels, speech at the Sportpalast, October 1, 1931.
25. Feder, *Der Deutsche Staat.*
26. Cited by Maurice Pernot, *L'Allemagne de Hitler,* 1933.
27. Cited by Konrad Heiden, *History of National Socialism* (German edition), 1933.
28. *Kampf gegen Hochfinanz,* collected articles and speeches.
29. Speech of W. Darre at Goslar, *Temps,* November 20, 1934.
30. Daunderer, *Die Ziele der NSDAP,* 1933.
31. Gregor Strasser, *op. cit.*
32. Tardy and Bonnefous, *Le Corporatisme,* 1935.
33. Karl Marx and Friedrich Engels, *Communist Manifesto,* 1848.
34. Martin Saint-Leon, *Histoire des Corporations de metiers,* 3rd edition, 1922.
35. La Tour du Pin, *Vers un ordre social chretien,* 1907.
36. Rocco, "Criso dello stato e sindacati," *Politica,* December, 1920.

37. Saint-Simon, *Du systeme industriel*, 1821.

38. *Doctrine de Saint-Simon, Expose, premiere annee*, 1829.

39. Proudhon, *De la capacite politique des classes ouvrieres*, 1864.

40. Paul-Boncour, *Le Federalisme economique*, 1901.

41. Henri de Man, *Corporatisme et Socialisme*, 1935.

42. Official text of the CGT plan.

43. "Le mensonage de l'Etat corporatif," *Le Mouvement Syndical Internationale*, January–April, 1934.

44. Ambrosini, "d'Annunzio et la constitution syndicale de Fiume," *Revue de Droit public*, 1926.

45. Mussolini, letter of April 23, 1918.

46. Moeller van den Bruck, *op. cit.*

47. Gregor Strasser, speech of July 20, 1925, in *Kampf um Deutschland*.

48. Feder, "Foundation of National Socialist Economy," in *Kampf gegen Hochfinanz*.

49. Daunderer, *op. cit.*

50. Program of the National Socialist Party, February, 1920.

51. Mathon, *Le Corporatisme, base de l'organisation economique*, 2nd edition, 1934.

52. Maurice Olivier, *Pourquoi, comment sauver l'economie nationale?*, 1935.

53. Lucien Laine, *Information sociale*, June 20, 1935.

54. Cf. Konrad Heiden, *Histoire du national-socialisme*.

55. Pierre Gerome, *Qu'est-ce le Fascisme?*, 1935.

56. Gorgolini, *op. cit.*

57. Gregor Strasser, speech of June 14, 1932, in *Kampf um Deutschland*.

58. Goebbels, *Revolution der Deutschen*.

59. Goebbels, *Die Zweite Revolution*.

60. Gorgolini, *op. cit.*

61. Mussolini, article concerning a speech by Salandra in Bari, cited by Gorgolini, *ibid.*

62. Proclamation issued the night of October 27, 1922.

63. Gregor Strasser, speech of September 15, 1929, in *Kampf um Deutschland*.

64. Winnig, *op. cit.*

65. Rossoni, March, 1925, cited by Hautecour, "Le Fascisme," *Annee Politique*, 1926.

66. Hitler, *Mein Kampf*.

67. Gien, *Unser Kampf gegen die Gewerkschaftsbonzen*, 1933.

68. Hitler, *Mein Kampf.*

69. Mussolini, September, 1920, cited by Nenni, *La Lutte de classes en Italie*, 1930.

70. Mussolini, speech of January 19, 1923, to the workers of the Motor Transport Company.

71. *Cronache Sociali d'Italia*, March–April, 1926.

72. Ugo Spirito, Report to the "Congress of Corporative Studies," Ferrara, June, 1932.

73. Gregor Strasser, *op. cit.*

74. Gregor Strasser is merely following a plan presented in 1920 to the commission for "socialization" by a Berlin industrialist, Kraemer, "a curious compromise that tries to protect both the rights of private property and collective rights." (Beaumont et Berthelot, *L'Allemagne, lendemains de guerre et de revolution*, 1922.)

75. Otto Strasser, *op. cit.*

76. Gorgolini, *op. cit.*

77. Walter Darre, *Neuer Adel aus Blut and Boden*, 1930.

78. Dr. Carl Hartwich, *Rittergut oder Bauerndorf?*, 1932.

79. *Temps*, July 29, 1933.

80. Konrad Heiden, *Geburt des dritten Reiches*, 1934.

81. Cited by the *Temps*, June 24, 1933.

Chapter 5

1. Silone, *Der Fascismus*, 1934.

2. A. Rossi, *La Naissance du Fascisme (L'Italie de 1918 a 1922)*, Paris, 1938.

3. Gorgolini, *Le Fascisme* (French translation), 1921.

4. Malaparte, *Technique du Coup d'Etat*, 1931.

5. Silone, *op.cit.*

6. Adolf Saager, *Mussolini* (French translation), 1933.

7. Gobetti, *La Revolution liberale*, November, 1924, cited by Borghi, *Mussolini en chemise*, 1933.

8. A. Rossi, *op. cit.*

9. Gobetti, *op. cit.*

10. A. Rossi, *op. cit.*

11. Malaparte, *op. cit.*

12. Gumbel, *Les Crimes politiques en Allemagne (1919–1929)*, (French translation).

13. Cf. Konrad Heiden, *Historei du national-socialisme*, (French translation), 1934.

14. Hitler, *Mein Kampf,* 1925.

15. Heiden, *op. cit.*

16. Hitler, *op. cit.*

17. *Ibid.*

18. Goebbels, *Kampf um Berlin.*

19. Pernot, *L'Allemagne de Hitler,* 1933.

20. Laurent, *Le National-Socialisme,* 1932.

21. *Battaglia Sindacale,* January 29, 1921; March 10, 1921, speech of Matteotti to the Chamber, summarized by Rossi, *op. cit.*

22. Kurella, *Mussolini ohne Maske,* 1931.

23. Turati, speech of June 24, 1921.

24. Rossi, *op. cit.*

25. Kurella, *op. cit.*

26. Silone, *op. cit.*

27. Rossi, *op. cit.*

28. Silone, *op. cit.*

29. Malaparte, *op. cit.*

30. Rossi, *op. cit.*

31. Hitler, speech to the Nuremberg Congress, September 3, 1933.

32. Goebbels, *op. cit.*

33. Rustico, "The Tragedy of the German Proletariat," *Masses,* June 1, 1933.

34. "Fascisme," *Bulletin d'information de la Federation Internationale des Transports,* Amsterdam, January 11, 1936.

35. *Humanite,* November 9, 1933.

36. Rustico, *op. cit.*

37. Gilbert, "La Catastrophe allemande," *Gauche Revolutionaire,* November 10, 1935.

38. Cf. Paul Faure, *Au Seuil d'une Revolution;* Sixte-Quentin, article in the *Populaire,* January 17, 1936.

39. Volpe, *op. cit.*

40. *Ibid.*

41. *Ibid.*

42. *Ibid.*

43. A. Rossi, *op. cit.*

44. Rocca, *Le Fascisme et l'antifascisme en Italie,* 1930.

45. Konrad Heiden, *op. cit.*

46. *Ibid.*

47. Cf. Otto Strasser, *Juni Sonnabend 30,* 1934.

48. *Tels qu'ils sont: Walter Darre*, Paris, 1934.
49. Giurati, speech in memory of Michele Bianchi, cited by H. Massoul, *La Lecon de Mussolini*, 1934.
50. Silone, *op. cit.*
51. Pietro Nenni, *Six ans de guerre civile en Italie*, 1930.
52. Silone, *op. cit.*
53. Cited by Rustico, *op. cit.*
54. *Leipziger Volkszeitung*, January 21, 1933.
55. *Rote Fahne*, September 15, 1930.
56. Thaelmann, speech to the Central Committee of the German Communist Party, February 19, 1932.
57. Cited by Rustico, *op. cit.*
58. *Rote Fahne*, end of January, 1932.
59. *Giustizia*, August 12, 1922.
60. Seelbach, *Das Ende der Gewerkschaften*, 1934.
61. Massoul, *op. cit.*
62. Konrad Heiden, *op. cit.*
63. All these details are taken from Konrad Heiden, *op. cit.*
64. Buozzi and Nitti, *Fascisme et Syndicalisme*, 1930.
65. Nenni, *op. cit.*
66. Mussolini, speech, July, 1924.
67. Cited by Rustico, *op. cit.*
68. Wels, speech of February 7, 1933, cited by Rustico, *ibid.*
69. Seelbach, *op. cit.*
70. D. Guerin, *La Peste Brune a passe par la . . .*, 1933.
71. *Humanite*, December 17, 1933.
72. *Humanite*, December 23, 1933.
73. Cited by Silone, *op. cit.*
74. Manifesto of January 16, 1927, printed in *Le Liberte syndicale: Italie*, Investigation by the League of Nations, 1927.
75. Cf. Seelbach, *op. cit.*

Chapter 6
1. Mussolini, speech in Naples, August 11, 1922.
2. Marx, *The Eighteenth Brumaire of Louis Bonaparte*.
3. Gorgolini, *Le Fascisme*, 1921.
4. Hautecour, "Le Fascisme," *Annee Politique*, 1926; Max Nomad, *Rebels and Renegades*, 1932.
5. Cited by Cambo, *Autour du Fascisme Italien*, 1925.

6. Ludwig, *Talks with Mussolini*, 1932.

7. Cited by Russo, *Mussolini et le Fascisme*, 1923.

8. Mussolini, speech to the congress of the Fascist Party, 1925.

9. Olivetti, article in the *Annuaire 1928 du Centre International d'etudes sur le fascisme*.

10. Cited by Manoilesco, *Le Siecle du Corporatisme*, 1934.

11. Volpe, *Histoire du Mouvement fasciste*, (in French), Rome, 1935.

12. Malaparte, *Technique du Coup d'Etat*, 1931.

13. Volpe, *op. cit.*

14. *Ibid.*

15. Silvio Trentin, *Antidemocratie.*

16. Cf. report of Starace, summarized in the *Temps*, December 31, 1934.

17. Cutelli, at the Congress of Ferrara, May, 1932.

18. Decree-law of October 19, 1934; *Temps*, January 11, 1937.

19. Aniante, *Mussolini*, 1933.

20. Silvio Trentin, *op. cit.*

21. Article of Heinz Heckel in the *Voelkischer Beobachter*, August 6, 1932, cited by Pernot, *L'Allemange de Hitler*, 1933.

22. Goebbels, *Der Nazi-Sozi*, 1931.

23. *Temps*, January 11, 1936.

24. *Humanite*, May 22, 1936.

25. Hermann Rauschning, *La Revolution du Nihilisme*, (abridged French translation), 1939.

26. Ferrari, *Le Regime fasciste italien*, 1928.

27. Trotsky, *What Next?*, 1932.

28. Quotations and facts taken from Silone, *Der Fascismus*, 1934.

29. Ludwig, *op. cit.*

30. Aniante, *op. cit.*

31. Silone, *op. cit.*

32. Cited by Kurella, *Mussolini ohne Maske*, 1931.

33. *Temps*, January 11, 1937.

34. Cited by A. Rossi, *La Naissance du fascisme (L'Italie de 1918 a 1922)*, Paris, 1938.

35. *Temps*, September 19, 1935.

36. *Temps*, February 5, 1938.

37. *Temps*, September 30, 1934.

38. *Temps*, December 21, 1934.

39. *Temps*, February 2, 1935.

40. *Paris-Midi*, May 10, 1936.

41. *Temps,* April 1, 1938.
42. *Temps,* December 21, 1934.
43. *Petit Parisien,* May 22, 1936.
44. *Temps,* June 10 and 11, 1938.
45. *Temps,* December 24, 1937.
46. Cf. Daniel Guerin, *La Peste brune a passe par la . . . ,* 1933.
47. Konrad Heiden, *Historie du national-socialisme,* (French translation), 1934.
48. *Temps,* July 13, 1933.
49. *Temps,* July 25, 1933.
50. *Temps,* July 5, 1933.
51. *Temps,* July 12, 1933.
52. Konrad Heiden, *op. cit.*
53. *Temps,* January 12, 1934.
54. Article of Heinz Ewald Bluhm in the *Reichwart,* cited by the *Temps,* February 15, 1935.
55. Ernst's "Testament" was published by the *Journal,* Paris, December 4, 1934.
56. Klaus Bredow, *Die bluetige Tragoedie des 30. Juni 1934,* 1934.
57. Konrad Heiden, *op. cit.*
58. *Temps,* January 22, 1934.
59. *Temps,* April 19, 1934; *Lu,* July 6, 1934.
60. Benoist-Mechin, *Historie de l'armee allemande,* 1938.
61. *Temps,* December 9, 1933.
62. *Temps,* July 2, 1934.
63. *Temps,* July 20, 1934.
64. Hitler, speech of September 10, 1934.
65. *Temps,* February 1, 1936; "Fascisme," *Bulletin d'information de la Federation Internationale des Transports,* Amsterdam, March 7, 1936.
66. *Temps,* September 12, 1934; *Lu,* September 14.
67. *Temps,* September 12, 1935.
68. *Temps,* April 14, 1935.
69. *Temps,* February 11, 1937.
70. *Temps,* December 3, 1934.
71. *Temps,* January 28, 1935.
72. *Temps,* August 4, 1935.
73. *Temps,* November 8, 1935.
74. Gentizon, *Temps,* July 6, 1934.
75. A. Leroux, *Populaire,* August 19, 1935.

76. Silone, *op. cit.*
77. "Fascisme," June 29, 1935.
78. *Temps,* December 22, 1933.
79. *Temps,* October 28, 1934.
80. *Ibid.*
81. Mussolini, speech of November 18, 1935.
82. Mussolini, speech of October 26, 1935.
83. Nenni, *Peuple,* July 21 and November 12, 1935.
84. Goebbels, speech of June 21, 1934.
85. Cf. Benois-Mechin, *op. cit.* and the *New Statesman and Nation,* July 8, 1934.
86. *Temps,* November 26, 1934.
87. *Das Neue Tagebuch,* August 24, 1935; *Temps,* September 12, 1935.
88. Cf. *Populaire,* March 3, 1936.
89. *Temps,* February 8, 1935.
90. *Temps,* April 21, 1936.
91. *Temps,* September 10, 1934.
92. *Temps,* November 9, 1934.
93. *Temps,* July 1, 1935.
94. *Temps,* July 21, 1935.
95. Hitler, speech at the Nuremberg Congress, September 13, 1935.
96. Hitler, closing speech at the Nuremberg Congress, September 16, 1935.
97. *Temps,* September 12, 1935.
98. *Temps,* February 7, 1938.
99. *Temps,* May 11, 1938.

Chapter 7
1. Marx, *The Eighteenth Brumaire of Louis Bonaparte.*
2. The expression is from Louis Dimier, *Les Maitres de la contre-revolution au XIXe siecle,* 1907.
3. Mussolini, speech of April 7, 1926.
4. Mussolini, *Le Fascisme, doctrine et institutions,* 1933.
5. Goebbels, *Revolution der Deutschen.*
6. Gregor Strasser, speech of June 14, 1932, printed in *Kampf um Deutschland.*
7. Cf. Jean Variot, *Propos de Georges Sorel,* 1935.
8. Mussolini, *Le Fascisme, doctrine et institutions,* 1933.
9. Edouard Berth, *Les Mefaits des intellectuels,* 1913.

10. Georges Sorel, *Les Illusions du Progres,* 1908.

11. Georges Sorel, article published in Italian in *Il resto del Carlino.*

12. Edouard Berth, *op. cit.*

13. Georges Sorel, *Reflexions sur la Violence,* 1907.

14. Mussolini, *Le Fascisme, doctrines et institutions,* 1933.

15. Mussolini, speech of October 24, 1922.

16. Volpe, *Histoire du mouvement fasciste,* (in French), Rome, 1935.

17. Mussolini, speech of July 9, 1934.

18. Paul Zillich, *Die Sozialistiche Entscheidung,* cited by Helvetus, "Le Mystique de la vie dans la revolution allemande," *Esprit,* January 1, 1934.

19. Professor Weber, cited by the *Temps,* February 1, 1935.

20. Rosenberg, *Der Mythus des XX Jahrhunderts.*

21. Gregor Strasser, *op. cit.*

22. *Temps,* June 27, 1934.

23. Hitler, speech of October 1, 1934.

24. Hanns Johst, *Schlageter,* 1933.

25. Georges Sorel, *Reflexions sur la Violence,* 1907.

26. Georges Sorel, interview in the *Gaulois,* January 11, 1910.

27. No. 1 of the *Cahiers du Cercle Proudhon,* January, 1912.

28. Georges Valois, *D'un siecle a l'autre,* 1924.

29. Mussolini, interview in the *A.B.C.,* cited by P. Dominique, *Les Fils de la Louve,* 1926.

30. Maurras, *Liberalisme et libertes, democratic et peuple,* 1906.

31. Maurras, *Enquete sur la Monarchie,* 1909.

32. The expression is from Mussolini's speech of October 24, 1922.

33. Mussolini, speech of October 4, 1922.

34. Mussolini, speech of September 20, 1922.

35. Mussolini, preface to Machiavelli, *The Prince,* (French trans.), 1929.

36. Mussolini, *Le Fascisme, doctrine et institutions,* 1933.

37. Rocco, cited by Georges Roux, *L'Italie fasciste,* 1932.

38. Rene Lauret, "Un ennemi de l'Etat: Oswald Spengler," *Temps,* December 26, 1934.

39. Spengler, *The Decline of the West.*

40. Goebbels, *Kampf um Berlin.*

41. Roehm, speech of April 19, 1934.

42. Moeller van den Bruck, *Le Troisieme Reich* (French trans.), 1923.

43. Sorel, *L'Avenir socialiste des syndicats,* 1898.

44. Maurras, *Liberalisme et Libertes,* etc., 1906.

45. Martinet, "Le Chef contre l'Homme," *Esprit,* January 1, 1934.

46. Maurras, *Enquete sur la Monarchie,* 1909.

47. Mussolini, speech to the Senate in 1926, printed in *La Reforme Syndicale en Italie,* (in French), 1926.

48. Mussolini, article written in 1917.

49. Rocco, cited by Georges Roux, *L'Italie fasciste,* 1932.

50. Malaparte, cited by Silone, *Der Fascismus,* 1934.

51. Hitler, *Mein Kampf.*

52. Hitler, report to the Nuremberg Congress, 1934: "Heroism, Race and Art."

53. Gentizon, *Rome sous le Faisceau,* 1933.

54. Cited by MacCabe, *Treitschke et la grande guerre,* (French trans.), 1916.

55. Pius XI, encyclical of June 29, 1931.

56. Mussolini, *Le Fascisme, doctrine et institutions,* 1933.

57. Rocco, "La Crise de l'Etat," *Revue des Vivants,* July, 1927.

58. Goering, statement to the German press, cited by *Lu,* July 6, 1934.

59. *Temps,* November 8, 1933.

60. Faulhaber, *Judentum, Christentum, Germanentum* (French trans.), Paris, 1934.

61. Rousseau, *Le Contrat Social.*

62. "Le nouveau naturalisme," *Temps,* August 25, 1935.

63. Nietzsche, *The Genealogy of Morals.*

64. Cf. MacCabe, *op. cit.*

65. Sorel, *Reflexions sur la Violence,* 1907.

66. Lenin, quoted by Gorki, *Lenine et le paysan russe,* (French trans.), 1924.

67. Mussolini, *Le Fascisme, doctrine et institutions,* 1933.

68. Mussolini, speech to the Fascist Grand Council, 1925.

69. Mussolini, speech of May 26, 1927.

70. Mussolini, speech of September 20, 1920.

71. Mussolini, speech of May 26, 1934.

72. Hitler, *Mein Kampf.*

Chapter 8

1. Mussolini, speech to the Senate, 1926.

2. Nicoletti, *Le Fascisme contre le Paysan,* 1929.

3. A. Rossi, *La Naissance du Fascisme (L'Italie de 1918 a 1922),* Paris, 1938.

4. Pietro Nenni, "La Faillite du syndicalisme fasciste," *Cahiers Bleus,* July 27, 1929.

5. Gorgolini, *Le Fascisme*, 1921.

6. Salvemini, "La Syndicalisme fasciste," *Nouvelle Revue Socialiste*, 1925.

7. Pietro Nenni, *op. cit.*

8. Kerillis, "Un Enquete en Italie fasciste," *Echo de Paris*, October 6–16, 1933.

9. Admission of the fascist leader Razza, October 3, 1933.

10. Valois, *Finances italiennes*, 1930.

11. Law supplemented by a regulation of July 1, 1926.

12. *Nuovo Avanti*, Paris, February 11, 1934.

13. Article in the *Popolo d'Italia* in 1929, cited by the *Peuple*, February 9, 1935.

14. *Universale*, Florence, April 25, 1933.

15. R. Bottai, "Ou mene la domestication des syndicats," *Revolution proletarienne*, May 25, 1934.

16. According to a speech by Mussolini, *Temps*, April 1, 1938.

17. *Temps*, February 1, 1936.

18. Cited by Jouhaux, "La Charte fasciste du Travail," *Revue des Vivants*, October, 1927.

19. Cited by Million, *Peuple*, August 2, 1935.

20. Decree of July 1, 1926.

21. Gaddi, *La Misere des travailleurs en Italie fasciste*, Paris, 1938.

22. Cf. J. Lazard, "L'Agriculture dans l'Italie du Nord," *Correspondant*, October 25, 1933.

23. Cf. Heiden, *History of National Socialism*, (German edition), 1933.

24. "Fascisme," *Bulletin d'informations de la Federation Internationale de Transports*, Amsterdam, January 11, 1936.

25. Hitler, speech of May 10, 1933.

26. Dr. Ley, article of November 15, 1933, printed in *Durchbruch der sozialen Ehre*, 1935.

27. "Fascisme," February 22, 1936.

28. "Fascisme," January 25, 1936.

29. Law Regulating National Labor, commentary by Dr. E. Schlichting.

30. "Fascisme," December 15, 1934, and No. 3, February, 1935.

31. *Temps*, January 11, 1937.

32. *Temps*, June 30, July 2 and 6, 1938.

33. *Ruhrarbeiter*, 5th edition of September, 1936.

34. Rossoni, article in *Lovaro d'Italia*, cited by Russo, *Mussolini et le Fascisme*, 1923.

35. Nenni, *La Lutte de classes en Italie*, 1930.

36. Cf. Rosenstock-Franck, *L'Economie Corporative Fasciste,* 1934.

37. *Il Lavoro Fascista,* July 1, 2, and 3, 1936, cited by "Fascisme," July 25, 1936.

38. "Fascisme," March 9, 1935.

39. *Temps,* October 9, 1934.

40. *Temps,* July 21, 1934.

41. *Temps,* December 22, 1934.

42. *Temps,* February 2, 1935.

43. *Corriere della sera,* March 29, 1932; *Lavoro Fascista,* March 27, 1932.

44. *Information,* May 22, 1937.

45. Cited by the *Temps,* February 18, 1935.

46. *Temps,* February 20, 1934.

47. Mussolini, speech of May 15, 1937.

48. *Temps,* August 12, 1935.

49. Cited by the *Temps,* January 28, 1936.

50. *Temps,* July 30, 1938.

51. Hitler, speech of October 1, 1934.

52. *Temps,* January 28, 1936.

53. "Fascisme," January 11, 1936.

54. *Temps,* February 26, 1938.

55. Dr. Ley, speech of November 27, 1936.

56. Report of the Chamber of Commerce of Essen for the year 1935.

57. Goering, speech in Linz, May 13, 1938, *Temps,* May 15, 1938.

58. *Peuple,* August 19, 1937.

59. *Wirtschaft und Statistik,* Nov. 23, 1935.

60. *Lavoro d'Italia,* April, 1921.

61. Rosenstock-Franck, *op. cit.*

62. Hautecour, "Le Fascisme," *Annee Politique,* 1926.

63. Modigliani, "La Loi Syndicale Fasciste," *Nouvelle Revue Socialiste,* 1927.

64. Cited by Fucile, *Le Mouvement Syndical et la realisation de l'Etat corporatif en Italie,* 1929.

65. Rocco, *La Nuova Disciplina.*

66. Cited in *La Liberte syndicale: Italie,* Investigation by the League of Nations, 1927.

67. Mussolini, speech of November 10, 1934.

68. Mussolini, speech to the members of the France-Italy Committee, September, 1933.

69. Mussolini, speech of October 6, 1934.

70. Mussolini, speech of March 18, 1934.
71. Mussolini, address of January 8, 1935.
72. *Vu,* August 9, 1933.
73. Rosenstock-Franck, *op. cit.*
74. Cf. Konrad Heiden, *Geburt des dritten Reiches,* 1934.
75. *Temps,* May 5, 1933.
76. Cited by Konrad Heiden, *Geburt des dritten Reiches.*
77. *Temps,* June 25, 1933.
78. Dr. Ley, speech in May, 1933.
79. Cited by "Fascisme," October 6, 1934.
80. Dr. Schmitt, speech of March 13, 1934.
81. *Temps,* September 7, 1935.
82. "Fascisme," March 7, 1936.

Chapter 9
1. Mussolini, speech of 1923, cited by Laporte, *Le Relevement financier de l'Italie,* 1924.
2. Mussolini, speech of March 18, 1923.
3. Mussolini, speech of September 20, 1922.
4. Perroux, "Economie corporative et systeme capitaliste," *Revue d'Economie Politique,* September–October, 1933.
5. *Temps,* February 12, 1933.
6. *Information,* September 13, 1933.
7. *Temps,* December 13, 1933.
8. *Temps,* December 19, 1933.
9. *Temps,* March 1, 1934.
10. *Information,* March 18, 1937.
11. *Information,* August 7, 1937.
12. *Peuple,* October 24, 1937.
13. *Correspondence Internationale,* March 15, 1937.
14. "Fascisme," January 26, 1935.
15. *Temps,* January 21, 1936.
16. De Stefani, speech of November 25, 1922.
17. Marini, *L'Impot sur le Capital en Italie,* 1928.
18. Don Sturzo, *L'Italie et le Fascisme,* 1927.
19. *Temps,* July 16, 1933.
20. *Temps,* April 20, 1934.
21. *Humanite,* March 9, 1935.
22. Cf. de Rousiers, *Les Cartels et les Trusts et leur evolution,* 1927; Hirsch,

Les Monopoles nationaux et internationaux, 1927.
23. Rosenstock-Franck, *L'Economie corporative fasciste,* 1934.
24. Cited by Perroux, *op. cit.*
25. Dr. Schmitt, speech of March 13, 1934.
26. K. Heiden, *Geburt des Dritten Reiches,* 1934.
27. Mussolini, speech of January 13, 1934.
28. *Temps,* January 9, 1934.
29. *Temps,* September 23, 1934.
30. Mussolini, speech of May 26, 1934.
31. Bottai, article in *Critica Fascista,* cited by the *Temps,* October 22, 1934.
32. Decree-laws of March 12, 1936, *Gazzetta Ufficiale,* March 16, 1936.
33. Mussolini, speech of March 23, 1936.
34. *Temps,* April 20, 1937.
35. A. Leroux, *Populaire,* July 7, 1937.
36. *Temps,* July 26, 1937.
37. *Bergwerkszeitung,* July 27, 1937.
38. Statement of General Hanneken to the German press, June 12, 1938.
39. *Deutsche Freiheit,* July 7, 1938.
40. Aquila, *Humanite,* December 11, 1934.
41. Annual Report of the Reichsbank, *Temps,* March 21, 1936.
42. *Temps,* January 30, 1934.
43. According to former Minister de Stefani.
44. Cited by Ed. Schneider, "L'Italie en Auto," *Temps,* August 18, 1935.
45. Bavarelli, *Politique des travaux publics du regime fasciste,* (in French), Rome, year XIII.
46. *Matin,* February 14, 1936.
47. Hitler, speech of December 17, 1937, *Temps,* December 19, 1937.
48. "Fascisme," March 17, 1936.
49. *Temps,* March 22, 1934.
50. "Fascisme," May 14 and 18, 1935.
51. Pietro Nenni, *Peuple,* December 21, 1935.
52. *Temps,* September 3, 1935.
53. Arias, *Popolo d'Italia,* February 3, 1938.
54. Thaon di Revel, speech of May 18, 1938.
55. *Populaire,* May 5, 1935.
56. Cited by *Information,* February 19, 1937.
57. Reinhardt, speech at the Nuremberg Congress, *Temps,* September 16, 1937.

58. *Temps,* December 19, 1935, and April 12, 1936.

59. *Temps,* August 18, 1935.

60. Dr. Dreyse's speech, *Pariser Tageblatt,* April 25, 1935.

61. Arias, *op. cit.*

62. Memorandum of the industrialists, published by *Information,* August 28 and 31, September 7 and 9, 1937.

63. *Temps,* August 18, 1938.

64. Decree-laws of March 12, 1936, *Gazzetta Ufficiale,* March 16, 1936.

65. Cited by *Lu,* December 20, 1935.

66. *La Loi du Reich sur le credit du 5 decembre 1934,* supplement to the *Bulletin Quotidien,* March 19, 1935.

67. G. Jeze, "Les Methodes financieres allemandes," *Das Neue Tagebuch,* September 13, 1935.

68. *Information,* October 28, 1937.

69. *Information,* September 30, 1937.

70. Rud. Lang, *Deutsche Freiheit,* July 21 and August 11, 1938.

71. *Information,* April 2, 1937.

72. Rud. Lang, *op. cit.*

73. *Temps,* August 18, 1938.

74. *Temps,* February 17, 1938.

75. Memorandum of the industrialists, previously cited.

76. Dr. Schacht, speech, *Temps,* April 22, 1937.

77. Communique of the "Supreme Commission for National Defense," February 20, 1935.

78. Cited by A. Leroux, *Populaire,* July 7, 1937.

79. *Temps,* October 28, 1937.

80. Mussolini, speech on May 15, 1937, *Temps,* May 15, 1937.

81. *Temps,* February 27, 1938.

82. *Temps,* March 24, 1938.

83. *Temps,* August 12, 1935.

84. *Voelkischer Beobachter,* October 21, 1936.

85. Memorandum of the industrialists, previously cited.

86. *Ibid.*

87. *Temps,* February 20, 1936.

88. General Serrigny, *Revue des Deux-Mondes,* April 1, 1936.

89. *Temps,* December 2, 1937.

90. Colonel Thomas, lecture, February 6, 1937, *Temps,* February 8, 1937.

91. *Temps,* July 3, 1935.

92. Funk, speech of May 24, 1938, *Temps,* May 28, 1938.

93. *Temps,* February 2, 1937.
94. *Temps,* November 28, 1937.
95. Memorandum of the industrialists, previously cited.
96. Goering, speech of December 6, 1935, in Hamburg.
97. Goebbels, speech of March 10, 1936.
98. Cf. Lucien Laurat, *Peuple,* December 13, 1936.
99. Rossi, *La Naissance du Fascisme (L'Italie de 1918 a 1922),* Paris, 1938.
100. Mussolini, speech of November 14, 1933.
101. Dr. Schacht, speech in Munich, *Temps,* January 30, 1935.
102. Dr. Schacht, lecture in Berlin, *Temps,* February 6, 1935.
103. *Temps,* March 21, 1935.
104. Law of February 4, 1934.
105. Dr. Schmitt, speech of March 13, 1934.
106. Cf. Guillaume, *Les Corporations en Italie,* 1934.
107. *Temps,* June 14, 1935.
108. *Temps,* December 31, 1935.
109. *Temps,* January 1 and 2, 1936.
110. *Giornale d'Italia,* May 22, 1934.
111. *Temps,* November 15, 1936.
112. Cited by Buozzi, *Peuple,* May 24, 1934.
113. *Temps,* January 7, 1936.
114. Rome, October 15, 1934; cf. *Temps,* October 21, 1934; "Fascisme," November 3, 1934.
115. Mussolini, speech of November 8, 1934.
116. Mussolini, speech of March 24, 1936.
117. Mussolini, article in the *Annales,* November 10, 1933.
118. Mussolini, speech of November 14, 1933.
119. Mussolini, speech of January 13, 1934.
120. Mussolini, speech of October 6, 1934.
121. *Voelkischer Beobachter,* November 14, 1934.
122. *Ibid.,* November 20, 1934.
123. *Fascisme,* June 27, 1936.
124. *Voelkischer Beobachter,* January 7, 1938, cited by *Syndicats,* February 16, 1938.
125. *Frankfurter Zeitung,* July 14, 1934.
126. *Temps,* April 29, 1935.
127. Cited by "Fascisme," August 11, 1934.
128. *Information,* January 21, 1938.
129. *Temps,* February 7, 1938.

130. Dr. Schacht, speech of December 4, 1935.

131. Dr. Schacht, speech, *Temps*, September 28, 1935.

132. Dr. Schacht, speech of November 30, 1935.

133. Funk, speech at the Koenigsberg fair, *Temps*, November 29, 1937.

134. *Populaire*, February 1, 1938.

135. *Temps*, February 9, 1938.

136. Colonel Thomas, lecture, *Temps*, April 20, 1936.

137. Cited by *Temps*, April 24, 1938.

138. *Temps*, December 21, 1936.

139. Cited by *Temps*, December 23, 1937.

140. Memorandum of the industrialists, previously cited.

141. *Frankfurter Zeitung*, November 28, 1937.

142. *Freies Deutschland*, July 28, 1938.

143. Edmond Landau, *L'Oeuvre*, January 18, 1938.

144. "Pas de retour en arriere," article in *L'Agence Economique et Financiere*, February 15, 1932.

145. Dr. Schacht, speech of November 30, 1935.

146. Gaddi, *La Misere des Travailleurs en Italie Fasciste*, 1938.

147. Cf. Landau, *op. cit.*

148. Volpe, speech of February 12, 1928, cited by Ferrari, *Le Regime fasciste italien*, 1928.

149. Cf. Gaddi, *op. cit.*

150. *Ibid.*

151. K. Heiden, *Geburt des dritten Reiches*, 1934.

152. *Temps*, April 13, 1934.

153. Landau, *op. cit.*

154. *Temps*, September 12, 1935.

155. Guillaume, *op. cit.*

156. *Pariser Tageblatt*, February 14, 1935.

Chapter 10

1. Cf. Saager, *Mussolini* (French trans.), 1933.

2. Silone, *Der Fascismus*, 1934.

3. Baravelli, *La Bonification Integrale en Italie*, (in French), Rome, 1935.

4. *Gazetta del Popolo*, December 13, 1934.

5. Rosenstock-Franck, *L'Economie corporative fasciste*, 1934.

6. *Ibid.*

7. Baravelli, *op. cit.*

8. Cf. Murat, *La Propriete agraire en Italie*, Lyon, 1936.

9. Rossoni, interview in the *New Statesman and Nation*, London, January 4, 1936.

10. Mussolini, speech of March 23, 1936.

11. Silone, *op. cit.*

12. *Temps*, November 19, 1935.

13. *Peuple*, August 19, 1937.

14. *Journal du Commerce*, June 29, 1933.

15. Walter Darre, speech of July 20, 1933.

16. Cf. Steinberger, *Die Agrarpolitik des Nationalsozialismus*, 1935; most of the information following is taken from this work.

17. Darre, *Neuer Adel aus Blut und Boden*, 1930.

18. Nicoletti, *Le Fascisme contre le paysan*, 1929.

19. Cited by Ricardo Bottai, "Ou mene la domestication des syndicats," *Revolution Proletrienne*, May 25, 1934.

20. Lachin, *La IVe Italie.*

21. Mussolini, speech of December 18, 1930.

22. *Corriere Padovano*, November 15, 1934.

23. *Oeuvre*, December 8, 1934.

24. Silone, *Fontamara* (English trans.), 1934.

25. *Lavoro Fascista*, October 23, 1934.

26. Silone, *Fontamara.*

27. Perroux, "Economie corporative et systeme capitaliste," *Revue d'Economie Politique*, September–October, 1933.

28. Ricardo Boatti, *op. cit.*

29. *Temps*, October 28, 1934.

30. According to the typical collective sharecropping contract for the province of Mantua *(Lavoro Agricolo Fascista*, January 24, 1932), Ricardo Bottai, *op. cit.*

31. *Temps*, April 21, 1938.

32. Steinberger, *op. cit.*

33. Cf. *Niederdeutscher Beobachter*, March 28, 1934.

34. *Reichsarbeitsblatt*, October 5, 1934.

35. *Der Deutsche Landarbeiter*, March 3, 1934.

36. *Temps*, April 9, 1934.

37. *Temps*, May 18, 1934.

38. *Nationalsozialistische Landpost*, September, 1933.

39. *Nationalsozialistische Landpost*, October 21, 1933.

40. *Etudes sur le Fascisme, Cahiers mensuels de l'Institut pour l'etude du fascisme*, No. 5–6, Paris, 1934–35.

41. Pietro Nenni, *Peuple*, April 9, 1935.
42. *Lavoro Fascista*, February 22, 1935.
43. Rosenstock-Franck, *op. cit.*
44. Cited by Gaddi, *La Misere des travailleurs en Italie fasciste*, 1938.
45. Steinberger, *op. cit.*
46. Silone, *Der Fascismus*, 1934.
47. *Assalto*, Bologna, October 15, 1932.
48. Baravelli, *op. cit.*
49. Rosenstock-Franck, *op. cit.*
50. J. Lazard, "L'Agriculture dans l'Italie du Nord," *Correspondant*, October 25, 1933.
51. *Temps*, January 9, 1938; *Information*, January 11, 1938.
52. Steinberger, *op. cit.*
53. *Temps*, December 25, 1936.
54. Steinberger, *op. cit.*
55. *Ibid.*
56. *Information*, August 14, 1937.
57. Steinberger, *op. cit.*
58. *Le Fascisme et les Paysans*, (pamphlet of the Comite de Vigilance des intellectuels antifascistes), Paris, 1935.
59. Gaddi, *op. cit.*
60. *Ibid.*
61. J. Lazard, *op. cit.*
62. A. Leroux, *Populaire*, May 28, 1934.
63. J. Lazard, *op. cit.*
64. Gaddi, *op. cit.*
65. Muret, *La Propriete agraire en Italie*, Lyons, 1936.
66. Edmond Landau, in *l'Oeuvre*, January 18, 1938.
67. *Freies Deutschland*, July 28, 1938.
68. *Peuple*, December 22, 1935.
69. Memorandum of the industrialists, published by *Information*, August 28 and 31, September 7 and 9, 1937.
70. Cited by Loutre, *Petit Parisien*, August 30, 1937.
71. *Temps*, March 25, 1937.
72. *Temps*, January 9, 1938.
73. Loutre, *op. cit.*
74. Rosenstock-Franck, *op. cit.*
75. *Information*, January 4, 1938.

76. Steinberger, *op. cit.*

77. Dr. Schacht, speech of November 30, 1935.

Conclusion

1. Cf. L. Magyar, "Qu'est-ce que le Fascisme?" *Cahiers du Bolchevisme,* December 15, 1933.

2. *Temps,* April 17, 1933.

3. Cited by Volpe, *Histoire du Mouvement fasciste,* (in French), Rome, 1935.

4. *Temps,* January 28, 1936.

5. Marx, *The Eighteenth Brumaire of Louis Bonaparte.*

6. Edouard Berth, "Enfin nous avons Hitler," *Revolution Proletarienne,* Nos. 161–162, 1933.

7. *Temps,* March 25, 1934.

8. *Temps,* January 2 and 3, 1935.

9. Trotsky, *What Next?,* 1932.

10. Mussolini, statement to an English journalist as reported by Kerillis, "Une Enquete en Italie fasciste," *Echo de Paris,* October 6–16, 1933.

11. Dr. Ley, press communique, April 27, 1935.

12. *Bulletin Quotidien,* May 14, 1935.

13. "Fascisme," *Bulletin d'Information de la Federation Internationale des Transports,* Amsterdam, January 11, 1936.

14. Cf. the Wuppertal affair in Germany, *Populaire,* February 24, and March 1936.

15. *Information,* April 20, 1937.

16. Mussolini, speech of May 26, 1927.

17. Volpe, *op. cit.*

18. Hitler, speech of June 18, 1933.

19. Hitler, speech of September 13, 1935.

20. *Temps,* July 13, 1933.

21. Gentizon, *Temps,* March 25, 1934.

22. Feroci, *Unser Wort,* middle of December 1933.

23. Nenni, *Peuple,* June 26 and December 31, 1934.

24. Cited by Gaddi, *La Misere des travailleurs fasciste,* 1938.

25. *Temps,* February 15, 1938.

26. Memorandum of the Industrialists, published by *Information,* August 28 and 31, September 7 and 9, 1937.

27. *Temps,* March 11, 1936.

28. *Temps,* January 11, 1937.

29. Spengler, *Decline of the West.*

30. *Temps,* March 29, 1936.

31. Marx, *op. cit.*

32. *Temps,* October 28, 1935.

33. *Temps,* March 29, 1936.

34. Article by Radek, cited by *Lu,* March 12, 1933.

35. Clara Zetkin, report to the plenary session of the Executive Committee of the Communist International, Moscow, June 1923.

36. Mussolini, speech of November 14, 1933.

37. *Voelkischer Beobachter,* June 7, 1936.

38. *Ibid.,* June 13, 1936.

39. Lenin, *Imperialism, the Highest Stage of Capitalism,* 1916.

40. Trotsky, *The Soviet Union and the Fourth International,* 1934.

41. *Ibid.*

42. Rosa Luxemburg, *Speech on the Program,* 1918.

43. Bela Kun, *Internationale Communiste,* August 15, 1933.

44. Don Sturzo, *L'Italie et le Fascisme,* 1927.

45. Nitti, *Bolchevisme, Fascisme et Democratie,* 1926.

46. Article of Decker in *Gesellschaft,* theoretical organ of the Social Democracy, 1929, II.

47. Martinov, at the Tenth Plenum of the Communist International, July, 1929.

INDEX

357

THE FIGHT AGAINST FASCISM

THE STRUGGLE AGAINST FASCISM IN GERMANY
Leon Trotsky

> Writing in the heat of struggle against the rising Nazi movement, a central leader of the Russian revolution examines the class roots of fascism and advances a revolutionary strategy to combat it. $32

THE SOCIALIST WORKERS PARTY IN WORLD WAR II
WRITINGS AND SPEECHES, 1940–43
James P. Cannon

> Preparing the communist movement in the United States to stand against the patriotic wave inside the workers movement supporting the imperialist slaughter and to campaign against wartime censorship, repression, and antiunion assaults. $24.95

THE JEWISH QUESTION
A MARXIST INTERPRETATION
Abram Leon

> Traces the historical rationalizations of anti-Semitism to the fact that Jews—in the centuries preceding the domination of industrial capitalism—emerged as a "people-class" of merchants and moneylenders. Leon explains why the propertied rulers incite renewed Jew-hatred today. $22

WHAT IS AMERICAN FASCISM?
James P. Cannon and Joseph Hansen

> Analyzing examples from the 20th century—Father Charles Coughlin, Jersey City mayor Frank Hague, and Sen. Joseph McCarthy—this collection looks at the features distinguishing fascist movements and demagogues in the U.S. from the 1930s to today. $8

LEON TROTSKY ON FRANCE

An assessment of the social and economic crisis that shook France in the mid-1930s in the aftermath of Hitler's rise to power in Germany, and a program to unite the working class and exploited peasantry to confront it. $25

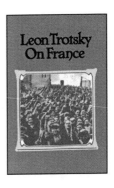

THE FIGHT AGAINST FASCISM IN THE U.S.A.

FORTY YEARS OF STRUGGLE DESCRIBED BY PARTICIPANTS

James P. Cannon and others

Lessons from the fight against incipient fascist movements since the capitalist crisis and labor radicalization of the 1930s. $8

REVOLUTION AND COUNTER-REVOLUTION IN SPAIN

Felix Morrow

A contemporary account of the revolution and civil war in Spain in the 1930s in which workers and peasants, betrayed by Stalinist, social-democratic, and anarchist misleaderships, went down to defeat under the blows of an armed fascist movement. $23

THE SPANISH REVOLUTION (1931–39)

Leon Trotsky

Analyzes the revolutionary upsurge on the land and in the factories leading to the Spanish civil war and how the Stalinists' course ensured a fascist victory. $31

COUNTER-MOBILIZATION

A STRATEGY TO FIGHT RACIST AND FASCIST ATTACKS

Farrell Dobbs

A discussion on strategy and tactics in the fight against fascist attacks on the labor movement, drawing on the experiences of the Minneapolis Teamsters movement of the 1930s. $8

Is Socialist Revolution in the U.S. Possible?
A Necessary Debate
MARY-ALICE WATERS

In two talks, presented as part of a wide-ranging debate at the Venezuela International Book Fairs in 2007 and 2008, Waters explains why a socialist revolution in the United States is possible. Why revolutionary struggles by working people are inevitable, forced upon us by the crisis-driven assaults of the propertied classes. As solidarity grows among a fighting vanguard of working people, the outlines of coming class battles can already be seen. $7. Also in Spanish, French, and Swedish.

Cuba and the Coming American Revolution
JACK BARNES

The Cuban Revolution of 1959 had a worldwide political impact, including on working people and youth in the imperialist heartland. As the mass, proletarian-based struggle for Black rights was already advancing in the U.S., the social transformation fought for and won by the Cuban toilers set an example that socialist revolution is not only necessary—it can be made and defended.

This second edition, with a new foreword by Mary-Alice Waters, should be read alongside *Is Socialist Revolution in the U.S. Possible?* $10. Also in Spanish and French.

www.pathfinderpress.com

Building a PROLETARIAN PARTY

The Changing Face of U.S. Politics
Working-Class Politics and the Trade Unions
JACK BARNES

Building the kind of party working people need to prepare for coming class battles through which they will revolutionize themselves, their unions, and all society. A handbook for those seeking the road toward effective action to overturn the exploitative system of capitalism and join in reconstructing the world on new, socialist foundations. $24. Also in Spanish, French, and Swedish.

Revolutionary Continuity
Marxist Leadership in the U.S.
FARRELL DOBBS

How successive generations took part in struggles of the U.S. labor movement, seeking to build a leadership that could advance the class interests of workers and small farmers and link up with fellow toilers around the world. Two volumes:
The Early Years, 1848–1917, $20; *Birth of the Communist Movement 1918–1922*, $19.

The History of American Trotskyism, 1928–38
Report of a Participant
JAMES P. CANNON

"Trotskyism is not a new movement, a new doctrine," Cannon says, "but the restoration, the revival of genuine Marxism as it was expounded and practiced in the Russian revolution and in the early days of the Communist International." In twelve talks given in 1942, Cannon recounts a decisive period in efforts to build a proletarian party in the United States. $22. Also in Spanish and French.

The Bolsheviks and the Fight against National Oppression

To See the Dawn

Baku, 1920—First Congress
of the Peoples of the East

How can peasants and workers in the colonial world throw off imperialist exploitation? How can they overcome national and religious divisions incited by their own ruling classes and fight for their common class interests? As the example of the October Revolution echoed around the world, these questions were addressed by 2,000 delegates to the 1920 Congress of the Peoples of the East. $24

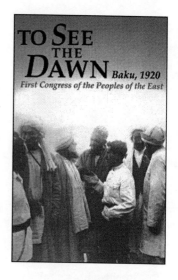

Workers of the World and Oppressed Peoples, Unite!

Proceedings and Documents
of the Second Congress
of the Communist International, 1920

Offering a vivid portrait of social struggles in the era of the Bolshevik-led October Revolution, the reports, resolutions, and debates—among delegates from 37 countries—take up key questions of working-class strategy and program: the fight for national liberation, the revolutionary transformation of trade unions, the worker-farmer alliance, participation in bourgeois parliaments and elections, and the structure and tasks of Communist Parties. Two volumes. $65

Lenin's Final Fight

Speeches and Writings, 1922–23
V.I. LENIN

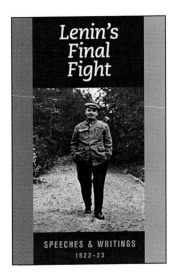

In 1922 and 1923, V.I. Lenin, central leader of the world's first socialist revolution, waged what was to be his last political battle. At stake was whether that revolution would remain on the proletarian course that had brought workers and peasants to power in October 1917— and laid the foundations for a truly worldwide revolutionary movement of toilers organizing to emulate the Bolsheviks' example. *Lenin's Final Fight* brings together the reports, articles, and letters through which Lenin waged this political battle. $20. Also in Spanish.

Lenin's Struggle for a Revolutionary International

Documents, 1907–1916; The Preparatory Years

In the years leading up to World War I, Lenin led the political battle within the leadership of the international workers movement for a revolutionary course to oppose imperialist war by organizing to lead the toilers in overthrowing the capitalist rulers. The articles and documents in this collection bring that debate alive. $38

Questions of National Policy and Proletarian Internationalism

V.I. LENIN

Why the fight of oppressed nations for self-determination is decisive in the worldwide proletarian struggle to take and hold power. Why workers and farmers in imperialist countries have a deep class interest in championing this right. $16

www.pathfinderpress.com

The Cuban Revolution and

Our History Is Still Being Written
THE STORY OF THREE CHINESE-CUBAN GENERALS IN THE CUBAN REVOLUTION

In Cuba, the greatest measure against racial discrimination "was the revolution itself," says Gen. Moisés Sío Wong, "the triumph of a socialist revolution." Armando Choy, Gustavo Chui, and Sío Wong talk about the historic place of Chinese immigration to Cuba, as well as more than five decades of revolutionary action and internationalism, from Cuba to Angola and Venezuela today. Through their stories we see how millions of ordinary men and women changed the course of history, becoming different human beings in the process. $20. Also in Spanish and Chinese.

From the Escambray to the Congo
IN THE WHIRLWIND OF THE CUBAN REVOLUTION
Víctor Dreke

The author describes how easy it became after the Cuban Revolution to take down a rope segregating blacks from whites in the town square, yet how enormous was the battle to transform social relations underlying all the "ropes" inherited from capitalism and Yankee domination. Dreke, second in command of the internationalist column in the Congo led by Che Guevara in 1965, recounts the creative joy with which working people have defended their revolutionary course—from Cuba's Escambray mountains to Africa and beyond. $17. Also in Spanish.

Renewal or Death
Fidel Castro

"To really establish total equality takes more than declaring it in law," Fidel Castro told delegates to the 1986 congress of the Cuban Communist Party, pointing to the revolution's enormous conquests in the fight against anti-black racism. "We can't leave it to chance to correct historical injustices," he said. "We have to straighten out what history has twisted." In *New International* no. 6. $16

World Politics

The First and Second Declarations of Havana

Nowhere are the questions of revolutionary strategy that today confront men and women on the front lines of struggles in the Americas addressed with greater truthfulness and clarity than in these two documents, adopted by million-strong assemblies of the Cuban people in 1960 and 1962. These uncompromising indictments of imperialist plunder and "the exploitation of man by man" continue to stand as manifestos of revolutionary struggle by working people the world over. $10. Also in Spanish, French, and Arabic.

Che Guevara Talks to Young People

The Argentine-born revolutionary leader challenges youth of Cuba and the world to study, to work, to become disciplined. To join the front lines of struggles, small and large. To politicize themselves and the work of their organizations. To become a different kind of human being as they strive with working people of all lands to transform the world. Eight talks from 1959 to 1964. $15. Also in Spanish.

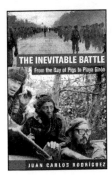

The Inevitable Battle
FROM THE BAY OF PIGS TO PLAYA GIRÓN
Juan Carlos Rodríguez

The U.S.-led invasion of Cuba in April 1961 was defeated in 66 hours by militia battalions composed of worker and peasant volunteers, along with soldiers from the Cuban armed forces. Cuban historian Juan Carlos Rodríguez explains that the human material available to Washington could not match the courage and determination of a people fighting to defend what they had gained through the continent's first socialist revolution. $20. Also in Spanish.

www.pathfinderpress.com

New International

A MAGAZINE OF MARXIST POLITICS AND THEORY

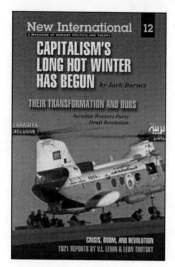

NEW INTERNATIONAL NO. 12

CAPITALISM'S LONG HOT WINTER HAS BEGUN

Jack Barnes

and "Their Transformation and Ours," Resolution of the Socialist Workers Party

Today's sharpening interimperialist conflicts are fueled both by the opening stages of what will be decades of economic, financial, and social convulsions and class battles, and by the most far-reaching shift in Washington's military policy and organization since the U.S. buildup toward World War II. Class-struggle-minded working people must face this historic turning point for imperialism, and draw satisfaction from being "in their face" as we chart a revolutionary course to confront it. $16

NEW INTERNATIONAL NO. 13

OUR POLITICS START WITH THE WORLD

Jack Barnes

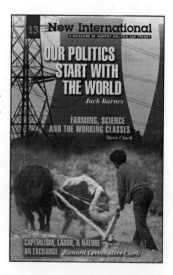

The huge economic and cultural inequalities between imperialist and semicolonial countries, and among classes within almost every country, are produced, reproduced, and accentuated by the workings of capitalism. For vanguard workers to build parties able to lead a successful revolutionary struggle for power in our own countries, says Jack Barnes in the lead article, our activity must be guided by a strategy to close this gap.

Also in No. 13: "Farming, Science, and the Working Classes" *by Steve Clark.* $14

THESE ISSUES ARE ALSO AVAILABLE IN SPANISH AND FRENCH AT
WWW.PATHFINDERPRESS.COM

EXPAND *your Revolutionary Library*

The Working Class and the Transformation of Learning

The Fraud of Education Reform under Capitalism

JACK BARNES

"Until society is reorganized so that education is a human activity from the time we are very young until the time we die, there will be no education worthy of working, creating humanity." $3. Also in Spanish, French, Swedish, Icelandic, Farsi, and Greek.

Problems of Women's Liberation

EVELYN REED

Six articles explore the social and economic roots of women's oppression from prehistoric society to modern capitalism and point the road forward to emancipation. $15

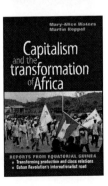

Capitalism and the Transformation of Africa

Reports from Equatorial Guinea

MARY-ALICE WATERS, MARTÍN KOPPEL

The transformation of production and class relations in a Central African country, as it is drawn deeper into the world market and both a capitalist class and modern proletariat are born. As Cuban volunteer medical brigades collaborate to transform social conditions there, the example of Cuba's socialist revolution comes alive. Woven together, the outlines of a future to be fought for today can be seen—a future in which Africa's toilers have more weight in world politics than ever before. $10. Also in Spanish.

PATHFINDER AROUND THE WORLD

Visit our website for a complete list of titles and to place orders

www.pathfinderpress.com

PATHFINDER DISTRIBUTORS

UNITED STATES
(and Caribbean, Latin America, and East Asia)
> *Pathfinder Books, 306 W. 37th St., 10th Floor,*
> *New York, NY 10018*

CANADA
> *Pathfinder Books, 7107 St. Denis, Suite 204,*
> *Montreal, QC H2S 2S5*

UNITED KINGDOM
(and Europe, Africa, Middle East, and South Asia)
> *Pathfinder Books, First Floor, 120 Bethnal Green Road*
> *(entrance in Brick Lane), London E2 6DG*

SWEDEN
> *Pathfinder böcker, Bildhuggarvägen 17, S-121 44 Johanneshov*

AUSTRALIA
(and Southeast Asia and the Pacific)
> *Pathfinder, Level 1, 3/281-287 Beamish St., Campsie, NSW 2194*
> *Postal address: P.O. Box 164, Campsie, NSW 2194*

NEW ZEALAND
> *Pathfinder, 4/125 Grafton Road, Grafton, Auckland*
> *Postal address: P.O. Box 3025, Auckland 1140*